SHAPING TOMORROW'S FAMILY

Volume 143, Sage Library of Social Research

RECENT VOLUMES IN
SAGE LIBRARY OF SOCIAL RESEARCH

shaping tomorrow's family

theory and policy for the 21st century

JOHN SCANZONI

foreword by JESSIE BERNARD

Volume 143
SAGE LIBRARY OF
SOCIAL RESEARCH

SAGE PUBLICATIONS
Beverly Hills / London / New Delhi

For information address:

SAGE Publications, Inc.
275 South Beverly Drive
Beverly Hills, California 90212

SAGE Publications India Pvt. Ltd.
C-236 Defence Colony
New Delhi 110 024, India

SAGE Publications Ltd
28 Banner Street
London EC1Y 8QE, England

Printed in the United States of America

Library of Congress Cataloging in Publication Data

Scanzoni, John H., 1935-
    Shaping tomorrow's family.

    (Sage library of social research ; v. 143)
    Bibliography: p.
    1. Family—United States—Moral and ethical aspects.   2. Twenty-first century—Forecasts.   3. Family policy—United States.   4. Right and left (Political science)
I. Title.   II. Series
HQ536.S337   1982   306-8'5'0973   82-16876
ISBN 0-8039-1920-4
ISBN 0-8039-1921-2 (pbk.)

FIRST PRINTING

CONTENTS

PREFACE

America is currently passing through a period of significant transitions. In the political and economic realms, we are feeling the effects of the so-called Reagan Revolution, and the precipitous decline of the New Deal, the Fair Deal, and the Great Society. In analyzing that decline, *New York Times* humorist Russell Baker (1981) recounts the biblical description of the death of King David: "Now David was old and stricken in years; and they covered him with clothes, but he gat no heat." Baker claims that progressive elements are similarly "old, stricken in years," and "gat no heat." They no longer, he says, possess any "recognizable ideas or philosophies worth sacrificing for." Implicit in his essay is the idea that it is time for progressives to do some fresh thinking if they are to face the critical challenges of the twenty-first century. A *New Republic* (1981) editorial echoes Baker's theme and expresses hope for a new "wave" of "public innovation" and "social construction."

Just as that sort of critical progressive reevaluation is desperately needed at the political and economic levels, it is equally needed at the social and cultural level—particularly with regard to family. According to pollster and psychologist Daniel Yankelovich (1981a), "A sweeping irreversible cultural revolution is transforming the rules that once guided American life." Nevertheless, many supporters of the conservative revival consider *saving* the conventional family a centerpiece of their agenda. Introduced into both houses of Congress, the

Family Protection Act vividly illustrates their aim of restoring the preeminence of the twentieth-century family (see Chapter 5). Outside of Congress, the so-called moral majority (surveys consistently show this group to be actually a statistical minority) is vigorously pursuing that same goal and trying to fill elective offices with persons sharing the group's vision.

The upshot is that the New Right has captured the "high moral ground" regarding family. Claiming to be the defenders of truth, goodness, and virtue, they have put progressives on the defensive. And, as in the political and economic realms, progressives tend to react by implicitly accepting conservative assumptions regarding family and then offering suggestions to make conservative agendas "work better." But it is ironic that in the case of family-related matters, the more progressives try to "patch up" the twentieth-century family, the more they are accused by conservatives of being morally bankrupt, because the overriding concern of conservatives is to return to what they consider a pristine state of family.

Consequently, the time is ripe for progressives to retake the high moral ground regarding family, and this book is one step in that direction. Fresh thinking is needed to give us a new image of family that is suited for a different century—a new age. This thinking must be morally and socially responsible, as well as attentive to the feminism and the individualism that Christopher Lasch (1977, 1978) castigates so severely. In this book I try to show why the twentieth-century family is not well suited to the kind of society emerging around us, and why this fresh concept of family contains the potential to make family a richer institution than it is right now. It is in this sense that the alternative image of family presented here is *moral*—it meets the *actual* majority of citizens where they are and provides guidelines for citizens, policymakers, and clinicians alike, helping them to fashion family in a responsive yet responsible manner to be in tune with the emerging realities of a new century.

In looking to the future, the *New Republic* (1981) editorial expresses hope that ideas for political change will be less "programmatic" and "palliative," and more "structural" and "radical." "Radical" sounds frightening until we define it as simply "going to the root of things." Being cosmetic or palliative or merely "programmatic" in order to solve family problems will no longer do. In this book, I go to the "root of things" regarding family in order to say that if we can adopt and adapt a fresh vision of what it's all about, family is indeed very possible.

I want to thank the many students and colleagues who over the past several years have discussed with me, and thus helped to sharpen, various issues and ideas appearing throughout the following pages. Special thanks are owed to Professor Gerald W. McDonald for an extraordinarily thoughtful critique of the entire manuscript. His comments and criticisms were expecially helpful in shaping the final version.

FOREWORD

This book takes us back to square one, to the "problem of order." It is a theoretical analysis, not in the form of a series of propositions or of generalizations of empirical data, but in the form of delineating the relevant questions and devising ways of analyzing and dealing with them. It reports on the struggle now in process between those the author calls "conventionals" and those he calls "progressives." He answers the basic question, "Is family possible?" in the affirmative. But, he warns us, don't count on its future being what you would like it to be. The family's future is not written in the stars. Much depends on who wins the battle of the Titans now in process. What are considered virtues by one side in this battle are seen as hazards by the other. If the winner were to be judged on the basis of suitability for modern society, characterized as it is by flux, the progressives would determine its future; if on the basis of firmness and stability, the conventionals would.

The solution to the problem of order, Scanzoni states, depends heavily on the way one conceptualizes society. On one side there is the so-called functionalist approach, often associated with the name of Talcott Parsons; on the other, there is the so-called conflict approach, associated by some, but not all, with Marxism. One emphasizes structure, the other process. One holds that "organisation is a *structure* which allocates individuals to specific parts of the total task which the organisation exists to perform, organisation is the scriptwriter of roles to which individuals find they become morally committed" (Burns, 1977: 261). The other sees organization as "a

process through which individuals are enabled to produce—
i.e., make what they do available to others, to socialize their
work; organisation is an essential instrument for the ac-
complishment of their individual ends and values."

The conventionals represent the organization-as-structure
point of view; the progressives, the process point of view.
Conventionals see society as a system of clearly defined roles,
each shaped to fit into other roles in a smoothly running
system. It is essential that all individuals be socialized into this
structure, be well versed in their obligations and prerogatives,
and live by them. The progressives see society, instead, as the
"outcome (network) of complex negotiations between
powerful interest groups in which each group maintains
preferred family patterns which seek to promote the interests of
that group."

The first conceptualization of society is "morphostatic," or
fixed, and anything that deviates from its goal of stability must
be exorcised so far as possible. The second, or progressive,
conceptualization is "morphogenetic," and anything that
rigidifies the system or interferes with its flexibility should be
reduced, if not eliminated. Proponents reject the so-called
Nuremberg argument, which calls on everyone to do whatever
he or she is told to do, or, in the present context, to do what the
role system calls for. There was a time when the conventional
conception prevailed almost unchallenged, but there has been a
shift in recent times.

Those of us who observed young people in the 1960s and
early 1970s saw the battle between proponents of these two
points of view not only in learned disquisitions in professional
journals, but in the minds of our students and children; we *saw*
it in living color before our very eyes. We saw the processes by
which these young people became disillusioned with the status
quo of the conventionals. We saw them shift from a functionalist society-as-benign to the society-as-exploitative viewpoint.
Thus, for example, until midcentury boys and girls took it for

granted that they were being prepared to "take their place" in society. The boy would get a job and know that he was to be part of the total productive system. Then there began to be a change. The young men were coming to see their jobs as a contribution, not so much to the economy as to the profits of corporations. They saw the corporations not as agencies to get goods produced but as ways to make money for shareholders. They were, in brief, coming to see society "as the outcome (network) of complex negotiations between powerful interest groups" and many wanted no part of it. This attitude, often labeled "antisocial," spread to other institutions; there was a powerful anti-establishment movement that challenged all institutions — governmental, educational, religious. These young men came to see the benign "society" they had been taught to accept willingly as indeed a congeries of cynical, exploitative, mercenary, self-serving interests.

The girls also went through similar disillusionments. They had taken it for granted that they would be in the work force for a few years after graduation from college, marry, have children, and be "taken care of" for the rest of their lives. But in the 1960s and 1970s many of them caught the disillusionment they found among the young men. Their conceptualization of "society" was also challenged. They no longer saw it as a protective, sheltering haven in which, if they obeyed the rules, they would be secure forever, but rather as an exploitative tyrant coercing them into marriages that were dysfunctional.

So much, then, for the "society" component of the "society-family" issue. Scanzoni is fair-minded and judicious in his review of the pros and cons of both the conventional and progressive points of view, though he makes no effort to hide where his own preference lies. He makes a strong case for the greater appropriateness of the progressives' perspective than of the conventionals' for this day and age and the kind of people it produces. He applies this distinction to one special kind of organization, the family. We turn here, then, to the family component, to the pros and cons of the family models that correspond to the two conceptualizations of society.

Weitzman (1981: xxii) has sketched the legal basis for conventional marriage: "It recognized the husband as head of the family and made him responsible for family support. The wife was responsible for the home and was obligated to provide domestic services and child care." In addition, religious norms prescribed permanence and sexual exclusivity. This model has many things in its favor, and Scanzoni states them succinctly. It has a long history; it is stable, fixed; it has taken the high ground of morality, goodness, virtue; it has the appeal of the functional point of view. Further, the conventional model has impressive credentials for taking care of men. Corporate and other employers much prefer "family men" when they are hiring. Insurance companies are strong supporters of conventional family life because it imposes a regimen on men that is good for their health and survival. It is demonstrable that married men are in better health and live longer than never-married men and men living in the status of divorce or widowhood. Voters seem to favor candidates with conventional families. In this sense the "society-family" issue favors the conventionals. If the conventional model is not so beneficial to wives, that is the way things are. Let them just grin and bear it. But increasingly women protest the demands made on them in this model, and with the growing proportion of two-earner marriages, the demands on them multiply.

This is a strong list of credentials; it cannot be discounted. Still, in addition to the shift noted above in the conceptualization of society among young people that rejects the society-as-structure view, the major weakness of the conventional model is that it is out of sync with the times—it does not conform to what is actually happening on the current scene. The present legal and religious structure of marriage, Weitzman (1981: xxii) notes, "ignores the current evidence concerning divorce, marriage in middle age and throughout the life cycle, childless marriages, more egalitarian family patterns, diverse family forms among ethnic minorities and the poor, and alternative family forms among homosexuals, communards, and others who live together without marriage.'' The attrition of the ground rule that the husband is the sole provider is illustrated by the rapid increase in two-earner families. The year 1980 may be taken as the "tipping point" at which the nonemployed wife became the nonconformist, the "deviant," a member of the minority (Bernard, 1981c). Official recognition of the end of the rule that the husband was "head of household" occurred in 1980, when the U.S. Census Bureau abandoned use of the term, which it had formerly automatically assigned to the husband, and substituted "householder," which members of the household themselves denominated. The fact that so many employed wives and mothers are in the work force means that unless household responsibilities and child care are shared by husbands, wives are subject to overload. The goal, if not the achievement, of shared roles in the family marks another step away from conventional marriage. The high divorce rate—it doubled in the decade between the mid-to-late 60s and the mid-to-late 70s—illustrates what has happened to the ground rule of permanence; and the growth of commercialized swinging—called the "fastest growing recreation today" (Bernard, 1982)—is only one example of what has become of the ground rule of sexual exclusivity in marriage. It is based on this kind of evidence that Scanzoni makes his case against the conventional model of marriage. It doesn't fit.

Many conventionals recognize these trends and bemoan them. They feel that the family is threatened by a congeries of forces, including the media, by courses taught in public schools, by books permitted in school libraries, by sex education that undercuts conventional mores, and by sex as portrayed on television, all of which they would like to see controlled.

In contrast to the conventional model, Scanzoni argues for "a model of family that is both theoretically and philosophically sound, that accounts for ongoing demographic trends, and yet is also practical and workable," one that "integrates changing preferences and behaviors into a coherent framework that would...eventually supplant it [the conventional] in dominance." This progressive model would facilitate intelligent options with respect to sex, marriage, and family. It presupposes that we would all be better off than we are now if our decisions were made with self-knowledge and "in terms of a new explicitly stated family philosophy." The current out-of-sync situation generates "ambivalence and uncertainty, often exacerbated by guilt, apprehension, and anxiety."

Unlike the conventionals, who want everyone to conform to the established and stable norms of society as they conceptualize it, the progressives present a model that permits a pluralistic view, one that allows many options: "Alternative views of family should be allowed to 'compete' in the marketplace, with nonaligned persons being allowed to gravitate toward those patterns suiting them best." It would roll with the punches and would have more flexibility in dealing with the punches to which modern life subjects it.

This book makes a strong case for the progressive model, but it does not refuse to recognize the weaknesses of that model. Scanzoni points out that the proponents of the progressive model are fragmented; there is little research to support the model. Progressives are defensive rather than aggressive. The conventionals seem to have the strong moral arguments. To overcome these deficiencies, Scanzoni urges the progressives to overcome their fragmentation and get their act together. He urges them to engage in fresh thinking rather than accept a mere tinkering approach to family. He states that they have not exploited the self-interest, positive advantages of their position to win over adherents. He recommends that the welfare of children be the positive cornerstone of the progressive model and that its inclusion be seen as part of the self-interest. He argues that progressives must derive a coherent alternative perspective on family, propagate it actively, compete with conventionals, cease to be defensive and apologetic, cease to let them have the high moral ground. A new morally responsible image is called for.

The position of this book with respect to equity for women will appeal to many feminists. Its strategic suggestions for progressives at the "meso" level, for example, are useful for feminists also. Scanzoni's critique of feminist strategies in dealing with ERA is also useful. His analysis of the family as oppressive of women is insightful. He recognizes that although progressivism and feminism are not identical, they are natural allies.

The problems with which this book wrestles are by no means simply academic. They resonate in the whole area of policy, for ideas have consequences. There is more consensus on current trends than on ways to deal with them. Some, the "macro" advocates, argue that efforts should be made by policy to turn back to the conventional pattern; others, the "micro" advocates, argue that more efforts should be expended on families themselves and the ways they are attempting to meet the issues created by the current scene. Scanzoni seeks to close the gap between family and society; he attempts to sketch the kinds of alternative families that would achieve this goal and policies to implement such a position.

In a book I published 40 years ago, I noted that change might occur in several ways. Norms might change and conformity to them follow. A law is passed—regulating automobile speed limits, for example—and most people conform. Or behavior might change and norms legitimizing it follow (Bernard, 1942: ch. 8). The conventionals lean heavily toward the first pattern of change; the progressives, toward the second. The progressives argue that, in the present context, behavior is following the demands of the times and, where suitable, should be legitimized by norms. This is not the same as thumbing one's nose at old norms. It is a matter of fitting the norms to the times. The fact that "everyone's doing it" does not mean that "it" should therefore become the law. The Kantian categorical imperative fits here.

Whichever model one favors, it must be recognized that both suffer from a challenge to which we have not yet found an adequate response, namely, the welfare of small children, whether in two-earner families or in female-headed households. The conventional model has been powerless to guarantee it; the progressive model does not promise it either. Combining the self-interest and the child-welfare "planks" in the progressive "platform," as Scanzoni recommends, will call for a good deal of thought. Many women will balk at it, since in their experience it has all too often been a male "self" whose interests were being served at the expense of the welfare of their children. Both conventionals and progressives will have to face up to the fact that we have not yet arrived at an adequate solution to this problem. This book does not pretend to.

This book does, however, provoke thought and provide food for it. It helps us understand the real issues underlying the political struggle for control of policy today. How much flexibility can we tolerate in our society? On how much stability do we have to insist? One need not be a confirmed proponent of either the conventional or the progressive model of family to profit from the analyses offered by this book.

— *Jessie Bernard*

PART I

WHERE WE HAVE BEEN
AND WHERE WE ARE

1

INTRODUCTION

As we close out the twentieth and anticipate entering the twenty-first century, many Americans acknowledge a sense of uncertainty and perhaps even unease. Thoughtful persons who are by no means alarmists or sensationalists ask us to reflect, for example, on the finiteness of fossil fuels. By what means will we power the engines of modern society once petroleum reserves are exhausted? What will be the cost to the environment of our western states if shale reserves are exploited? And while industrial societies scramble for energy to maintain their favored positions, what about developing nations seeking to establish theirs? What will be the effect on the hierarchy of nations as the peoples of the Third World step up their competition to reap some of the gratifications possessed in such abundance by the industrialized nations? And, to complicate the horizon still further, the specter of nuclear blackmail perpetrated by a few reckless terrorists leads the pessimistic among us to speculate whether the twenty-first century will mark the end of Western civilization as we now know it. Less extreme than the threat of nuclear warfare is the nonetheless grotesque prospect of worldwide financial crises leading to political crises—runaway inflation curbed through the iron fists of dictators in the mold of Adolph Hitler.

One does not have to imagine the worst possible scenario among these and a score of additional realms to accept the proposition that the twenty-first century is likely to be characterized by profound worldwide changes in the ways that governments and people alike organize their relationships. To be sure, change is the essence of modern life. What is more, categories we label as "centuries" are totally arbitrary. We say the nineteenth century was markedly distinct from the eighteenth century, as is the twentieth from the nineteenth. But, in reality, the forces that shaped the nineteenth century evolved relentlessly out of the eighteenth. Similarly, the twentieth century has its roots deep in the nineteenth; and the origins of the twenty-first century are being fashioned right now. Consequently, to speak of profound changes is not necessarily to imply radical discontinuity (nuclear holocaust excepted) or that societies and persons will automatically be either "better" or "worse" off than at present. Instead, to characterize changes as *profound* means no more nor less than that the present course of things is shifting toward very different stages in the development of Western societies.

With this understood, we must also go on to describe the specifics of the changes, explain why they are occurring, and evaluate them, and on the basis of that critique we must ponder the extent to which we can participate in the shaping of these changes. Use of an evolutionary analogy to describe social changes sometimes suggests that forces beyond the control of persons and groups are at work. But social forces are, after all, generated, maintained, interrupted, and finally destroyed by human beings. We are not the absolute prisoners of these forces, possessing no recourse whatsoever to influence the course of ongoing changes. How much influence we ultimately have depends, of course, on the realm in question, how well we grasp what is actually transpiring, and the risks we are prepared to take to assert our influence.

Nowhere do those conclusions apply with greater force than in that part of society we call "family." Although family changes have been occurring for several hundred years (Stone, 1977), some observers wonder if family is changing itself out of recognizable existence as we approach the twenty-first century.

As with the kinds of issues cited above, it is not at all clear where family is headed and what it will be like two, three, four, or more decades hence.

Indeed, will it "be" at all? "Is family possible?" is a question posed by many observers. Given the numerous forces in modern societies that seem to impinge on family, can it "survive"? Does it make sense for it to survive? Can we divide up certain tasks now being performed by family, and parcel them out efficiently to other parts of society? Some observers cringe in horror at these prospects and assert that family as we know it must survive. Somehow, they argue, ways must be found to shore it up.

My purpose is to explore whether family is possible and, if so, how. Phrasing the question in this particular fashion makes plain my debt to Georg Simmel's classic 1908 essay, "How Is Society Possible?" (Levine et al., 1976). The reasoning Simmel used to answer his question becomes the starting point to answer mine. Asserting that family *is* possible (which I do) is one thing; but discerning the shape it will take is much more difficult and thus quite another thing. In 1963, Goode said that the "classic farm family of nostalgia" was largely a myth, and a good deal of historical research since that time appears to have proven him correct (Laslett, 1977). The ideal of several generations sharing the same household, spending their days working as a unit, and then lounging together during the evenings was evidently rare indeed. And while certain observers were mourning the passing of that nostalgic fantasy, and by implication simultaneously being critical of the newly emerging late-nineteenth-century and twentieth-century family, the future of that "new" family was itself gradually becoming problematic. Thus to suggest that family is possible is most assuredly not to assert that *the* family of twentieth-century vintage is either necessary or sufficient for the well-being of society or of individuals. Instead, what is possible is a new image of *family* in synchronization with the twenty-first century, supplying benefits to both society and individuals.

This issue of the *mutual* well-being of society and individuals is the central principle of this book. As we shall see, after one distills what the various critics say about what is happening to *the* family it finally comes down to what Lasch (1977) describes as narcissism, or excessive individualism. The critics allege that people are pursuing their own rights at the expense of social responsibility. That issue is ancient. Socrates asked, "How can social organization be made highly advantageous to a person, and a person made so aware of these advantages that he will always act socially?" (Bogardus, 1960: 113). In more recent times, Talcott Parsons has described the perennial dilemma of balancing the interests and well-being of the whole and its parts as the "problem of order." Failure to resolve that "problem" may result in authoritarianism on the one hand, or chaos and anarchy on the other. If the twentieth-century family is indeed trapped by that sort of dilemma, then it is not "possible"—that is, it can no longer exist as a viable entity in society. My intention is to show, in contrast, that certain emerging family patterns do provide a means to balance society's interests with those of individuals. By rephrasing Socrates in contemporary terms, Yankelovich (1981b: 248) describes this balance:

> The genius of a great social ethic [for example, pertaining to family patterns] is neither to suppress desires indiscriminately nor to endorse them indiscriminately.... A social ethic may assume a variety of forms, changing when objective conditions change, but always responsive to the requirement that individuals fulfill themselves through advancing goals that are good for the society.

In contrast, the twentieth-century family described in Chapter 2 as the "conventional family" no longer appears capable of solving the "problem of order" because, in Socrates' terms, it is ceasing to be "advantageous" to many persons, and thus there is little reason for them to "act socially." Thus it should come as no puzzle or shock that its future is bleak. Decades ago it apparently was a reasonably effective vehicle to facilitate the interests of both society and individuals simultaneously. But as we move into the twenty-first century, that seems less and less to be the case. Applying Yankelovich's (1981b: 248) notions, it would appear that the conventional family seems increasingly less able "to make the goals of society responsive to fundamental human yearnings and at the same time to socialize the individual so that he wants to achieve society's goals and thereby create the best forms of human existence that economic and historic conditions permit."

Partly in reaction to its decreasing effectiveness, considerable attention has been paid of late to ways to ameliorate the "worsening condition" of *the* conventional family. And so in the following pages not only do I explore the relative advantages of conventional and emerging families in balancing social and individual well-being, I simultaneously consider the matter of practical application—what are the connections among emerging family patterns and social and legislative policy, programmatic efforts aimed at family-related matters, and clinical approaches to family? While at first glance it might seem that practical application is thus disconnected from the general question of order—of balancing mutual interests—in reality it is not. A compelling feature of the problem-of-order perspective is that inherently it combines the themes of *understanding* and *application*. If one traces the history of social thought from the ancient Greeks to the late nineteenth century, one finds that these dual themes have seldom been divorced. It has only been in this century that some social and behavioral scientists have pleaded for a "value-free" or "objective" science. Whatever the merits of these recent arguments, thinking in terms of the problem of order subverts the dichotomy of understanding and application. As we shall see (Chapter 3), even Talcott Parsons, a strong advocate for value-free science, promulgated an implicit agenda for the practical application of his ideas.

Boulding (1976) displays great perception in suggesting that empirical research must simultaneously be kept distinct from and yet connected with practical applications. In Chapters 5 and 9, I discuss this thorny issue more fully, but in any case it is a difficult tightrope to walk, although there are recent precedents (Giele, 1978: Bernard, 1981b; Weitzman, 1981) suggesting that it can be done effectively.

This sort of "balancing act" seems requisite, not only because family research has often been devoid of practical application, but because family policy has been devoid of organizing principles—general guidelines by which to evaluate ongoing and proposed practical applications. When guidelines are applied, they most often tend to be derived from conventional family models, resulting in the irony that many practical applications have been geared to situations that are becoming increasingly irrelevant. But viewing family from a problem-of-order perspective simultaneously supplies understanding as well as the guidelines from which to derive relevant applications. The understanding consists of identifying the conditions necessary to achieve a balance of individual and societal interests; and, accordingly, the applications would seek to implement those conditions.

However, attempts to ameliorate family conditions have recently been beset by a more severe problem than lack of systematic guiding principles. Family policy and applications have become front-page political issues. Highly organized, well-financed interest groups—many with fundamentalist religious convictions—have launched crusades to "save the family," meaning the conventional family, which they perceive to be under siege. During the 1980 presidential and congressional campaigns these right-wing groups flexed a great deal of political muscle in efforts to elect persons sharing that siege mentality. It was these groups who, once they discovered the ease with which the Equal Rights Amendment was being passed by the states, launched a campaign that effectively sealed its doom (Boles, 1979). The successes of these interest groups are a clear signal that any systematic efforts to shape family policy, programs, or therapy in directions other than conventional ones will be met by powerful political resistance. They simply do not accept the notion that changes in family patterns are not automatically negative. The prospect of a twenty-first-century family substantially different from the conventional one is for them horrifying indeed. For them family is not "possible" unless it is *the* family with which they are familiar.

However, one does not have to be an extremist to wonder how family is possible if it is not organized along familiar, often comfortable, lines. Many thoughtful people share misgivings about the future of family. Nevertheless, in spite of these misgivings, family continues its inexorable course of change. Consequently, the most prudent course of action is, first, to try to understand these changes. Once we do that, we are likely to be persuaded that family is possible in the twenty-first century, though it is likely to be very different from what we now experience. Second, having shaken our misgivings as to family's basic viability, the next course of action is to try to participate in those changes so that we can shape them as fully as possible to be socially responsible as well as personally satisfying. This book is an attempt to follow both courses of action. We want to understand because that is intrinsically satisfying; we want to apply our understanding because that is socially responsible.

2

THE MAKING OF THE CONVENTIONAL FAMILY

Divorce and Individualism

In pondering whether family is "possible" or not, a factor that immediately springs to the minds of many people is divorce. According to O'Neill (1967: 34), this connection was first generated by an 1889 Bureau of Labor report, which described how common divorce had become. For several decades thereafter, a number of influential people, whom O'Neill (1967: 45) labels "divorce-conservatives," made the connection between divorce and the deterioration of the family explicit in the public mind by arguing that "divorce was inspired by an individualism rooted in Protestantism and the English common law that treated man as an individual and not as a member of the family." In contrast to "self-interested individualism," the conservatives argued for "an appreciation of social order" and for "socializing the will and embedding the individual in a web of 'altruistic interest'" (O'Neill, 1967: 45). To the conservatives of a century ago, divorce "involved an apparent conflict between the public welfare and individual rights" (O'Neill, 1967: 47); because of its child-rearing function, the family was considered the foundation of society.

Consequently, since the conservatives were convinced that divorce destroyed the family, they believed that society was doomed. Thwing and Thwing (1887: 97-98) represent the prevailing sentiments of that era when they assert: "It is in the family...that...moral qualities...essential to the preservation of the State, may be most carefully and completely trained. If Rome had maintained the early strength and purity of her domestic institutions, she might have remained the mistress of the world." To the Thwings and other conservatives of that era, "modern men and women put too much stress on happiness...and...individual rights were being exalted at the expense of the common welfare" (O'Neill, 1967: 86).

As Stone (1977: 151) acknowledges, "Individualism is a very slippery concept to handle." Stone (1977: 151) claims that individualism seeped into English (and thus American) family life during the late seventeenth century and the eighteenth century; he defines individualism as "a demand for personal autonomy and a corresponding respect for the...right to privacy, to self-expression, and to the free exercise of...will within limits set by the need for social cohesion." He elaborates by stating that individualism involves "a recognition that it is morally wrong to make exaggerated demands for obedience, or to manipulate or coerce the individual beyond a certain point in order to achieve social or political ends." Stone (1977: 151-152) reminds us that most societies, both historically and currently, "despise and deplore" individualism because it is "equated with narcissism and egocentricity, a selfish desire to put one's personal convenience above the needs of the society as a whole, or those of sub-units such as the kin or the family."

In short, the late nineteenth- and early twentieth-century conservatives explained divorce as a result of narcissism, egocentrism, and selfishness, or, as May (1980: 2) interprets the conservatives, "individual depravity." However, based on her examination of Los Angeles County divorce records, May (1980: 46-47) concludes that pre-1900 divorces were mostly the result of persons unwilling to live with the *costs* of their spouses' unfulfilled obligations: Husbands who were not good providers or who philandered or drank; wives who were nonmaternal, nonsubservient to husbands, unconcerned with care of children and household, or who drank and indulged in public amusements. While their parents and grandparents had tended to accept such costs without resorting to divorce, the last of the victorians refused to endure them. Their emerging individualism was expressed in their desire to shift marital relationships—to terminate those that were costly, and to seek new ones from which those costs were absent.

May (1980) claims that after 1900 the divorce records reveal a subtle but highly significant shift in the way individualism was expressed. No longer were persons divorcing merely to escape costs; an increasing number divorced and remarried to gain valued *rewards* as well. May's (1980: 76) studies of 1920s divorce records suggest that men and women were seeking "the self-contained privatized home geared to personal happiness." She concludes that "personal life seems to have become a national obsession in 20th century America" (p. 163). "Women wanted their mates to be good providers as well as fun-loving pals; men desired wives who were exciting as well as virtuous.... Couples hoped that marriage would include fewer sacrifices and more satisfactions" (pp. 90-91). And since marriages cannot fulfill completely "the great expectations for individual fulfillment...divorce is likely to [continue] with us" (p. 163).

Thus twentieth-century individualism was moving people not only to avoid marital costs, but to seek richer satisfactions as well. But, as May (1980: 88) observes, the "complicating factor" in this new quest "was inevitably children." What had not altered since the nineteenth century were intense pronatalist pressures characterizing women with "no desire for children [as] irresponsible [and] unnatural" (May, 1980: 88). Nevertheless, May (1980: 89) suggests that during the twentieth century the "strict discipline of the nineteenth century geared to raising pure and moral individuals gave way to indulgence as mothers focused their own need for amusement on their

children. With little else offering sustained personal involvement, women turned with intensified commitment to
home and family.... Childrearing took on new meaning in
order to fit the 'fun morality' of the leisure lifestyle.''

The Fading and Reappearance of Hierarchy

The marriage and divorce patterns May describes are a far
cry from the sixteenth-century English family, which was
"hierarchical, authoritarian and inquisitorially collectivist"
(Stone, 1977: 409).[1] And, says Stone, the family of that day was
a carbon copy of society. But throughout the seventeenth and
eighteenth centuries democracy and individualism began to
spread so that "neither the absolute monarch nor the
patriarchal father was any longer necessary for the maintenance of social order" (Stone, 1977: 411). However, toward
the close of the eighteenth century, Stone (1977: 422) says that
"a strong revival of moral reform, paternal authority and
sexual repression...[arose] among the middle classes...and
continued for over a century." The forces of individualism
were being stymied by the birth and development of what came
to be known as the *Victorian* family. Part of the reason for this
brake on individualism was the fear, stimulated by the French
Revolution, that the "impoverished and alienated masses in the
industrial cities would rise up in bloody revolution" (Stone,
1977: 422). Thus two powerful religious interest groups, "the
Evangelicals and the Methodists,...[combined to bring about]
the enforcement of patriarchy and obedience, and the crushing
of the libido" (Stone, 1977: 422). Since both of these groups
were strong in America as well as in England, similar consequences occurred on both sides of the Atlantic. Cott (1979:
164) argues that "the [Victorian] ideology of [female]
passionlessness was tied to the rise of evangelical religion [in
America] between the 1790s and the 1830s." Prior to that era

she concludes (as does Blauvelt, 1981) that women were viewed by "Anglo-Americans" as *"especially* sexual" (Cott, 1979: 163).

In his analyses of the impact of evangelical religion on American society during that same era, Mathews (1977: 111) argues that their "commitment to 'women's sphere'...came out of the early Evangelical perception of the cosmic conflict between the church and the world." Evangelicalism, as a *sect,* was rebelling against the established churches, as well as against the larger society in general. Troeltsch (1931) describes the sect posture as a "we-they" mentality, based on constant fears of "their" encroachment on "us." Furthermore, the leaders of this eighteenth- and nineteenth-century sect held a world-and-life view; their aim was to create "an 'enlightened and refined people.' The early Evangelical movement had created a self-conscious people who rejected the cultural and social hegemony of traditional elites" (Mathews, 1977: 111). As the dominant religion of the emerging nineteenth-century middle class, Evangelicalism criticized the manners and morals of the aristocracy and also of the lower class:

> To supplant the sinful power of the aristocratic ideal of womanhood [or what Stone described as eighteenth-century family individualism], Evangelicals began to shape a model of behavior and ideals which was peculiarly the possession of women and was based on their unique contribution to the ideal community....Evangelical women, it was believed, were endowed with a capacious piety...they were assumed to be more emotional and affectionate than men [Mathews, 1977: 111, 113].

Thus the idea that women were especially *sexual* became replaced by the radically different notions that they were especially *affectionate* and *pious*.

In any case, the essential point to keep in mind—and it is central to the discussion of later chapters—is that what eventually became the predominant family model in the late nineteenth and early twentieth centuries was born in what Mathews calls "social conflict." That is, a particular religious interest group emerged and, among other things, repudiated the family patterns of existing segments of society, and then, as Mathews says, "self-consciously" set about establishing its own unique arrangements.

At the same time that the emerging nineteenth-century Victorian family effectively repudiated women's sexuality, it also reduced women's economic and occupational activities. Cott and Pleck (1979) point out that prior to industrialization farm wives worked just as many hours and just as hard as their men. Women were in fact requisite to their men's economic survival; Hareven (1977) describes it as an "economic partnership." In addition, there is evidence that eighteenth-century women were considerably more active than nineteenth-century women in mercantile and other urban economic activities (Cott and Pleck, 1979). In contrast, the nineteenth century witnessed the development of a substantial middle class, throughout which it became normative to try to imitate selected aspects of the upper-class lifestyle. For instance, middle-class husbands who could afford it began to "keep" their wives at home as a sign of their economic success. While it may seem ironic that Evangelicals were censuring upper-class manners and morals at the same time they were adopting this particular custom, they adopted it because it jibed with their notion of women as "the moral and mental preceptors of the family" (Mathews, 1977: 112). Freedom from outside labor enabled them to emphasize "one of the most important distinctions between themselves and worldlings. Repudiated was the presumed carelessness of worldly women, who were said to be lackadaisical about child care" (Mathews, 1977: 112). In brief, unlike aristocratic women (both in England and America), who did not use their economic freedom to care for their own children but instead utilized nannies and boarding schools (and in contrast to lower-class women, who were with their children fewer hours because they worked out of necessity), middle-class women adopted the ideal of "full-time motherhood."

According to Hareven (1977), the Industrial Revolution forged the sharpest ecological and physical cleavages ever experienced between work place and domicile. Also historically unique was the emergence of the role of "full-time mother"—a phenomenon that is now "only one century old" (Hareven, 1977: 109). Hareven uses expressions such as the "cult of motherhood" (p. 109) and the "glorification" of motherhood (p. 104) to describe the "new" idea (which Lasch, 1977, seems to assume had been fixed forever) that the nineteenth-century family became a haven—"a domestic retreat from the world of work" (p. 104),[2] and that the woman was its "custodian." As the roles of husbands and wives became ever more segregated *(he,* the provider; *she,* the homemaker and child caretaker), "the old economic partnership" (p. 104) between spouses disappeared. And even though throughout the nineteenth century working-class white people and many black Americans, along with most European immigrants, could not initially afford the luxury of women not being gainfully employed, as quickly as they could they apparently adopted the urban white middle-class lifestyle as "the family norm" (Cott and Pleck, 1979; Modell and Hareven, 1978: 267-268), just as the middle class itself had earlier imitated the upper class. This conclusion is drawn from the fact that by the end of the nineteenth century only 5 percent of American married women living with their husbands were gainfully employed (Campbell, 1893).

Paradoxically, at what appeared to be the zenith of its acceptance the rigid patriarchal features of the Victorian family began to diminish to some degree (Hareven, 1977: 105) during what O'Neill (1976) describes as the late nineteenth-century "Progressive Era." Renascent individualism (in the form of increasing divorce frequency) was beginning to seep into the emerging twentieth-century family (Halem, 1980). In protest, critics on both sides of the Atlantic were censuring its individualistic tendencies—especially the proclivity toward divorce described above by May (1980) and O'Neill (1967). Thus after being dormant throughout the nineteenth century, family individualism was emerging once more. Nevertheless, as we can see from the following description of what Rapoport et al. (1977: 349) call the twentieth-century "conventional" family, individualism's parameters were explicitly declared and severely limited for both sexes.

> The elements of the previously dominant paradigm (which we call the conventional model of the conjugal family) are as follows:
>
> 1. The male head of the household, the father, is the sole economic provider.
> 2. The female head of the household, the mother, is the homemaker, and is responsible for domestic care and the socialization of the children. She is a helpmeet to the husband providing support for him in his struggle for the family's survival.
> 3. The children are helpless and dependent, vulnerable and malleable. They must be nurtured full-time by the mother (or mother-surrogate) only, as emotional stability is essential.
> 4. The family is a private institution and within it individuals can fulfill their most important needs. This fulfillment is based on the foundation of the economic income provided by the husband (where necessary, supplemented by the state). Only when economic and material needs have been met do expressions of psychological and social needs for love, esteem, self-expression and fulfillment emerge within the family.
> 5. Healthy families produce healthy individuals, who adjust to social roles.

When I use the term "conventional family" in subsequent chapters, the preceding model is what I have in mind. Since I frequently compare it to what I describe as "emerging" or "progressive" models of family, one could gain the impression that I am offering a simple dichotomy of conventional versus progressive. This is not the case. Beginning in Chapter 3, where

I discuss the "drift" of the "unaligned majority," and continuing throughout the book, I repeatedly emphasize the many shades of differences that exist with regard to family norms and behaviors. Sharply contrasting conventional twentieth-century models with emerging twenty-first-century possibilities is chiefly a heuristic device. In Chapter 9, for example, when I discuss research possibilities, I make the point that the distance between "conventional" and "progressive" is actually spanned by a continuum consisting of rigorously operationalized variables.

Summary

Late nineteenth-century social critics expressed considerable anxiety over observable increases in divorce reflecting, they alleged, a suddenly rampant individualism. Actually, however, that individualism had lain dormant for about a hundred years after its eighteenth-century nadir. As eighteenth-century Evangelicalism emerged, one aspect of its world-and-life view was to transform family, and it self-consciously entered into conflict with other segments of existing society in order to do so. Over time, and in conjunction with the forces of industrialization and urbanization, it achieved that aim in large measure. Consequently, the *conventional* family model that has prevailed throughout the twentieth century has its roots in that complex set of historical circumstances.

NOTES

1. It is not my purpose to present a detailed and exhaustive review of the conflicting bodies of scholarship pertaining to family changes that have been developed in recent years by social historians. Interested persons should consult the works of historians

cited in this and later chapters. In particular, Albin and Cavallo (1981: 2) attempt to supply balanced perspectives on "historians of the family [who] have engaged in heated debates about the structure of families in the past." My purposes here are to draw on the areas of apparently greatest consensus among historians and to stress the religious roots of the conventional family. Persons desiring to explore the myriad complex subtleties involved in the issue should examine the ongoing debates among family historians.

2. Historians Albin and Cavallo (1981: 236) argue that the "myth" that "the family is a haven of love and security, and a 'place' that values the person because of who he is rather than for what he has achieved [is] . . . to a great extent . . . nonsense."

3

DRIFTING FROM THE
CONVENTIONAL FAMILY

In spite of the assumption underlying the conventional model that individualism should be restricted by strict normative parameters, as the twentieth century progressed it became apparent (from such things as increases in wife employment, divorce, nonmarital sexuality, and so forth) that increasing numbers of adults were drifting away from conventional patterns, often in response to individualistic interests. In the midst of this surge of adult individualism, many observers wonder what the consequences will be for children, and thus for succeeding generations. From the problem-of-order perspective, is the individualism pursued by adults detrimental to family as an institution, and to the larger society? Hence a major facet of the question "Is family possible?" is whether adult individualism is engulfing children's interests, and thus burying family and society.

In 1964, even before the full implications for the conventional family of renewed feminism were realized, an interdisciplinary symposium was convened to consider "the family's search for survival." To introduce it, Farber et al. (1965: viii) state that "with regard to social and cultural possibilities, the family is very apt to constitute a limitation upon the potentialities of the individual." Having recognized that side of the problem-of-order question, they go on to raise the other side of the dilemma: "It would seem that no other social structure is able to assume the most important function of the traditional family, the nurture of the young." A resolution of the dilemma appears to have escaped them, because they suggest, "We seem to be witnessing the rapid dissolution of an institution which is yet indispensable.... The uncertain future of the modern family is, of course, generally acknowledged."

The Parsonian Perspective

One of the participants in this symposium was Talcott Parsons (1965), who by no means shared the pessimism of its conveners. Parsons (1965: 38) believed that the central concept in explaining whether or not groups, including families, are "possible" is *solidarity*. By "solidarity" he means that group members accept their "common belongingness as members of a...system [in which they depend on each other]." Second, they *"trust* each other to fulfill mutual expectations." Not only did Parsons hold that solidarity (in terms of a sense of belongingness and trust) was necessary for family order, he also believed that it was requisite for societal order. Parsons asks, "How is it possible to develop solidarity and...trust [in the larger society]?" He responds to his own question by telling us to think of "the family [as] the 'primordial' solidarity unit of all human societies" (Parsons, 1965: 38). He continues, "Family solidarity is the primordial basis of social solidarity...'guaranteed' by the personal security of the individual" (p. 39).

In other words, the child first experiences solidarity, in terms of belongingness and trust, within the family. Hence not only is the family benefited because of orderliness, but, simultaneously, individuals develop sound mental and emotional health, which make them psychologically secure. It is this security that enables people to trust others, not only in the family, but outside the family in community and formal organizations such as schools and businesses. Throughout the larger society, trust stimulates and is stimulated by a sense of belongingness. The result? Solidarity and social order. Thus, in Parsons's view, to the degree that family fails to generate solidarity not only is it unclear whether or not family is possible, but the possibility of society is equally uncertain.

Given that family solidarity is so essential to family and society, how are its components—belongingness and trust—generated? Parsons (1937: 89) agrees with seventeenth-century social philosopher Hobbes that people are ultimately "ruled by their passions." As people seek their goals in an individualistic manner, "there is nothing to prevent their pursuit resulting in conflict [often employing the use of] force and fraud" (Parsons, 1937: 89-90). To prevent individualism from subverting solidarity, Parsons concludes that families and societies must possess shared norms prescribing and proscribing behaviors. Since these "rules of deportment" (Birenbaum and Sagarin, 1976: 15) guide mothers, fathers, and children in their behavior toward each other, individualism is curbed, and belongingness, trust, solidarity, and, finally, order are achieved. Note that Parsons rejects Socrates' view on how to achieve order because, according to Parsons, an inevitable result of that view is "allowing" each person to decide for him- or herself what is "prudent" or "best" or "advantageous" for him or her (see Chapter 1).

In Parsons's view, and that of conservatives[1] generally, society "decides" what is best for individuals, and individuals should conform. One of Ibsen's (1970b) characters makes a statement that embodies the conservative indictment of deviance: "You have an inveterate tendency to go your own way.... And in a well-ordered society, that's...inexcusable. The individual has to learn to subordinate himself to the whole—or, should I say, to those authorities charged with the common good." According to Parsons, society must "decide" and individuals submit because people are too selfish to make choices other than those that will benefit them, the ultimate result being social chaos and anarchy. For example, Pitts (1964: 76), one of Parsons's expositors, tells us that "society" says the following regarding the conventional family:

> Male superiority is a basic theme of the structure of the nuclear family in all known societies. This...[means] that...the community roles in which he participates...have a priority over most family roles—at least that the family roles "stretch"...in order to maximize the capacity of the husband to participate in community roles.

Why does the husband but not the wife participate in community (specifically occupational) roles? According to Pitts (1964: 103), "Psychologically, there can be some debate as to whether women's personality systems permit as thorough a socialization into professional patterns." He goes on to argue that the "function" of having women in low-status "expressive"-type jobs (secretary, receptionist) "is to dilute the competitive strain bearing upon the men" (p. 103). Furthermore, he says that working women must be content with lower-prestige jobs so that the family is not disrupted: "Another functional requirement is that final [family] authority [based on the husband's greater prestige and income] should be assigned without ambiguity" (p. 103). Pitts's notions are illustrated by another of Isben's (1970c) characters, who says that "marriage has to be accounted almost a kind of miracle. The way a woman little by little makes herself over until she becomes like her husband." When a female character asks if "a man could also be absorbed that way, over into his wife," he responds, "No, because a man has his vocation to live for.... He has a calling in life."

Why would people allow "society" to "tell" them to behave in terms of these conventional patterns? According to Parsons (1951: 37), it is because of the socialization I described earlier, whereby people learn "internalized need-dispositions to conform with value-standards independently of any significant consequences of that conformity." Thus order is achieved not because of self-interest, but "from a principle beyond self-interest.... This principle requires compliance with norms which run counter to individual self-interest" (Ellis, 1971: 696). In short, Parsons supplies a coherent theoretical and philosophical base for the twentieth-century conventional family: People should conform to it, not primarily because doing so would benefit them, but because they have learned what Ellis calls a "moral" obligation to do so. In other words, conforming is the *correct* thing to do—it is best for social order—for something larger than oneself and one's own petty interests. Note how sharply this view contrasts with Yankelovich's (1981b) blend of order based on individual fulfillment *and* societal goals (see Chapter 1).

Adding considerable bite to the motivation to conform are the religious roots of the twentieth-century family described in Chapter 2. Although the twentieth-century family is less hierarchical and less libidinally restrained than was the Victorian family, the conventional model differs merely *in degree,* not in kind, from what Stone (1977), Cott and Pleck (1979), and Mathews (1977) say was strongly promulgated 200 years ago by religious conservatives.[2]

Religious Perspectives

To many Americans who take their Judeo-Christian heritage seriously, the twentieth-century family is not merely one more stage in an ongoing evolutionary process. Even more unthinkable for them is the notion, suggested in the pages following, that particular family forms are essentially creatures of competing interest groups. Instead, since these Americans believe that this model of family represents the divine will, they see conforming to it as indeed the "right" thing to do; it is a moral obligation. The interests of maintaining the model are much greater than any self-interests. In recent years the so-called moral majority, alongside related fundamentalist and evangelical religious groups, has become exceedingly vocal about conventional family "moral obligations" in such areas as abortion, homosexuality, divorce, heterosexual ethics, sex education, and so forth.

A recent national sample survey (Connecticut Mutual, 1981) tried to measure "religious commitment" of individuals,[3] and then sought to relate this measure to their views on family matters. A total of 50 percent of the sample ranked "low" or "lowest" in commitment; 26 percent ranked "highest" or "high" (Connecticut Mutual, 1981: 43). Between these extremes was 24 percent of the sample, those who ranked "moderate" on commitment. Hence, to the degree that the commitment measure is valid and the sampling representative, we can conclude that American adults are divided into three broad camps: half who are not very religiously committed and a quarter who are, plus a quarter somewhere in the middle. Significantly, the study found that the "very committed" tended to: be older, live in the South, be black, be female, have lower incomes and education, and live in small cities and rural areas (Connecticut Mutual, 1981: 49).

The study then attempts to show how religious commitment is related to the kinds of matters the "New Right" or "moral majority" is transforming into what the authors call "America's new political issues": adultery, hard drugs, homosexuality, adolescent sexual activity, lesbianism, pornography, abortion, marijuana, cohabitation, and premarital sex (Connecticut Mutual, 1981: 86). Only 24 percent of the sample for this study said that all of these things are "morally wrong," thus leading the researchers to conclude that there is no such thing as a moral *majority* but, instead, there is a moral *minority*: "those who are strictest in their definition of what is morally wrong [and who] are significantly more religious [committed], and older... [and] slightly more likely to be less educated" (Connecticut Mutual, 1981: 99). In short, according to this study the New Right is a minority of religiously committed people (who are older and less educated)—the heirs of the Evangelicals and Methodists of 200 years ago. And, like their forerunners, they tend to be vocal and powerful beyond their numbers.

Religiously committed people hold definite norms regarding the conventional family, and they make those norms known. For example, "the most religious are much more likely than the least religious to favor a traditional marriage (41% versus 16%)" (Connecticut Mutual, 1981: 135). "Traditional" was defined for the respondents in terms of points 1 and 2 of Rapoport et al.'s (1977: 349) description of the conventional family (see also Chapter 2). The religiously committed rejected the idea of "an equal *marriage of shared responsibility* in which the husband and wife cooperate on working, homemaking and child-raising" (Connecticut Mutual, 1981: 132). It therefore follows that, compared to the least religious, the most religious are: more likely to feel that an unhappy marriage should be reconciled at all costs (27 percent difference); less likely to approve a woman earning money if her husband can support her (25 percent difference); more likely to want divorce to be made more difficult (33 percent difference); more likely to say an unhappy couple should stay together if they have young children (34 percent difference); more likely to say a mother of young children should not work outside the home unless it is a financial necessity (27 percent difference); and more likely to believe that "living with someone before marriage is morally wrong" (73 percent difference; Connecticut Mutual, 1981: 88, 135-136).

Organic Versus Interest Group Perspectives

Thus far, I have been using O'Neill's (1967) term "conservative" to describe persons adhering to one version or another of the conventional family. However, care must be taken to distinguish between religiously committed conservatives on the one hand, and social scientists, applied professionals, and clinicians who follow some version of the conventional model on the other (see Lasch, 1977).[4] A major distinction, for instance, is the righteous zeal with which the former propogate their views and pursue their ends in the political arena. But in spite of significant differences, family conservatives of all stripes tend to share—often implicitly—a particular view regarding the link between society and the family. They view society as a kind of organic entity, analogous to the human body. *The* family is, of course, an integral part of this organism.

In effect, in the view of family conservatives, society is allegedly one organic whole, and one subset of it is called "the family." In contrast to the organic perspective, the following pages develop a different perspective derived from ideas initially presented in Chapter 2. Recall that Stone (1977) argues that certain religious organizations, or what Dahrendorf (1959) calls "interest groups," were successful in implementing their norms and behaviors regarding family. From this interest group perspective, society is not an organic whole with merely *one* form of family. Instead, contemporary society is composed of numerous groups, some of which are competing to implement *their* family, that is, their own ideals and goals as to what family *should be*.

Outside the United States, the closest analogue to the notion of "family interest groups" is what Lory (1980) describes as "family unions." Found in Quebec, Canada, as well as in France, Belgium, Spain, and Germany, "these family movements are particularly dedicated to presenting demands concerning the economic situation of families and changes in family allowances" (Lory, 1980: 115). Lory goes on to remark that "they devote themselves" to improving the levels of services supplied by government but, significantly, "they do not sufficiently pursue social innovation." In short, these family unions focus almost exclusively on economic matters, in contrast to the full range of family-related issues that concern American conservative and progressive interest groups. These issues will be discussed more fully in Chapters 6 and 9.

1960s Family Policy

Parsons, of course, was a prime spokesman for the organic perspective in which family change—if there was any—occurred in gradual *evolutionary* fashion over long periods of time. But even he was very much aware of "a very substantial residual group...failing to meet...the minimum generally acceptable standards" of *the* family (Parsons, 1965: 47). To correct that deviancy from *the* family (including "poverty," "juvenile delinquency," "broken families," and so forth), Parsons gave assent to the kinds of federal programs that, during the mid-sixties, were being incorporated into the "Great Society" (Aaron, 1978).

Thus at the federal level, family social policy was being aimed primarily at *poor* people—children in particular, but also adults—with the goal being to extricate them from poverty and enable them to conform to "minimum acceptable standards"—in other words, the conventional family model. Since most poor people were black, they were, as Hareven (1977: 110) notes, the prime targets of these policies. In a widely publicized document, Moynihan (1965) described *the* American black family as both victim and cause. According to Moynihan, because of social and economic deprivation, blacks were unable to conform to prevailing familial norms; consequently, there was a great deal of "disorganization" throughout black society. This theme became the basis of numerous federal programs to assist disadvantaged families.

Most often implicitly, but sometimes explicitly, the ultimate goal of these policies and programs was to enable persons to conform to conventional family norms—the types of norms that some scientists and practitioners, and conservatives in general, feel are essential if *the* family is to be "possible." Phillips (1981: 166), for example, observes that throughout the 40-year history of AFDC (Aid to Families with Dependent Children) there have been 6 policy objectives aimed at "trying to get low-income people to conform to conventional structures of financial support patterns.... [These are] preventing family breakup, encouraging single parents to marry, discouraging illegitimate births, discouraging childbearing by women who receive AFDC, encouraging fathers to pay child support, and [most recently] requiring mothers to work.''

State Legislation

Most observers agree that, apart from AFDC and related programs (most of the related programs are now defunct), the United States has had no federal family policy as such (see Monroney, 1979). Nevertheless, there is a shared national family policy if one considers state laws regarding marriage, divorce, sexuality, children, and so forth (Sachs and Wilson, 1978; Weitzman, 1981). By and large, it can be said that most state family law reflects the views of the most conservative segments of the population. Most of the laws were originally formulated during the nineteenth century, when the Victorian and (later) conventional family forms were virtually unchallenged.[5] And when late-nineteenth-century ''challenges'' arose, such as artificial birth control, states responded by passing strict laws prohibiting them (Himes, 1936). Similarly, Halem (1980: 34) points out that civil divorce codes became more restrictive during the late-nineteenth-century ''progressive era,'' precisely when divorce frequency first began to be noticed. Starting in Connecticut and spreading throughout other state legislatures, conservatives succeeded in forcing repeal of more lenient divorce laws, and in imposing instead very rigid and inflexible divorce requirements.

An analogous pattern of movement in state laws from considerable leniency to total rigidity occurred with regard to abortion. During the first half of the nineteenth century abortions were fairly simple to obtain because of vague and ambiguous statutes (Mohr, 1978). Moreover, regular (male) physicians did not have the monopoly on such procedures that they subsequently obtained. Indeed, it was in part to obtain that legal and economic monopoly over obstetrics in general that physicians successfully spearheaded a late-nineteenth-century crusade to pass strict state laws regulating abortion (Mohr, 1978: 160). However, another reason physicians crusaded for these laws was that "most regular physicians were white, native-born, Protestants of British and North European stock...[and] were among the most defensive groups in the country on the subject of changing sex roles" (Mohr, 1978: 166-168). Mohr (1978: 168) cites one of their spokesmen as saying that "I would not transplant [women] from their proper and God-given sphere" to anywhere else. As part of that *sphere*, the "chief purpose of women was to produce children"; abortion "interfered with that purpose," and consequently it could not be tolerated (Mohr, 1978: 169).

Today, no state provides explicit legal recognition of the idea of a male being supported by his wife, of homosexual marriages, or of cohabitation, although some recent state court actions appear to give limited financial rights to cohabiters.[6] Moreover, across states there is some variation in family policy because a few allow "no fault" divorce, and several have appended "equal rights" amendments to their own constitutions. But virtually all the liberalization of state laws occurred prior to the recent emergence of vocal conservatives, that is, the statistical minority cited above. In any case, the thrust of state family laws continues to support the conventional family model.

Contrasting Policy Viewpoints

In a recent survey of family policy in 14 industrialized countries, Kamerman and Kahn (1978: 14) identified 3 prevailing viewpoints toward family and social order. From the conservative viewpoint, "what is occurring is the disintegration of the family. They fear the breakdown in traditional family patterns.... Family policy is viewed as a...strategy for returning to the previous status quo." Kamerman and Kahn's second category is made up of those who "vehemently deny that the family is dying." They offer as an example of the people in this category Bane (1976: 70), who, chiefly on the basis of demographic analyses, states unequivocally, "American families are here to stay." As indicated above, many scholars and activists who identify with this second category placed enormous faith in "Great Society" programs (Abt, 1980). Consequently, many persons in this "moderate" category seldom appear to question the conventional family assumptions that underlie past government policy. Instead, they wish to reexamine "existing [family] policies . . . in order to make these policies more responsive to the needs of different and changing families" (Kamerman and Kahn, 1978:14).

In all fairness to Bane, however, it must be said that in her discussion of "sexual equality and family responsibility," she advocates policies that would inevitably lead to reevaluation of conventional family norms (Bane, 1976: 75ff). Perhaps the most crucial feature connecting conservatives and this second category of "moderates" is their overriding "interest in helping children per se" (Kamerman and Kahn, 1978: 13). Recent publications by Keniston et al. (1977), sponsored by the Carnegie Council on Children, and Aldrich (1976), sponsored by the Advisory Committee on Child Development of the National Academy of Sciences, are illustrative of Parsons's reasoning regarding the links between *the* family and society. That is, moderates tend—at least tacitly—to share Parsons's view of society as an organic whole, which subsumes a subpart called "the family."

While Kamerman and Kahn (1978: 10) found that "all the countries" they surveyed view the family as the central institution for the economic support, nurture, care, and socializing of children," they also unearthed a subtle emerging nuance: "Interest in helping children per se appears to be of less importance in generating family policy exploration" (p. 13). This change is most evident in the third category they identify— the category I call "progressives."" According to Kamerman and Kahn (1978: 14), people in this category are "concerned about problems of [societal] inequality and recognize that inequality has a 'family component.'" This family component is evident in two kinds of inequality: that found in the parent-child relationship (children vary in the amounts of tangible and intangible benefits received from parents); and that found in the husband-wife relationship (current arrangements tend to limit women's occupational and men's expressive options). Many progressives believe that "there is no way to eliminate [inequalities] without in some way affecting the family situation" (Kamerman and Kahn, 1978: 14).

Vedel-Petersen (1978: 318-319) provides specific descriptions of Kamerman and Kahn's three major categories in Denmark. First, he says that "relatively few" and "strongly conservative" persons support the notion that family policy should promote "the traditional family with a working father and a mother who stays home and looks after the children." However, in "broad, moderately conservative circles" the idea is that public policy should "remain neutral" toward all family-related issues. A second major category ("women's liberation extremists and far left wing extremists") promotes public policy that "aim[s] at dissolution of the traditional family." The third category is "the broad center of the Danish political spectrum [who feel that] the family must be helped to make its way in a modern society...by liberat[ing] both parents and let[ting] them both get out to work, [and] by looking after and educating the children during the day."

In their responses to the question "Is family possible?" Americans in these three categories differ significantly. Conservatives say that family is not possible unless the conventional form is revived and renewed. American moderates claim the question is moot—from demographic data they conclude that the family is alive and well, though undergoing some evolutionary modifications. And, they say, practical applications should reflect those realities. Meanwhile, American progressives find themselves torn. This group tends not to include the "extremists" to which Vedel-Petersen refers, nor does it aim at dissolution of the conventional family. American progressives share the pessimism of the conservatives regarding the current state of the twentieth-century family, but they reject as unrealistic the notion that it can be revived

(Shorter, 1975). Simultaneously, they share the optimism of the moderates that over the long term family is likely to be a viable institution. However, they feel that the moderates are naive in failing to grasp the depths and the gravity of the changes that family is experiencing. The differences in these three perspectives are linked with contrasting views of individualism and family order. Present-day conservatives (see Lasch, 1977, 1978; Bronfenbrenner, 1972) are as negative about individualism as critics of a century ago. They are doubtful that present trends toward increased individualism can result in anything other than family disorder. On the other hand, progressives such as Yankelovich (1981b) view enlarged individualism as a sign of vitality, although they are keenly aware of its potential for disruption. In between, the moderates tend not to concern themselves very much with theoretical issues of individualism, order, and so forth. Their focus is more on demographic descriptions; they have little apparent interest, as Feldman (1979) observes, in critiquing the assumptions that underlie family patterns and interactions.[8]

The progressives' pessimism regarding the twentieth-century family and the group's affinity for individualism are the reasons for the change reported by Kamerman and Kahn (1978)—the edging away from children's well-being as the *overiding* focus of practical applications. More specifically, Kamerman and Kahn (1978: 13-14) report that "increased female labor, and the drive for greater equality for women constitute together the most important influences on the growth of interest in family policy everywhere." Most assuredly, progressives are not oblivious to children's well-being; instead, they elevate the spousal relationship to at least the same level of significance, both for purposes of understanding and application. Whereas the conservatives contend that children are best served if spousal roles remain conventional, and moderates merely acknowledge the changes in spousal roles and look for ways to adapt to them in order to serve children, progressives take an additional step and contend that fostering certain changes in spousal roles is actually the best means available to assure children's interests.

Feminist Perspectives

The fact that analysts taking the progressive position often write from a feminist perspective (see Safilios-Rothschild, 1974) should in no way suggest a necessary and inevitable equation of feminism with what I call "progressivism." There is considerable overlap, to be sure, but those whom Jaggar and Struhl (1978) label "radical" or "Marxist" feminists may not find themselves comfortable with such an equation, and neither Eisenstein (1981) nor Sokoloff (1980) would find it agreeable. On the other side, some progressives may feel that while their concerns embrace feminist goals of autonomy for women (and men), they hold wider goals as well. Some progressives believe that while feminists (of both genders) have eloquently and forcefully argued for greater individualism, they have not sufficiently addressed the other half of the problem of order— the well-being of family as an institution and the well-being of society itself. Consequently, feminists have not generally been able to respond adequately to thoughtful critiques of individualism by observers such as Lasch (1977) and others. While the conservatives have emphasized the *responsibilities* of women and men to family and society, many feminists have emphasized *rights*—especially those of women. However, it may be that not enough has been said about a *balance* of rights and responsibilities in the context of social order.

Bernard (1972: 309ff) addresses this matter by asking such questions as "Are there intrinsic limits to the forms of marriage in the nature of society (and of culture) itself?" In a subsequent work, Bernard (1974: 360ff) quotes Erikson in calling for "a new balance of Male and Female, of Paternal and Maternal." Her argument is that as both sexes adopt both instrumental and expressive characteristics and behaviors, they will be better off and so will families and societies. Elaborating, she says that, "the outside world...is no longer the same world as that of early industrialism; the individualism is no longer permitted to be so rugged.... Technology...had the gentling effect" (Bernard, 1974: 361-362). Her conclusion is that as both genders adopt androgynous personalities, a more suitable "fit" will emerge between families and society. Giele (1978) makes a similar argument in asserting that the work place is becoming more humanized while the family is becoming more "rationalized." Hence, she asserts, men and women alike need to cultivate androgynous personalities in order to function optimally in both spheres. In essence, the conclusion at which Bernard, Giele, and other feminists arrive is that as persons are allowed untrammeled pursuit of the full range of their human potential, societies will be the better for it. By this means, individualism makes its contribution to the common good (Giele, 1978: 32).

A Conservative Image of Society and Family

Why doesn't the sort of reasoning discussed above speak to critiques of contemporary family made by thoughtful conservatives? Because conservatives hold a very different view of society and family than do nonconservatives. The conservative view is that of society as an organic whole, as discussed above. What is more, conservatives perceive that whole to be in serious trouble. Lasch (1977) eloquently expresses their fears by describing society as "heartless" and, more important, as undergoing a breakdown of *moral norms* and the authority they convey. And not only is American society gripped with narcissism (see Lasch, 1978) but "relations within the family have come to resemble relations in the rest of society" (Lasch, 1977: 174). And what are these relations like? "Authority deserves to be regarded as valid only insofar as it conforms to reason.... Most rules exist only to be broken." The result, according to Lasch, is that "the administration of justice gives way [both in society and family] to a complicated process of negotiation.... In learning to live by the law, therefore, the child actually learns how to get around the law, in the first place by getting around his parents."

Lasch's image of society is the very one against which Parsons warned so strongly: the substitution of individualistic bargaining for moral norms. The deep-seated fear is that in this sort of milieu it is every man or woman for him- or herself, and the "devil take the hindmost." Thus it should come as no surprise that when feminists argue for profound and far-reaching changes in both society and family, the reactions often range from dismay, uncertainty, and confusion to anger and open hostility. The torpedoing of the Equal Rights Amendment is powerful evidence that feminists and others interested in family change have not spoken effectively to the issue of group solidarity—the issue of the well-being of family and society. They have not convinced the "unaligned" majority of citizens that "family is possible" at the same time that women's (and men's) autonomy is enhanced. Instead, the anxiety of many persons seems to be that "the dissolution of authority [based on traditional family norms] brings not freedom but new forms of domination" (Lasch, 1977: 184).

This anxiety helps define for us what contemporary conservatives fear most when they anticipate *the* family's future. Moreover, it is this anxiety that feminists such as Giele fail to address when they forecast continued societal evolution away from traditional gender patterns. While nineteenth-century conservatives may never have traced through to its conclusion the logic of the assertion that "if you destroy the family, you destroy society," modern conservatives believe that they have a clearer conception of what that means. In their view, twentieth-century totalitarian regimes (especially of the left) have closely involved family in their efforts to control society. Thus when they allege that *the* family is disintegrating, conservatives do not necessarily perceive that functions now performed by family (reproduction, socialization, expressiveness, consumption, and status placement) would forever go unperformed, or that chaos and total anomie would predominate indefinitely. Instead what they fear is that as conventional norms continue to lose their moral force, a strong central government will eventually step in and impose its will on family through regulation, manipulation, or even "outright violence" (Lasch, 1977: 184).

Control of Child Socialization

While Lasch analyzes this profound conservative fear in terms that suggest a sophisticated Orwellian *1984* approach, spokespersons for the so-called New Right are far less subtle. Pointing to the alleged menace of worldwide "communism and socialism," they perceive that these "godless and atheistic" forces have already begun to influence government policy regarding family. The crux of the issue is control of child socialization (see Chapter 4). Many citizens, including those who are not part of the New Right, are concerned about their seeming inability to socialize their own children in "proper fashion." New Right parents go beyond that feeling and contend that their children are already being exposed to "mind control" and that this "insidious manipulation" can only grow. An example of this subversion is found, they say, within public school biology curricula. Most texts and teachers describe Darwinian and "big bang" notions as possible explanations of physical reality. But around the country, groups of parents (from the "moral minority") are organizing to bring pressure to bear on school boards, legislatures, and the courts to force schools to teach fundamentalist creationism alongside evolution. Unless that is done, say the parents, their religious values and those of their children are being undermined.

Similar arguments regarding the subversion of religion and morals are used by this same minority to prevent schools from introducing comprehensive programs dealing candidly with sexuality and gender roles, to say nothing of extensive contraceptive delivery systems. In short, some persons perceive not only an erosion of religious, moral, and "traditional family" values, but also their simultaneous replacement by "secular humanist" values,[9] aided, allegedly, by the schools and the federal government. The drift away from the conventional family is creating a vacuum that, in the view of even thoughtful observers such as Lasch, is being filled by government—government intent on maintaining itself and its image of social order. Thus conservatives fear that the only family that will eventually be "possible" is one designed by federal government bureaucrats and planners.

Needless to say, the people who were involved in shaping Great Society "family programs" have been quite startled to discover that they were part of a sinister conspiracy to reshape family in some Orwellian fashion. Instead, they would affirm Kamerman and Kahn's (1978: 10) cross-national findings that policy planners tend not to have any family "master plan" in mind and that "there is no evidence of a universally accepted theory of family policy" (p. 483). While this is undoubtedly true, we have learned that one concrete aim of policy planners is to assist poor families to escape poverty and achieve conventional family status. Furthermore, if there is anything like a philosophy that subsumes the views of most American family policy planners on nonpoverty issues, it is caught by Bane's (1976: 141) observation that "the most workable approach to sexual equality is probably to enforce the political and economic rights of women, and to rely on families to work through the power shifts and changing division of labor that political and economic equality imply." (By way of contrast, European nations tend to make gender equality itself a much more central feature of their social policies; see Steiner, 1981: 179.) Interestingly enough, the most strongly supported recommendations of the 1980 White House Conference on Families (flextime, job sharing, and so on) reinforce Bane's seemingly modest philosophy (see Tucker, 1980).

Conservatives, on the other hand, do not consider government enforcement of gender equality "modest," and, since they also reject Monroney's (1979: 463) view that "no one family type is superior to another or should be favored over others," they see increasing rates of divorce, illegitimacy, nonmarital sexual activity, abortion, cohabitation, and so on in a particular light. They perceive these phenomena as reflective of a growing societal drift away from conventional family values and patterns. And, as the drift continues, they perceive government planners to be intervening in ways detrimental to conventional values. Conservatives' conception of this intervention is illustrated by two of Ibsen's (1970b) characters: One says, "Isn't it a citizen's duty to inform the public if he comes on a new idea?" The other responds, "Oh, the public doesn't need new ideas. The public is best served by the good, old, time-tested ideas it's always had."

One example of the differing perceptions of conservatives and government planners can be found in their approaches to the problem of illegitimate births: Most planners advocate more comprehensive contraceptive and abortion programs to curb this problem; conservatives advocate sexual abstinence as a solution (Baldwin, 1977). This divergence of opinion returns us to the problem-of-order question and the question of one's image of society. Conservatives believe that family and societal order are achieved through a reaffirmation of conventional family norms. They perceive grave threats from the individualism expressed by persons who implicitly drift away from those patterns, as well as from activists, such as Bane or Giele, who explicitly express preferences for change. Since in the conservative view society and family constitute one organic whole, any change in the nature of that whole is by definition a threat. Giele (1978) and other feminists counter by proposing an evolutionary model of change, so that the whole gradually develops into something else. But many conservatives reject *any* development away from the conventional model because of their view that it is a *given*. While some conservatives may not attach metaphysical connotations to the model, they are convinced that change away from it represents decline of one sort or another.

A Prevailing Paradox

The mid-1980s reveal a curious paradox. At the formal level, laws and "official" pronouncements (those of governments, churches, schools, and the like) reflect the conventional model. Moreover, conservatives have demonstrated substantial political power in crippling sex education programs, halting ERA, influencing the 1980 White House Conference on

Families, electing persons who share their views on abortion, and so forth. At the behavior level, however, there is increasing evidence (Connecticut Mutual, 1981; Masnick and Bane, 1980) that ordinary citizens are tending to ignore the conventional model. Yet, in spite of this paradox, progressives have failed to articulate a coherent alternative perspective, or philosophy of family, that speaks to the problem of order and that would appeal to that 75 percent of the population not aligned with conservatives. Such a philosophy could serve as a basis for changes in state laws, and perhaps eventually could serve as a basis for formulating national family policy. Initially, it would primarily be a means to weld together those majority segments of the population in terms of a philosophy that "makes sense" to them (that is, meets their individual interests, yet simultaneously achieves the common good) as they enter the twenty-first century. During the early nineteenth century, Alexis de Tocqueville *(Democracy in America)* "observed that cultural behavior and unspoken beliefs typically change long before people openly concede to each other that times have changed. Lip service is given for years—generations—to ideas long since privately abandoned. No one conspires against...these beliefs, Tocqueville said, so they continue to have power and discourage innovators" (Ferguson, 1980: 34).

There are numerous reasons (which I will discuss more fully in later chapters) that progressives have not yet articulated a coherent and appealing alternative to the conventional model. One obvious reason that deserves mention here is lack of agreement among progressives themselves. Those progressives (often feminists) who, for instance, assume an interest group (rather than an organic) model of society are criticized by their peers on the grounds that such an image is not particularly reassuring to the unaligned majority. Take Giele (1978: 4-5), for example, who characterizes the interest group image as "not...particularly helpful," and instead offers an evolutionary (organic) model of change derived from 1960s functionalism.

In short, many progressives tend to be fearful of approaching contemporary changes in family from an interest group perspective. The very term "interest group" has all sorts of unfortunate connotations—especially in conjunction with an institution supposedly devoted to furthering intimacy. In addition, many progressives wish to disassociate themselves from what they consider to be the ideological excesses of certain "radical feminists" and "Marxist feminists." Meanwhile, although many progressives might prefer the kinds of gradual evolutionary changes envisioned by Giele, conservatives have capitalized on progressives' temerity and "thrown down the gauntlet" by resisting all "gradualism" away from the conventional model. It is the conservatives who have made the question of family one of competition between *their* conventional family and all other varieties of families.[10] At the same time, conservatives possess an enormous advantage because their long-standing philosophy of family pervades most segments of society, so that, even for those unwilling or unable to conform to the conventional model of family, it is extraordinarily difficult to articulate an alternative viewpoint. And it is more taxing still to transmit an alternative to one's children.

However, the fact of family change seems inexorable—63 percent of persons surveyed said they preferred the "equal marriage of shared responsibility" described earlier, and 71 percent rejected the traditional or conventional form of marriage (see Connecticut Mutual, 1981: 132).[11] Thus the majority of citizens seem to prefer something other than the twentieth-century model, but the full implications of those preferences are not totally clear, even to them. The upshot is that in spite of changes in expressed preferences as well as in certain behaviors, conventional family philosophy lingers on, dominating both professional (applied and basic research, and clinical work) and public discourse. The twentieth-century family is the one existing coherent model against which all emerging behaviors and norms are evaluated; it is the touchstone of "appropriate" family patterns. It is my argument that the twenty-first century requires a new touchstone—a model of family that is both theoretically and philosophically sound, one that accounts for ongoing demographic trends, yet is also practical and workable.

There seems, in brief, no alternative but to make explicit a family philosophy that integrates changing preferences and behaviors into a coherent framework that would operate in much the same way the conventional framework has operated, and would perhaps eventually supplant it. A chief purpose of that framework would be to help people to make behavioral choices regarding family, sex, and marriage as "intelligently" as possible. No one believes that all aspects of all current family-related changes are necessarily beneficial, either to individuals or society. Certain current behaviors may need to be modified, but persuasion for that is likely to come more readily from a new Socratic rather than an old (Parsonian) perspective on family. It can be seen readily that "making intelligent behavioral choices" is simply another way of stating Socrates' conception regarding the resolution of the problem of order. The assumption is that individuals would be better off, both psychologically and socially, behaving self-consciously in terms of a fresh explicitly stated family philosophy than they are under the current situation of ambivalence and uncertainty which is often exacerbated by guilt, apprehension, and anxiety. Concomitantly, both family and society should profit accordingly. But in order to bring about this individual and social "profit," progressives must possess a coherent alternative perspective on family; and, what is more, they must be willing to propogate it by entering the "competition" the conservatives have established. Progressives can no longer afford to remain on the defensive and allow conservatives to claim the "high moral ground" as they aggressively promote *their* family.

Summary

The issues involved in exploring family and the problem of order are numerous, varied, complex, and highly interrelated. Of pivotal concern is the trend toward individualism. How much individualism is possible before the twentieth-century family and societal well-being are threatened? And, in reaction to potential disorder, what would be the consequences of imposing authoritarian solutions from either the left or the right? A more concrete, underlying issue in this debate is that of children. For a hundred years conservatives have argued that the adult pursuit of individualistic goals (divorce in particular) is harmful to children. In turn, *the* family is harmed, and ultimately the entire society. Federal public policy, though not necessarily designed or managed by conservatives, has reflected this preoccupation with children's interests (especially those of poor children). The most sophisticated analysis of precisely why child socialization is so critical to the well-being of society conceived as an organic whole has been presented by Parsons (1965). A sense of solidarity in *the* family, he contends, is a necessary prerequisite to the development of solidarity throughout the remainder of society — its numerous organizations and institutions. Representing the conservative perspective, he asserts that solidarity in family and society is achieved through *conformity* to particular moral norms.

Latter-day conservatives perceive a falling away from those conventional family norms; they urge a return to the conventional family lest the resulting disorder produce government-imposed authoritarian family patterns. In response, some scholars and activists contend that *the* family is not disintegrating, it is merely changing. Using demographic trend data to support their claim, they espouse government policies to assist disadvantaged families in coping with changes. These advocates strongly resist the conservatives' assertion that their proposals smack of "secular socialism" or in any way subvert conventional family norms. Closely allied with, but moving a significant step beyond these analysts are feminists, who explicitly argue that we are already moving away from conventional family patterns and suggest additional ways to facilitate that process. It is this position, probably more than any other, that has generated considerable opposition from conservatives, who fear contamination of their children, their family form, and society.

The majority of citizens are not at all clear as to which of these viewpoints, if any, is the "right" one. They are aware that family is changing—that people are not behaving in quite the same ways they once did with regard to divorce, cohabitation, work, sex, marriage, children, and so forth. Because these people share a concern that their children be socialized in ways that will benefit both the children and the larger society, they are, in effect, raising the problem of order at a very pragmatic level. While their own parents and grand-parents never questioned the twentieth-century family philosophy—a philosophy that spoke to the problem of order and was shared by most citizens, and that was written into public policy in the form of state laws—many Americans are questioning it now. At this time there is no coherent "guiding philosophy" of family that seriously rivals the one underlying the conventional model. As we enter the twenty-first century, such a philosophy—addressing itself in the Socratic fashion to the ancient problem of balancing the good of the whole and the good of its parts—becomes requisite.

NOTES

1. As Merton (1949: 38-47) argued during functionalism's heyday, it is a theoretical approach and not a sociopolitical philosophy that can be characterized as "conservative" or "liberal." And while a distinction must be made between types of conservatives, critics then and now have observed a clear overlap between functionalism's theoretical notions and maintenance of the sociopolitical status quo.

2. In another place (Scanzoni, 1982), I have characterized the pre-nineteenth-century marital situation as an *owner-property* arrangement; many nineteenth- and twentieth-century marriages can be labeled as *head-complement,* while marriages in which wives are employed outside the home can be labeled as *senior partner-junior partner* (SP-JP) arrangements. An additional marriage type can be labeled *equal partner-equal partner*; the bases of this type of marriage are discussed in Chapters 6 and 7.

3. The authors reported that the following eight items constitute a Guttman-type scale of religious commitment: "feeling that God loves you, engaging in prayer, attending religious services, reading the Bible, having something you call a religious experience, participating in a church social activity, encouraging others to turn to religion, listening to religious broadcasts" (Connecticut Mutual, 1981: 291).

4. Besides the differences drawn in the text, there is the obvious one of a metaphysical versus a secular foundation for their viewpoints.

5. Exceptions included "utopian experiments" such as the Oneida Community.

6. For a discussion, see Scanzoni and Scanzoni (1981: 222ff).

7. This is a term coined by O'Neill (1967) and also used by Novak (1977).

8. For a recent exception to that pattern, see Masnick and Bane (1980).

9. See Krauthammer (1981).

10. As I show in Chapter 6, they did so in response to perceived organized threats on the part of progressives.

11. The difference in these figures can be accounted for by 8 percent of the respondents, who said that they prefer either to "remain single" or "to live with someone and not marry."

4

THE OUT-OF-PHASE
CONVENTIONAL FAMILY

"Several points of view have at times seemed promising [for our understanding of] the family...but have gradually disappeared. The structural-functional [approach] was a major school of thought in the 1940s and 1950s, but was generally abandoned in the 1960s and 1970s" (Holman and Burr, 1980: 733). So goes a ˙scholarly assessment of Parsons's functional attempts to explain the family and its impact on social order and, accordingly, to fashion practical applications for its well-being. But simply because researchers no longer rely on Parsons's ideas to understand family by no means implies that all of them necessarily doubt the tenacity of what I am calling the twentieth-century conventional family. And it most certainly does not indicate that most citizens have necessarily given up on it either.

In a recent classroom discussion of these matters, one student reported that she wished to emulate her mother—a traditional housewife who "drives her husband to the train station each morning in her station wagon, then goes off to her tennis club, and also chauffeurs the children to their various activities during the afternoon." A second student, however, responded that he thought that "if younger people want to do things differently, there will be some changes in marriage."

A third student reflected the dilemma sensed by many college students (see Bardwick, 1978; Sexton, 1979) and most adults:

"I think most of us have our feet planted on both sides." She was specifically referring to a series of questions used to measure persons' gender-role preferences.[1] In this series of questions, each item is bisected by the response, "mixed feelings." Responses that fall to one side of "mixed feelings" reflect conventional preferences; those that fall to the other side indicate nontraditional preferences. This student was commenting on the fact that many of her peers responded to the questions in ways that were seemingly inconsistent—in both conventional and nontraditional ways. More generally, her metaphor graphically conveys the ambivalent situation in which many Americans find themselves when they ponder contemporary family patterns and trends. Whether one is reflecting on behavioral experiences (one's own or those of others) or being philosophical, the sense seems to be that while there may be much "good" (benefits, rewards) to be had by retaining the best parts of the old, there may also be something to be said for the promises of the new. As the classroom discussion continued, yet another student concluded that "what our parents had was security, but we don't have that any more."

This perceived lack of "security" is linked to the "drift" and "paradox" described in Chapter 3. As mature persons "drift" from conventional family norms, younger onlookers may gradually develop the notion that the norms themselves are basically "out of phase" or "out of sync" with the realities of modern society; hence, the sense of insecurity. In this chapter I want to consider, first, parent-child relationships and, second, adult relationships, in order to identify some of the specific characteristics of this apparent lack of synchronization between the conventional family and contemporary society.

Parent-Child Relationships

The "out of phaseness" of the twentieth-century family has been discussed most fully in connection with the husband-wife relationship. Feminist and other literatures have argued strongly that since the patterns for this relationship are inherently unjust, both individual fulfillment and ultimately the public good have suffered (Safillios-Rothschild, 1974). But, as noted above (in Chapter 3), the conservative reply to this argument has been that those particular pleas for change are self-serving, with little actual consideration for the common good. Perhaps the most common charge conservatives use to make their point is that advocates of change focus on adult relationships to the *exclusion* of parent-child relationships. The common good, they say, is benefited most when the younger generation is "properly outfitted" to become the society of tomorrow. The rampant individualism they perceive in the behaviors of adult family members is seen as negative for children because children's interests are not being taken into account. Farber et al. (1965: viii) express a conviction held by many citizens: "The most important function of the traditional family [is] the nurture of the young." If this is so, how does the "out of phaseness" of the conventional family hinder the performance of that function?

Socialization within the conventional family tends to be thought of in *morphostatic* terms. I shall us this word frequently, because it conveys a sense of sameness and resistance to incursions and change—even in the face of fresh new inputs (Buckley, 1967: 58). That which is morphostatic has the tendency to maintain a "steady state" or equilibrium against all efforts to "disturb" it. For example, although there are social-class variations in many kinds of norms and behaviors that parents pass on to children, and although there is increasing realization that offspring can and do influence parents (Lerner and Spanier, 1978), Yankelovich (1981c) concludes that a great deal of explicit socialization for occupation, sexuality, dating, marriage, parenthood, and so on remains "script oriented." Although the scripts are based on the norms and roles that make up the twentieth-century family, the irony is that as parents transmit them, they often appear to hold little confidence that their children will be willing, able, or motivated to carry them out (Rapoport et al., 1977). Thus if there is anything like a sense of adult uncertainty regarding child rearing, it stems from parental inability to convince children that (1) the conventional scripts are the most desirable and (2) that the parents are unambivalent about and behaviorally committed to those scripts. It also stems from an underlying awareness on the part of many parents—an awareness that is often not verbalized, but may be—that the scripts may actually be out of step with the emerging realities of modern society.

Yankelovich (1981c: 6) argues that "many...parents are increasingly uncomfortable with the sweeping permissiveness that their own pursuit of permissiveness has created for young people." He says that his national data show that "even the most untraditional parents...raise their children according to traditional moral precepts." He sees "them as hedging their bets. Uncertain and confused about the full import of their own values, they fall back upon simpler, less individualistic, less *ad hoc* principles." In short, among the unaligned majority of ordinary citizens, there is a keen sense that children represent their area of greatest risk. One can "gamble" or "experiment" or "explore" with one's own life, but how "proper" is it to experiment with a child's life? Consequently, adults tend to opt for the "sure thing," namely, the traditional scripts. And they make this choice because they have not yet found viable (individually fulfilling and socially responsible) alternatives to those scripts.

In the face of these realities and the sense of inadequacy they generate, many parents, according to Berger and Callahan (1979: 5), become immobilized and yield their initiative to what has come to be known as the "professionalization of parenthood." Underlying this concept is the idea that social workers, psychiatrists, educators, and the like have established standardized criteria identifying the "good" or "effective" family. As Berger and Callahan describe it, parents not achieving these criteria are labeled as "less than successful"; however, they then proceed to show how professionals differ among themselves as to the appropriate criteria for child-rearing "success." According to Berger and Callahan (1979) conflicting opinions among professionals have led the middle-class family to "abdicate...its child-caring role in favor of the child-care industry." And the effects of the "professionalization of parenthood...on the non-middle-class segments of the population" have been "devastating" (Berger and Callahan, 1979: 6). The ultimate point made by these authors is that in view of burgeoning research findings regarding parent-child interaction, it is extremely risky to establish criteria purporting to assess "effective parenting." Today's success criteria may be obsolete by tomorrow. Furthermore, the notion of establishing standarized, concrete criteria for effective parenting reflects the penchant for morphostasis noted above. Inherent within our understanding of twentieth-century (and earlier) families is the idea of predictable structure. Whether in the area of gender roles, occupational behaviors, sexual patterns, or whatever, many parents believe that they are "good" and "successful" parents if they can convey particular information and values to their offspring and then witness their conformity.

Morphostasis is central to the conservative view of child training, and certainly to Parsons's analysis of socialization. The "good society," Parsons says, is a stable, organic whole. Such a society is characterized by conformity to "dominant values" based on a shared consensus that those values and norms are "morally right." Individuals conform to the norms out of a sense of belonging to a common whole and out of a sense of trust that others are doing the same. This model of consensus, belonging, and trust, along with strict conformity to fixed values and norms, is learned initially in the family and then, according to Parsons, transferred into the larger society.

Yet as wholesome, desirable, and worthy as this image may be, the reality is that society is not organized around moral consensus but, instead, around competing interests and efforts at negotiating a participatory democracy (Collins, 1975). Consequently, it is characterized by often unexpected and rapid changes. Nevertheless, in spite of the likelihood that training children to fit a consensus model does them no apparent service, socialization within the twentieth-century family is often based on consensus assumptions. *By definition, therefore, this mode of socialization would appear to be out of phase with the essence of modern societies.*

For many years, some sociologists in the Parsonian tradition identified adolescent peer groups as subverting parental socialization because they exposed children to "deviant" norms. But, viewed from a less morphostatic perspective, peer groups may have the positive "function" of bridging the out of phaseness of formal parental socialization with the realities of modern societies. Furthermore, recent research (Troll and Bengston, 1979) suggests that the "generation gap" between parents and children may be somewhat exaggerated, giving further indication that many parents may be unable and/or unwilling to press very strongly for conformity to conventional values and norms. That is, to the degree parents become aware that the out of phaseness of the scripts they are "supposed" to transmit makes their task exceedingly difficult, they may place correspondingly less priority on the conventional scripts and be more flexible regarding their children's beliefs and behaviors. In this manner, potential "gaps" are avoided. Additionally, argue Troll and Bengston (1979), some parents may actually become *re*socialized over time through their children's norms and behaviors. That is, for some parents the ambivalence Yankelovich (1981c) identifies may become resolved as they witness the newer patterns "working reasonably well" in their children's lives.

Tension between the conventional and the emerging is probably nowhere more salient than in the area of gender roles and in the related area of sexuality (Pogrebin, 1980: 247-273; Brown, 1981). Depending on their educational level, marital status, employment status, and religion, parents vary in the extent to which they seek to obtain conformity to traditional gender roles from their children (Scanzoni and Fox, 1980). White, working-class fathers may be most insistent that their boys and girls behave in the "proper" gender-typed fashion. If fundamentalist religion is added to the equation then the insistence takes on an additionally grave dimension—the divine will. In contrast, upper-middle-class mothers and fathers (blacks perhaps more so than whites) are more willing to tolerate or, on occasion, even encourage their children to behave in other than stereotypical modes. Parents wishing to obtain adolescent conformity in *both* gender roles and sexuality face the most serious contradictions. Available studies (Scanzoni and Fox, 1980) suggest that adolescents are much more willing to experiment sexually than they are to experiment with modern gender roles. And, in spite of the media blitz inundating young persons with the pleasures of sex, virtually nothing is communicated regarding contraceptive responsibilities (Byrne, 1979). Proposed efforts to increase communication in this area, such as television advertising for condoms (to say nothing of realistic sex dialogues in the schools), are forbidden, largely due to pressures from conservatives (Scales, 1982).

The evidence suggests that most parents communicate almost nothing of substance to their children regarding sexuality except notions that it is somehow "wrong to do it" before marriage (Baldwin, 1977; Fox, 1979). Nonetheless, the evidence also shows that adolescent sexual activity is steadily increasing at all social class levels and among whites faster than among blacks (Zelnick et al., 1981). Interestingly, the less gender-role traditional *adolescent* women are, the less likely they are to be sexually active (Fox, 1979). Thus parents who are indifferent to or who encourage gender-role changes in their adolescent daughters are, paradoxically, more likely to see them conform to conventional sexual behavior. By sacrificing one aspect of traditional scripts—gender roles—they maintain another. In contrast, parents who insist on both aspects (traditional gender roles and traditional sexuality) run the risk of sacrificing the one aspect (sexual abstinence) that, if they had to choose, they would probably consider more significant.

In short, it appears unworkable to try to maintain both aspects of traditionalism simultaneously. Conventional family scripts are simply too out of phase with the prevailing sexual climate to permit it. As Pogrebin (1980: 270-271) puts it, "The best sex education you can offer your children...is anti [traditional] sex role education." However, this is not to imply that parents who are willing for their children to manifest gender-role changes (to say nothing of that smaller minority of parents willing to accept changes in gender roles *and* sexuality) necessarily find themselves in total synchrony with their milieu. In most cases, communities, friends, religious groups, kin and so on are not likely to be strongly supportive of overt changes in traditional gender-role (and sexuality) scripts. Thus, for example, in training their children to be gender-role "modern,"[2] parents run the risk that their children may have relatively few peers who share their innovative preferences. Consequently, these parents might have to live with the discomfort induced by contributing to that most abhorrent (to many American parents) of all outcomes—the "socially maladjusted child." In order to avoid this outcome, even progressive parents seem more willing merely to *accept* peer-induced gender-role modernity in their children than they are to try to actively *generate* it themselves, although they certainly do not encourage traditionalism. The upshot is that even though some parents may sense that traditional scripts are not in the best *long-range* (occupational, marital) interests of their children, they hesitate to question the scripts explicitly so as not to sacrifice their children's apparent *short-range* (peer-acceptance) interests. This potential sacrifice of children's long-term interests may be construed as yet another indication of the out of phaseness of twentieth-century traditional family patterns with the realities of modern life. Furthermore, if long-term interests actually are harmed, aren't these patterns subverting the well-being of both individuals and society?

As indicated above, the fundamental contradiction between traditional socialization patterns and the exigencies of modern societies is that those patterns are morphostatic—a term conveying the notion of a more or less permanent arrangement or structure. Some have compared it to "Newtonian physics," in which it was thought that the universe could be understood as fixed and orderly patterns. In a very real sense, Parsons's views of society and of family are a type of Newtonian physics. Similarly, in the minds of many parents the task of socialization is essentially a Newtonian one—it is an attempt to shape children to "fit" and actually become part of a steady-state pattern, even though some parents perceive that the state is no longer as steady as they might like. As Degler (1980: 471-472) concludes his history of women and family since the American Revolution he identifies the contradiction in these terms:

> The central values of the modern [conventional] family stand in opposition to those that underlie women's emancipation.... Where the women's movement has called for...individualism, the family has insisted upon subordination of individual interests to those of the group.... The...values for which the family stands are at odds...with those of today's world. Democracy, individualism, and meritocracy...are conspicuous by their absence from the family.... The family...is an anti-individualistic institution.

Whereas Stone (1977) sees contemporary family as strongly permeated by individualism, Degler (1980) views it as still gripped by familism.[3] However, the reality is that there is not one organic entity called "*the* family," as Degler and many citizens seem to believe. Instead, the familism Degler describes is indeed intrinsic to the conservatives' own family model. Conversely, the democracy, individualism, and meritocracy he and Stone identify are clearly more compatible with the contrasting progressive vision of family. In short, Degler badly misconstrues the situation by failing to take account of the interest group perspective in explaining competing images of family.

While many parents may be unable to conceptualize the dialectic in terms of competing images of family, it nonetheless affects their socialization efforts, in the ways described above as well as in numerous other ways cited in later chapters.[4] On the one hand, there is enormous social pressure and support for parents to shape their children according to conventional patterns. On the other hand, some parents are becoming increasingly and often painfully aware that those patterns are out of synchrony with a fast-paced modern society. Even when they are "successful" in eliciting the desired behavioral conformity from their adolescents, parents know that when offspring leave home they often tend to follow less conventional patterns of sexuality, living arrangements, marriage, divorce, children, occupational behaviors, and so forth. Throughout the past hundred years or so of gradual shifts in these kinds of patterns, many parents may have reasoned that although their efforts to achieve *permanent* child conformity to conventional behaviors were somewhat unrealistic, they were determined to strive for it anyway, because the behaviors were "risk free' and "right," in the Parsonian sense of "moral obligation." Today, however, increasing numbers of parents seem to be taking a more pragmatic view of their socialization tasks and questioning how it is possible to *best* prepare children for the realities of the twenty-first century. To the degree such questioning occurs, it makes the fundamental contradiction between the conventional family and modern society more vivid, because alongside the questioning comes realization that there are no longer any clear and certain answers. Becoming apparent are the sorts of conclusions drawn by Rapoport et al. (1977: 348, 361, 364) from their exhaustive cross-national review of the parenting literature:

> The different [disciplines] all operated according to a model of "conventional" family life [which is] at variance with new developments in the experiential world of parents as people. We are at what seems to us to be a pivotal point in history, in

which new models of family life itself and the relationship between family and society are required.... A new formulation is required about the nature of men and women and of the family.... The new formulation should be a dynamic [in contrast to a morphostatic]...one.... The reality of contemporary life points to the impression that many ordinary families are in trouble...because they have inherited conceptions of family life that are inadequate to cope with the requirements of modern living.... A central issue confronting [parents] is how to function in a society such as ours, with its conflicting and rapidly changing directives.

Adult Relationships

Recall Kamerman and Kahn's (1978: 13) observation that while much previous thinking about family social policy has focused on children, they now detect a subtle shift in the direction of giving comparable emphasis to husband-wife interaction. Rapoport et al. (1977: 364) stress this point as well, but also add that policies are required "that will take into account the predicament of ordinary families, not just deprived or pathological ones." In short, atheoretical policies aimed primarily at the needs of children (poor or nonpoor) do not, in the long run, serve them or the larger society in optimal fashion. Comprehensive theory and policy are required that, *at the least,* give "equal time" to adults. Indeed, if one elaborates the assumption underlying that conclusion—that adult and spousal relationships are foundational to parenting relationships—one might even go so far as to assert the primacy of adult patterns. But I shall not do that; I concur with Rapoport et al. that families, society, and individuals are best served by a systematic integration of adult and child interests.

Just as we saw that "out of phaseness" tends to characterize parent-child relationships in the twentieth-century family model, we find that it characterizes adult relationships as well—at least to the degree those relationships are founded on efforts to conform to norms that tend not to be in synchrony with modern societies. However, in contrast to socialization patterns with children, for adults the problem is not how to transmit these norms to others, but how to fulfill them for oneself. Hence, whether it has become more difficult to be a parent or a spouse is hard to say. According to Swidler (1980) and Lerner and Spanier (1978), the contradiction between the morphostatic and the dynamic may be sharper and more severe in the realm of husband-wife relations than in that of parent-child relations. At least in the latter there has always existed some sense of change; the child development school has always studied the progression from infancy into the scripts of adulthood. However, until recently, prevailing wisdom had it that once they were locked safely into the scripts, adults required little investigation except when undergoing biologically based changes connected with birth, menopause, and death. Now this static notion is gradually being turned on its head: Adulthood is coming to be viewed as "a time in which change is continuous, interspersed with occasional quiescent interludes" (Pearlin, 1980: 174).

EXPRESSIVE ISSUES

According to Swidler (1980: 125), love plays a "central symbolic role [for adults] in integrating the issues of individual identity, moral choice, and social commitment." Arguing that a society's view of love is related to its conception of the problem of order, Swidler (1980: 125) observes that characterizations of love supply important clues regarding the "nexus of individual identity with social commitment": "Individual rebellion and social commitment [both exist] in bourgeois romantic love...[and] embody the tension between individual and social demands." On the one hand, for instance, "the individual must be able to convince himself that the next step is up to him and...he always has the choice of leaving or turning in the opposite direction"; on the other hand, the reality, as Swidler (1980: 126) sees it, is captured by phrases such as

" 'trapped' into marriage; work is a loss of freedom, a shameful 'settling down.' "

According to Swidler (1980: 126-127), "In the current period...love...is undergoing a change.... The balance of elements...is shifting...[toward] the rebellious, free, individualistic side of...love." Furthermore, this shift corresponds with the sorts of changing definitions of adulthood described by Pearlin (1980), that is, continual flux.

"Choice versus commitment" is the *first* of the four dimensions along which, according to Swidler, love (or intimacy) is being significantly reevaluated. The traditional idea of love as commitment (fixed, unswerving loyalty—"my partner right or wrong, no matter what the costs") clashes head on with "the demand for continuing growth and change in adulthood.... True love is not a love to which one is committed, so much as a love in which one can have complete communication.... The value of love, and its challenge, is that it must stimulate and absorb perpetual change.... The ideal of permanence [for its own sake] is undermined. What is good about a relationship is not the commitment...but how much a person learns about himself" (Swidler, 1980: 128-129).[5]

The ascendence of continuing evaluations and choices above a once-and-for-all commitment (based on permanence for its own sake) is quite foreign to the conventional model of marriage described in Chapter 3. The whole basis of the Parsonian view of family is that there are fixed norms to which one is morally obliged to conform for the sake of family and society. Prime among these norms is the notion that permanence is *inherently superior* to impermanence. And although this notion has been critiqued by no less than John Milton (1963), and in recent years by Farber (1964) and McCall (1966), it maintains a strong hold in traditional thought (Halem, 1980). Even among the "unaligned majority" of citizens who are already behaving contrary to that perspective, there appears to be considerable ambiguity as to whether "permanence for its own sake," or "continuity with stimulation" is a more desirable norm to hold and propagate (Connecticut Mutual, 1981). In any case, exploring unknown and uncharted individual interests was inconceivable to the Parsonian mind-set, and that is why Parsons (1965), along with other traditionalists, held that a "a love that ended was a failure, a sign of some terrible mistake" (Swidler, 1980: 129). But if the emerging view is that exploration supersedes permanence for its own sake, then love's termination is not seen as failure at all, but as a lesson in growth and development, even though it may be exceedingly painful.

In passing, it should be noted that while Swidler's insights are useful, she tends to overstate her case. For example, juxtaposing her work with that of Yankelovich (1981b), we find that they are both saying that the traditional notion of commitment based on self-sacrifice (permanence even in the face of severe costs) is being replaced by what Yankelovich calls a "*new* ethic of commitment." As I describe it more fully in Chapter 7, this "new ethic" steers a middle course between self-sacrifice and the self-indulgence for which Swidler could be criticized.

In Swidler's (1980) analysis, "rebellion versus attachment" is the *second* dimension along which love is undergoing reevaluation. By "rebellion," Swidler (1980: 131) means feelings of "restlessness" in quest of a sense of meaning. "Attachment" means precisely the opposite—whether in work or love, one conforms to social expectations and accepts their limitations, settles down, and "toes the line." But, Swidler (1980: 133) observes, "those occupations with the greatest prestige and interest are also those which require the greatest readiness for continuing change." The person aspiring to those occupations discovers no respite from a "demanding society." By analogy, Swidler reasons that modern adults increasingly find no respite from the "demanding lover." Thus issues of work and love are not as distinct in modern societies as some observers had thought; instead, "both problems become the same problem, that of the restless self" (Swidler, 1980: 134). Love is no longer expressed through silent, unswerving loyalty, but through "continual negotiation and renegotiation of personal relationships.... To 'make them work'" (Swidler, 1980: 134-135; compare Scanzoni and Szinovacz, 1980). The "old concern with personal virtue [is replaced by] a new passion for honesty, fairness, equality" (Swidler, 1980: 135).

Here too it is plain how different is the idea of "rebellion," or the restless quest for meaning, from conceptions inherent in the conventional marriage model. At one time there was probably no greater cultural ideal than the "American Dream," in which the male strove with all his energies and finally reached a plateau called "success." Having "made it," he could relax and enjoy his life and his family. They, along with he, feasted contentedly on the fruits of his labor. The male success theme, and his family's participation in it, were complementary and inseparable elements. For instance, in a classic study of white, middle-class suburbia, Seeley et al. (1956) conclude that the husband is the "earner of the income on which rests the whole structure of family life."

Although Parsons wrote a great deal regarding the primacy of male achievement in Western society, it was left to another functionalist, Merton (1949), to comment on its "boundlessness." Achievement and success in work are marked by potentially infinite expectations, and since that infinity is gradually being transferred to the expressive aspects of marriage and family as well, there is now potentially no respite from the range of expectations spouses hold for each other, either in the expressive realm or in the instrumental realm (for example, facilitation of work opportunities for both spouses, and so forth). In a trenchant analysis of this developing infinitude, Bernard (1981a) concludes that the consequences of the decline of the male "good provider role" (Seeley et al., 1956), combined with women pressing men for increased intimacy, greater female work place activity, and greater male domestic activity, are not at all clear.

Swidler (1980: 136) calls the *third* area of love's reevaluation "self-realization versus self-sacrifice." Traditionally, spouses held "the obligation to sacrifice oneself for [one] another." Of course, the definitions of sacrifice and service were clearly spelled out by twentieth-century gender-role norms (Scanzoni, 1978: 116-117). The male served his family through paid employment; the woman served through domestic work and child care. Now, according to Swidler (1980: 136), those conventional notions are being "replaced by the duty to respect the other persons' separateness, to recognize the other's needs for growth and change, to give to the other in return for what one receives." Thus *to love* is to allow one's partner optimal potential for self-realization; *to be loved* is to receive that benefit from one's partner. Significantly, Swidler's insights were anticipated by Ibsen (1970c) in his *Lady from the Sea,* in which, after a long struggle between his wife and himself, Wangel finally says to her, "Our contract's dissolved. Right now, this moment. Now you can choose your own path—in full freedom.... I mean it with all my miserable heart." She responds, "You can let this *be?*" And Wangel says, "Yes, I can. Because I love you so much."

Furthermore, comments Swidler (1980: 136), "the emerging cultural view of love...emphasizes exchange. However, her definition of exchange—"what is valuable about a relationship is 'what one gets out of it' " (p. 137)—is grossly narrow, as is her notion that "exchange metaphors...imply impermanence" (p. 137). Roloff (1981: 14), for instance, defines exchange as "the advancement of both parties' self-interest," suggesting that partners may be on a quest for maximum *joint,* rather than *individual,* profit. And, under his "new ethic of commitment," Yankelovich (1981b) observes that sacrifice is not relegated to oblivion, nor is it chiefly the province of women; instead, it becomes a *negotiated* phenomenon. Both partners may expect to sacrifice, not because of fixed conventional norms prescribing what those sacrifices should be, but because of the dynamics of what Yankelovich calls "giving and getting compacts," which will be described in Chapter 7.

However, Swidler's (1980:137) point is well taken that love no longer primarily implies "self-sacrifice but self-development"; once more it is plain how alien that notion is to the form of marriage that has predominated throughout the twentieth century. In Parsons's and Pitts's (1964) analyses of marriage, women accepted subordinate status positions because that was "healthy" for family, society, and developing children. Men, likewise, unquestioningly accepted the status of achiever-provider, or Bernard's "good-provider" (even if they disliked the pressure to achieve, or the frustrations of eventually having to come to terms with an imposed achievement ceiling), because that too was thought to be "functional," that is, beneficial for others.

Swidler calls her *final* dimension of love's reevaluation "libidinal expression versus restraint." According to Swidler (1980: 139): "The ideals of virginity before marriage and fidelity afterward demanded sexual restraint. Sexuality sealed the intimacy of lovers; sexual restraint made their bond exclusive and inviolable." However, "in the contemporary period," says Swidler (1980: 139) "the ideal of sexual restraint has weakened.... Individual development has entered the sexual sphere, condemning relationships that limit individual growth or possibilities for new experiences." She goes on to say that while sex once got people into marriage and sealed their commitment, now "it must also sustain satisfaction and closeness within those relationships.... Sexual experience has come to symbolize the expansion and fulfillment of the self—the continuing capacity to grow, learn, and appreciate experience" (p. 141).

In direct contrast to Swidler's analysis of emerging sexual patterns, Pitts (1964: 97) portrays the conventional situation: "The boundary for the couple...is very sharp and is maintained through the exclusiveness of sexual love.... The main reinforcement is to restrict the social life of the married couple either to same-sex affairs, occupational peer-group activities, 'lunch with the girls,' or couple-to-couple relationships which split off into same-sex interaction.... In the upper-middle class, there may be flirtation and extramarital necking at...parties." After arguing that sex is strongly regulated in these ways, Pitts verifies Swidler's contention that conventional patterns supply little leeway for sexual experience as a means to enhance personal adult development: "Romantic love...is seen as being...abnormal for grown men. Once it has welded the marital bond, it is not supposed to burn again in the heart of the man: his occupation should be his passion." Seeley et al. (1956: 177), for example, found that successful suburban husbands actually feared significant emotional involvements with their wives and children lest such involvements somehow hindered their continued achievements. At the same time, by not even bothering to discuss the "control" of romantic love among adult women, Pitts lends tacit acceptance to the Victorian notion persisting into the twentieth-century family that women are indeed "passionless" (Cott, 1979). Similarly, Seeley et al. (1956: 178) support the then prevailing notion that men's and women's sexual passions differ by asserting that "food, sex, and interesting activity must be provided by the wife to please and attract the husband." However, one looks in vain throughout their report for any discussion of what Swidler and others mean by intimacy: self-disclosure, vulnerability, sharing of one's deepest feelings, fears, anxieties, emotions, desires, and so forth.

By foreclosing the possibility of males ever behaving more expressively, Pitts and Seeley et al. reinforce conventional norms in the face of changes occurring throughout the larger society. For example, in reviewing the 1970s, Pleck and Pleck (1980: 40) observe that some "men were entering nontraditional jobs, from nursing to midwifery, or were drawn to work with young children in day care centers and kindergartens. Some men, taking fathering more seriously than men had in the past, wanted to be present in the delivery room, sought paternity leaves from their jobs in order to spend more time with their children, and were seeking to raise sons and daughters free from many of the traditional definitions of masculine and feminine behavior.... National surveys...began to find that men with employed wives were spending increasing amounts of time in housework."

In analyzing her four dimensions, Swidler is not implying that conventional notions are by any means quiescent. On the contrary, what she has called "commitment" (permanence for its own sake), "attachment," "self-sacrifice," and "libidinal restraint" are very much alive and vigorous throughout segments of the population that strive to maintain twentieth-century marriage patterns (see Chapter 3). And even among that growing segment beginning to experiment with changes in gender roles the shifts are apparently occurring more rapidly in *instrumental* areas—paid occupations, household chores, child care, and so on. Among many citizens there is evidently greater resistance to change in Swidler's *expressive* areas and change in those areas is taking place more slowly.

Swidler's analysis is valuable for several reasons. First, it helps us to grasp more firmly the morphostatic nature of conventional marriage: "Identity, commitment [permanance for its own sake], self-realization, and intimacy, once achieved were simply supposed to last a lifetime. Moral meaning lay in being able to stick to what one had chosen, to continue to be animated by the commitments one had made" (Swidler, 1980: 142-143). Second, similar to our examination of parent-child socialization and our consideration of the contradictions many parents experience as they try to fit new children to old scripts, Swidler's paradigm identifies some of the struggles many adults have as they seek to reconcile conventional scripts with their own emerging orientations. Third, her paradigm focuses our attention squarely on the problem-of-order question. She herself cites Lasch's criticisms of what, to conservatives, are the outlandishly extreme lengths to which Stone's "affective individualism" are being carried: choice, rebellion, self-realization, and libidinal expression. How can marriage, much less children and family, be "possible" if "moral significance" is sought "in acts of choice, in attempts to discover, clarify, or deepen the self, whether or not these choices lead to or remain within a commitment" (Swidler, 1980: 143)?

To the degree that a shift is actually occurring from Swidler's conventional to her emerging paradigm, the out of phaseness of the twentieth-century family is plainly underscored. However, as I noted earlier, Swidler pushes the pendulum too far in the self-indulgence direction, without taking account of the middle ground suggested by Yankelovich (1981a). Based on his compilation of national sample surveys from the 1950s to the present, Yankelovich (1981a: 36) maintains that Americans are indeed fashioning a "cultural revolution that is transforming the rules of American life and moving us into wholly uncharted territory.... This cultural revolution is as fateful to our future as any changes in the economy or politics." However, as I suggest in later chapters, the "revolution" focuses on his new "ethic of commitment," and not on a repudiation of the commitment notion per se.

INSTRUMENTAL ISSUES

While Swidler's analyses focus on the expressive side of adult relationships and on some of their underlying assumptions, there is yet another, more familiar and somewhat less controversial, side to the matter of synchrony between modern society and the twentieth-century family. I refer, of course, to *instrumental* issues connected with paid employment, child care, and household chores. As Degler (1980: 443) puts it, Betty Friedan's 1963 "polemical book *The Feminine Mystique*...was an angry outburst from a...woman who suddenly recognized that for too long she had accepted the idea that middle-class woman's proper place was at home with her children even when that role was neither fully satisfying nor totally occupying.... Friedan urged women to make a life for themselves outside of, and in addition to, their homes and families.... Literally hundreds of thousands of women could make a connection between their lives as workers now, after years as wives and mothers, with what Friedan was saying. Many men, too, could see the...claims of women."

In the last two decades increasing numbers of married women have been entering the paid labor force under what Lapidus (1978: 341) calls an "assimilationist" model: "Its fundamental premise is that women, but not men, have dual roles.... Women are guaranteed equal legal and political rights and equal educational opportunities...[and] are also assigned the primary responsibility for homemaking and child care." The universality of this model throughout the United States and in other Western countries, and in Eastern European and Russian societies is well documented (Lapidus, 1978; Jancar, 1978; Heitlinger, 1979). Rather than the husband and wife being "head" and "complement," respectively, as in the conventional arrangement described in Chapter 2, they are now *partners*—except that he is the senior partner, and the employed wife is the *junior* partner (SP-JP). He is the senior partner because, although they are both now wage earners, nothing has been done to alter fundamentally the morphostatic nature of their relationship—it is merely a variation on the basic twentieth-century family theme. When the wife adopts a "career" rather than a "job," and also defines herself as "co-provider" (Scanzoni, 1978), the possibilities for altering this essential morphostasis are increased, but by no means guaranteed (this issue is elaborated in Chapter 6).

The overlay of the SP-JP pattern onto conventional forms brings into bold relief the contrasting ways in which conservatives and progressives evaluate the "drift" described in Chapter 3. On the one hand, "conservative psychologists like Urie Bronfenbrenner" (Degler, 1980: 451) view the growing popularity of the SP-JP pattern as far too radical and threatening.

'America's families and their children are in trouble,' warned Bronfenbrenner in 1972. 'Trouble so deep and pervasive as to threaten the future of our nation.'...A mother's continual presence in the household during a child's growing up, Bronfenbrenner insisted, was essential. He deplored the increasing tendency of women to be employed away from home even if they had small children [Degler, 1980: 451].

Hence, when Kamerman and Kahn (1978: 12) assert that "by far the most significant change [in twentieth-century family structure] is the increased labor force participation rate of women in all industrialized countries," conservatives react with the counterassertion that this trend is yet another indication that family has moved too far too fast, and that such radical change is damaging to family, society, and individuals.

On the other hand, progressives view this type of shift as inadequate and insufficient and, owing to the essentially morphostatic nature of the SP-JP pattern, as remaining out of synchrony with a dynamic society:

> Starting with the premise that biological differences have only limited relevance for the allocation of social roles, it [the progressives' preferred model] rests on the assumption that in modern society there are neither male nor female roles but only human ones.... Family and work have an important place in the lives of men and women alike. This model envisages the opportunity for men and women to participate fully [outside family and within family] [Lapidus, 1978: 342].

In contrast to Bane's (1976; see Chapter 3) position, Lapidus (1978: 343) goes on to say: "Public policy in this model [explicitly]...assumes the obligation of both men and women to support themselves, as well as to jointly share in the responsibilities of parenthood."

Figure 4.1 suggests different ways we can view men and women in the labor force and in their connections to family. The far left panel of the figure illustrates the SP-JP pattern, in which women and men are both "workers" or "earners"— each holding *jobs*. Within the middle or "transition" panel, both partners have "careers," or are "achievers."[6] However,

Figure 4.1   Statuses of Women and Men in the Labor Force and in the Family

Dual Worker (Earner)	Dual Career (Achiever)	Equal Partner
husband usually works full time wife may work either full time or part time	both partners are usually employed full time	all work and domestic arrangements are open to negotiation and continual renegotiation (see Chapter 6)

since the pattern portrayed in the second panel does not guarantee that morphostatic assumptions are being questioned, we must move to the third panel. In this pattern, such assumptions are indeed severely critiqued; this critique is carried out in Chapter 6.

The overall thrust of this discussion confirms Swidler's proposition that within emerging family patterns the instrumental and expressive are woven out of the same cloth. Expressively, she argues, partners who are basically independent and autonomous exchange emotional gratifications. Women are no longer the unique "emotional hub" that they are in the conventional family. Men, as much as women, are expected to be able to provide nurturant rewards—to participate fully in intimacy. Simultaneously, men are no longer the unique "instrumental hub" that they are in the conventional family. Either partner can earn money and engage in child care (along with other household duties). Furthermore, even if no (subsequent) partner is found for one or both sets of continuing exchanges, the person is not thought to be any less a "whole" or "complete" or "autonomous" person. He or she is presumably able to care for him- or herself economically, to parent effectively, and to "grow" emotionally (Stein, 1981).

In contrast to this idea of women and men being equivalent or *interchangeable*[7] in both the expressive and instrumental realms, *specialization* and ultimately (female) dependence is the essence of the conventional family. To many conservatives, specialization and social order go hand in hand. Thus they fear that autonomy and interchangeability indicate a level of individualism that could make family order exceedingly problematic. It is indeed ironic that American religious conservatives, who fear what individualism will do to the established order and also condemn "atheistic socialism and communism" because they "destroy the family," should find themselves in concert with communist leaders, who also fear individualism's impact on the public order.

Family-Society Sync in Communist Societies

While conservatives are aware that "the emancipation of women was one of the central goals of the Russian Revolution, and all communist leaderships since then have pledged themselves to achieving sexual equality" (Jancar, 1978: 2), they have not bothered to discover that communist governments have uniformly imposed strict limits on the degree of individualism they will tolerate. Indeed, individualism as defined by Stone (1977) is not tolerated at all: "What is not allowed either sex is sufficient space to develop according to individual inclination" (Jancar, 1978: 207). While communist governments have aggressively established social policies shifting family from the head-complement model to a dual-worker—even dual-career—status, they have decidedly not done so in the name of individualism, since they fear individualism as much as American conservatives do. "From the very beginning," Soviet family policy made "a critical distinction between mobilization and liberation.... The emphasis in Western liberal thought on elimination of obstacles to full participation was replaced in Russia by an emphasis on the obligation to contribute.... An effort [was made] to harness all available human energies—male and female alike—on behalf of national development" (Lapidus, 1978: 337-338). "Marxism as an ideology of economic revolution has proved wanting as a conceptual vehicle for feminism" (Jancar, 1978: 206) because the Soviet

Union and the Eastern European communist governments solved the problem of order in society and family by imposing their own rigid hierarchy in place of the previous ones.

In contrast to Western feminists, such as Giele (1978), who argue that the aim of social policy should be to encourage *individuals* (women and men) to develop their abilities, communist leaders assert that "the sole aim established for both sexes is service to the state" (Jancar, 1978: 207). Because these leaders believe that "class rather than sex [is] the crucial social division" (Lapidus, 1978: 338), production and economic development of the society—the larger whole—are infinitely more important than individual development. Seen in this light, the insistence of communist leaders that married women participate in the work force and that family structure shift from a head-complement to a dual-worker model makes good sense; and resistance of these leaders to female individualism, in their view, makes equally good sense. Having established a new social order based on the overriding goal of rapid economic development, communist societies cannot tolerate the conflict and disruption that is likely to occur if individualistic demands are pressed by interest groups opposed to Communist Party policy. Consequently, they strongly favor Lapidus's (1978) "assimilationist" model but vehemently oppose her "humanist" model; they also oppose Jancar's (1978) decidedly more radical notions, discussed in Chapter 6. At this juncture a distinction must be drawn between communist leaders and American conservatives. As observed in Chapter 3, American conservatives fear that a "left-leaning" government, with the goal of development of a social-ist society, might emulate the communist states by imposing a variation of the senior partner-junior partner pattern of family. Conservatives argue for a "return" to the head-complement pattern of family, which they contend is in harmony with the free-enterprise, capitalist system that they believe "made America great" during the nineteenth and early twentieth centuries.

While Western societies have not imposed the dual-worker pattern, the Kamerman and Kahn (1978) conclusion makes plain the fact that our citizens have been adopting it in steadily increasing numbers. And Jancar's (1978: 206) conclusions regarding communist societies could, in most essentials, be applied to the situation in the West: "Communist regimes have opted for a high degree of traditional role-playing in...the nuclear family. The emphasis on the woman as first mother and then worker has created tension between the demands made upon her at home and those made at work. The guaranteed right to work has meant that women must perform a minimum of four roles—wife, housekeeper, childrearer, and worker." Jancar (1978: 207) adds that "every Communist country puts this special responsibility...of producing the next generation...ahead of a woman's development as an individual." "Producing," in this context, means not only reproducing, but also assuming prime responsibility for child development. Consequently, "the experience of Eastern Europe shows that a state-socialist transformation [aimed at mobilization and economic development] is insufficient to bring about the liberation of women" (Heitlinger, 1979: 203). Thus, in contrast to Sokoloff (1980) and certain other feminists who identify capitalism as a prime factor in women's subordination, Jancar (1978: 208) contends that "sexual equality" must be analyzed in a way "that is independent of 'capitalist' or 'Communist' " labels; this point is developed in Chapter 6.

For now the conclusion is that, in both East and West, married women have been streaming into the paid labor force at a much more rapid rate than married men have been assuming domestic responsibilities. Communist governments have actively recruited women into the labor force, but have done virtually nothing to advance, and sometimes have subtly opposed the recruitment of men into the home. Most Western governments have not vigorously recruited in either direction, and America's legal statutes (see Chapter 8) do not encourage and often inhibit this two-way flow (Sachs and Wilson, 1978; Weitzman, 1981). Sweden's government is one exception, in that it has officially established policy aimed at the cessation of gender-typed division of labor. According to Lapidus (1978: 343), this policy reads: "A decisive and ultimately durable improvement in the status of women cannot be attained by special measures aimed at women alone; it is equally necessary to abolish the conditions which tend to assign certain privileges, obligations, or rights to men. No decisive change in the distribution of functions and status between the sexes can be achieved if the duties of the male in the society are assumed *a priori* to be unaltered." It is precisely this kind of social policy that communist governments strongly oppose, because they perceive its individualistic implications to be detrimental to the greater good of their societies. Not only do conservatives in the United States employ the same reasoning, some of them move a step backward in time, to argue for a return to the early twentieth-century family.

INDIVIDUALISM AND SOVIET CHILDREN

It was mentioned in Chapter 3 that conservatives express a great deal of anxiety over the allegedly negative impacts of the public schools on the family, on marriage, and on the sex norms of children. Their core complaint is that conventional scripts (their morphostatic image of family) are being undermined in the public schools in favor of ideas that will, in the conservatives' view, eventually destroy family and society with it. Some conservative parents have formed private schools in order to protect their children from these ill effects; in these schools, curriculum materials are employed that convey the valued traditions of conservatives. Typical of these institutions are a number of schools in Virginia built around *McGuffey's Readers*.[8] More than simply tools for teaching children how to read, these *Readers* are designed primarily to convey certain kinds of moral ideas and ethics in both instrumental and expressive realms. Thus education in these institutions is not merely academic, but *moral*—and the morality represents the nineteenth-century context from which *McGuffey's Readers* sprang. There is nothing in the *Readers* that prepares children to grapple with the complexities of this century and the next; they contain no information on how to balance individual and social interests pertaining to family.

It is interesting that the conservatives' passion to influence their children's education so as to ensure acceptance of conventional hierarchical patterns is matched, and indeed far exceeded, by the Soviets. Given recent conservative agitation to influence school libraries and curricula, it seems plain that the sort of control exercised by the Soviet government over children's literature (O'Dell, 1978) is a model to which American conservatives aspire in form, though obviously not in specific content. For example, the type of anti-individualism described by Jancar (1978) and Lapidus (1978) is impressed on Russian children very early in their development. In what they are allowed to read, *"man must be portrayed as being basically a social animal"* (O'Dell, 1978: 7; emphasis in original). The "Soviet hero," according to O'Dell (1978: 7), may act in an individualistic fashion for a brief period of searching, but eventually will see that his greatest good, as well as that of the society, comes from conforming to its "true and glorious path." The "basic tenet" that Russian children discover in their literature is "that society rather than the individual is of central importance." In concert with that "basic tenet," Soviet children's literature fosters the *legitimation* of the government's authority (O'Dell, 1978: 175). O'Dell (1978: 175) characterizes efforts in Western societies to establish the "rightfulness" of the government's demands in the minds of children as "much more haphazard."

In contrast to the West, where occupational achievement has been the prime virtue, the Soviets systematically impress upon their children that "patriotism is...the prime virtue. It is subordinate to no other quality, whereas all the others hinge on it. It is...the supreme embodiment of collectivism" (O'Dell, 1978: 186). Children are taught that the characteristic that supports patriotism is "a necessary submission to a higher authority.... The children are told that collective decisions are the correct ones.... The stress is inevitably on subordination of self to duty.... The implication is also one of submission to something more important [than] oneself" (p. 186). That "something" is the "Motherland" and the requirement to serve her through productive labor: "Work is a joyful service of the Motherland" (p. 177); that is, work that promises greater social good, not work that furthers individual development.

Because of their perceived disruptive consequences, literary treatments of sex are considered especially pernicious by the Soviets. Children and adolescents are refused access to any writings that might in any way discourage "strong sexual self-discipline.... Young people are discouraged from practicing (or even reading about) sex so that they can concentrate on study and on becoming more economically productive citizens" (O'Dell, 1978: 185). The pursuit of sexual gratifications, in short, is viewed as simply one more manifestation of an individualism that tends to interfere with economic development, and thus with social well-being. In this vein, it is worth noting that American religious conservatives are very much at home with the notion of unquestioned submission to a higher authority—as long as the authority represents their views on various issues. Moreover, their arguments against sex education in the schools suggest, as do other things, that conservatives are very comfortable with Soviet ideas regarding libidinal restraint (see Chapter 8).[9]

In any event, from childhood onward Russian children learn that individualistic interests, whether they be expressive (affectionate, sexual) or instrumental (achievement by either gender), are properly subordinated to the larger production interests of the state. Systematic socialization is thus one means used by communist governments to resolve the problem of order in favor of the larger society. However, communist governments have also recently used force to suppress their own dissident feminists, who are attempting to form interest groups and challenge communist order by arguing that the SP-JP model is inadequate (Morgan, 1980). Dissident feminists are considered as much a threat by those governments as other dissidents who, in recent years, have sought a broad range of enlarged human and political rights. As a result, "an independent feminist movement of the current Western type...cannot legally emerge in the communist countries to campaign against male domination or for fundamental changes in the sexual division of labor" (Heitlinger, 1979: 76).

While the communist countries maintain calculated efforts to enforce male privilege in the name of social order, these sorts of official overt acts are generally absent throughout the West, including the United States. It is difficult to tell what the long-term consequences might be for the communist countries of their efforts to impose order through suppression. Perhaps the concentration on children's socialization in these countries will render feminist stirrings miniscule and ineffectual. However, the major focus of this book is with more complex situations in countries such as the United States, where, first of all, laws (and formal endorsements) tend to express one type of family pattern (the conventional model), but, second, actual behaviors are shifting in the senior-junior partner direction, and, third, there are strong stirrings on the part of some to explore the models of family depicted in the second and (especially) third panels of Figure 4.1. The shifts in Western patterns are clearly not the result of deliberate government efforts but, in large measure, of a powerful individualism, which is, after all, the phenomenon that exists at the root of Western democracies—individualism, however, tempered by the need for social responsibility on the part of interest groups promoting it.

Consequently, the contrast between East and West family-society synchrony is striking. In communist countries there is apparently little, if any, out of phaseness, or lack of synchrony, between the larger society and family *qua institution* since both are structured largely along traditional, authoritarian, hierarchical, and morphostatic lines. Communist governments, though formally committed to family change and women's emancipation, have clamped strict limits on the degree to which both phenomena are permitted to occur. Thus central government control achieves synchronization between society and family at the expense of individualism. Ironically, American conservatives, so unutterably opposed to communist family experiments, nevertheless unwittingly concur with communist governments in their fear of the impact of individualism on family and society. The upshot is that in the West, and in the United States in particular, as many realms throughout the larger society become increasingly dynamic and nontraditional, family continues to be organized *formally* (that is, legally, along with symbolic pronouncements by elected officials, educators, parents, and clergy) in morphostatic terms. Alongside that lack of society-family synchrony, and in part as a result of it, many persons are quietly drifting from and ignoring those morphostatic patterns. This gap, or absence of synchrony, between the formal and the actual (the actual as manifested both in terms of trends in the larger society *and* in people's family behaviors) is the family's Achilles' heel—that is, the nature of its out of phaseness—and the reason the twentieth-century family no longer appears to be "possible."

Summary

My argument is that the Achilles' heel of the twentieth-century conventional family is its out of phaseness with the essence of what modern Western societies are all about. While most Western societies are experiencing dynamic flux based on participatory democracy, family continues largely to be morphostatic and to be based on various hierarchical modes. From the conservative viewpoint, family members have merely gotten out of sync with conventional "moral norms," and it is this departure that accounts for alleged contemporary family crises. From the nonconservative perspective, however, out of phaseness can be demonstrated, first of all, in terms of parent-child relationships: Many parents are struggling to prepare their children for participation in a dynamic society using scripts that are essentially morphostatic. Second, the contrast between morphostatic scripts and emerging realities can also be seen with regard to both expressive and instrumental aspects of adult relationships.

At the expressive level, the contrasting emerging versus conventional views of love are described by Swidler (1980) as choice versus commitment, rebellion versus attachment, self-realization versus self-sacrifice, and libidinal expression versus libidinal restraint.

Within the instrumental dimension, I have compared Western societies with communist societies to illustrate differences in society-family synchrony. In the East, hierarchical, nondemocratic governments insist on family structures (with regard to women's employment, child care, and household duties) that operate in the same hierarchical mold for the greater good of the state, not of individuals. However, the participatory democracy characteristic of Western governments (and the dynamic character of those societies in general) is only minimally present within its family structures, accounting in part for inequities between the sexes in terms of employment opportunities as well as household task performance. In contrast, communist countries are characterized by synchrony between hierarchical arrangements throughout the larger society as well as in family. Thus there are gender inequities in both types of societies, but for different reasons. At present, the lack of family-society synchrony in American society is caused by the gap between formal, morphostatic laws and policies and the dynamic character of the larger society, including the drift of many persons from that morphostasis.

NOTES

1. For examples, see Scanzoni and Szinovacz (1980: 17): "A married woman's most important task in life should be taking care of her husband." Respondents have the following choices: "strongly agree," "agree," "mixed feelings," "disagree," "strongly disagree."

2. "Modern" simply means the opposite of "traditional." For example, responses of "disagree" or "strongly disagree" to the item in note 1 would indicate "modern" thinking. In another place (Scanzoni, 1975: 29), I observe that "a 'modern' emphasis [indicates] reduced commitment to the notion of the subordination [to males] of wife [or female] interests. . . . A 'traditional' emphasis [indicates a] greater commitment to superordination [primacy] of husband and child interests [above those of the woman]."

3. "Familism implies that obligations and duties to the larger group . . . take precedence . . . over concerns about individualistic costs and rewards" (Scanzoni, 1975: 188).

4. See especially Chapters 7 and 8.

5. Interestingly, a recent study of 35 California couples married at least 50 years revealed a great deal of dissatisfaction with their situations even though they were quite pleased with the fact that they had "made it" that long (Greensboro [North Carolina] *Daily News,* July 8, 1980; from the *Los Angeles Times-Washington Post* News Service).

6. Serious conflict occurs, of course, if partners define themselves, or each partner fails to define the other, in different ways.

7. The notion of "interchangeability" is developed further in Chapter 7 as one of four critical moral norms.

8. See the *Washington Post* (March 29, 1981: A-1).

9. A recent report quotes a Russian sailor who often visits American shores as saying, "The bottom of Kaliningrad Harbor is lined with *Playboy* magazines." The writer (Brendan Murphy, in the Greensboro *Daily News,* July 19, 1981; *Los Angeles Times* News Service) suggests that Russian sailors are not as impervious to American views on sexuality as their leadership might hope.

5

RESPONSES TO THE
OUT-OF-PHASE FAMILY

If the argument in Chapter 4 is valid, namely, that society and the conventional American family are out of sync, then, logically, *at least* two responses are possible. One is a surface response, aimed merely at trying to "relieve" symptoms of the out of phaseness; the other is more "radical" (in the sense of "going to the root of things") and seeks to redress the out of phaseness itself. This chapter examines the first, or symptomatic, response; subsequent chapters examine the second.

In recent years, three major applied family strands have appeared: legislative, programmatic, and clinical. All three have been primarily addressed to symptoms, and could be collapsed into two major categories—macro- and micro-level perspectives. While representatives of the macro perspective have sought to assist families in preventing or curing symptoms through legislation and bureaucratic regulation, those at the micro level have relied on school curricula and voluntary community or religious programs to prevent or cure symptoms, and also on counseling/therapy for cures. However, many macro and micro advocates fall largely into the category of what I earlier called "moderates," that is, persons who tend not to address the basic theoretical and philosophical (or "root") assumptions underlying contemporary family.

Macro/Policy Responses

When I assert that macro advocates are responding to a certain out of phaseness of the family, it must be understood that the type of "nonsync" they tend to perceive is substantially different from that perceived by many other family advocates. As Aaron (1978) points out, the genesis of most recent federal family-relevant legislation was in the Great Society thrust of 1964-1968. The very specific nonsync perceived by politicians, social scientists, and advocates of that era was *economic*. While the majority of white society was living in relative affluence, a substantial proportion of black society (and a small part of white society) was engulfed in poverty. It was this particular incongruity that Great Society family-type programs set out to correct. But the emphasis was never on family *qua unit*. The prime issue was economic disadvantage—How could more Americans as individuals share more fully in the "American Dream"? "Sharing" came to be defined in terms of comparable levels of education, job status, and income. Thus bringing poor people into greater sync with an affluent society meant devising laws and programs to try to achieve comparability in all three areas. And for some advocates of equity and justice (mostly economists), that particular goal was sufficient. Apparently they gave little or no thought to any actual family-type issues, and certainly not to such abstract matters as individualism-familism and the problem of order. As Abbott (1981: 200) puts it, they were possessed by a "Service State" mentality that, while perhaps useful in trying to help meet the basic economic needs of poor *individuals*, did virtually nothing to address the larger issue of *family* in general.

In time, however, advocates with broader perspectives joined the ranks of the macro policymakers (Aaron, 1978). Their particular concern was the *children* of poor families. They contended that enlarging the family incomes of the poor would benefit their children in particular ways, such as increasing infant birth weight (Kehrer and Wolin, 1979), enhancing children's school performance (Maynard and Murnane, 1979), and enhancing adolescents' school and employment decisions (McDonald and Stephenson, 1979). These kinds of arguments, along with the notion that enlarged incomes might reduce the high rates of marital instability among the disadvantaged (it was also thought that stability itself benefited children), gave rise to ambitious social experiments known as "family income-maintenance programs" (Tallman, 1979). Apparently, advocates of these programs reasoned that if children benefited in the above-mentioned ways, so, ultimately, would the larger society. Moreover, one of the prime assumptions underlying these programs was the notion that divorce is a *failure*, and that couples who stay together are *successful* (Parsons, 1965). There seems little doubt that the "selling" of income-maintenance programs to Congress was facilitated by the seemingly unassailable objective of enhancing marital stability.

The notion that such phenomena as marital instability, out-of-wedlock births, and female-headed households represent family "breakdown" and "disorganization" probably reached its peak during the mid-1960s discussions surrounding urban black families. A government document known as the Moynihan Report (1965) described these phenomena as evidence of the "pathology" of black families and, what is more, as the *cause* of their other social and economic difficulties. One of the results of the controversy that ensued over that report was the establishment of Great Society programs to relieve black family poverty. However, certain blacks (and whites) asked what family forms lower-class blacks would adopt if and when they were ever able to escape poverty in significant numbers (Glazer, 1966). The assumption of many white legislators and policymakers was that the female-headed household was "dysfunctional" (Zimmerman, 1978, says it was a "transitional" stage enroute to the conventional family), but since blacks asserted that it was vital on grounds of black pride not merely to imitate whites, it was not at all clear that conventional family patterns should be their ultimate aim.

With increasing disenchantment over Great Society anti-poverty programs (Aaron, 1978), the idea evolved during the early 1970s that family programs ought to focus on the non-poor as well as on the poor. Impetus in this direction came mostly from those advocates who were concerned in part over the consequences of shifts at all social class levels from the head-complement model of marriage to various forms of SP-JP marriage arrangements (see Figure 4.1). These people were particularly anxious about the impacts on children of mothers' employment, and also the impacts of nonparental and nonkin child care arrangements (Bronfenbrenner, 1975; Keniston, 1977). In the view of many observers, these emerging work and child care patterns represented significant departures from the twentieth-century family model; one of the federally funded studies that took place as a result of concern over these departures was the National Day Care Study (Travers, 1980). Cognitive development and language-skills acquisition among nonpoverty as well as poverty children, both in and out of day care facilities, was also investigated. The push for government policy to cast a net beyond the poor was heightened as a result of "the 1973 Senate hearings on 'American Families: Trends and Pressures,' and...[Senator] Mondale [who said]...'We must start by asking to what extent government policies are helping or hurting families'" (Johnson, 1981: xii). The proposed legislation stimulated what eventually came to be known as "family impact analyses."

Such analyses are basically evaluation research aimed at determining the broadest possible range of consequences (impacts) for families of *any* type of federal program at any social class level (Zimmerman, 1978: 454). Although never federally financed, the Foundation for Child Development provided funds to support research conducted by the Family Impact Seminar. However, according to Steiner (1981: 32), the "seminar offers little promise for resolving the dilemmas that beset all efforts to strengthen families while acknowledging their diversity and pluralism." And part of the reason for that disappointment may lie with the seminar's apparently tacit acceptance of the conventional model. For example, while listing the seminar's investigative aims, its director (Johnson, 1981: xii) places first, "Does the policy encourage or discourage marital stability?" More important, his essay in no way critiques the conventional model, nor does it appear sensitive to any broader issue than describing policy consequences, the major theme, incidentally, of the 1980 White House Conference on Families, discussed later in this chapter. The seminar's results, according to Steiner (1981: 32), are "exhortations to 'think family,'" but contain little in the way of "informed prediction."

The notion that macro-level family-related objectives have rarely addressed fundamental issues is reinforced by an examination of the social circumstances of the people most closely connected with those efforts. In his analysis of Great Society programs, Aaron (1978) observes that many social scientists (economists, in particular) rotated between government and the universities, promoting various aspects of these programs. Furthermore, he contends that while it is inevitable that their own career interests were at least as important to them as the interests of those persons and families they were trying to assist, they often opted for policy "suggestions" that placed their own interests ahead of citizens' interests. And part of enhancing their own interests lay with making policy recommendations that tended to avoid basic theoretical and philosophical issues (Aaron, 1978: 158), a point to which I return shortly.

Simultaneously, outside government and the universities, an "applied research contract industry" emerged in response to the huge sums of federal dollars available for policy research during the 1960s and 1970s. Writing from his perspective as one of the leaders of this "industry," Abt (1980: 157) concludes: "There is a theory gap between the empirical results of social experiments and their implications for social change." He goes on to say that "we are not learning as much or as quickly as we could about what really works in improving our society." He concludes that government officials are suffering from "data poisoning"—they are overwhelmed with information that has never been integrated in any systematic, theoretical fashion.

It is both ironic and heartening that Abt should make these judgments after his 20 years "in the business"—ironic in that the kinds of private contract centers he represents have contributed enormously to the gap; heartening in that his admission makes all the more urgent the necessity to be explicit regarding the basic assumptions underlying applied efforts to "improve" family and society. For instance, note his seemingly innocuous yet undefined reference to "improving society." Presumably, Abt includes "family" under "society"; however, the conservative's definition of "improvement" is vastly different from the progressive's. Hence, although Abt (1980: 157) cites Einstein's belief that "there is nothing more useful than theory," he supplies his own case study of the confusion and uncertainty that arise when one's theoretical assumptions are not made explicit.

Perhaps part of the reason for the failure of macro-level advocates to make their underlying assumptions explicit is lack of a clear alternative to the twentieth-century family model. In contrast to Great Society researchers and policymakers, conservatives possess a clear conceptual model of family—or some variation thereof. "Good families," in the conservative view, are those that conform as closely as possible to the *morphostatic* image described earlier; "good" policy promotes that conformity. Nonconservatives, on the other hand, seem able to concur on only one point: "Defining a 'family' in concrete terms might tend to exclude many families and to implicitly favor certain types of families. If this were to happen, it would be counterproductive. A more useful approach would be to recognize variant forms of families and to work toward strengthening these forms" (Monroney, 1979: 463). Kahn and Kamerman (1979: 3) say the same thing by dismissing what they call a "monolithic" perspective in favor of an "essential pluralism" based on "fami*lies* policies" that "encourage diversity, or at least [are] neutral among a variety of acceptable alternatives in style, roles, direction...including female-headed families with young children—whether created by divorce, desertion, widowhood, or out-of-wedlock birth."

However, beyond this rejection of the uniqueness and primacy of the twentieth-century family, many nonconservatives appear unwilling or unable to express what "healthy" families or "good" social policy are. This uncertainty exists in spite of the fact that these nonconservatives have promoted most of the family and child legislation of the past fifty years, laws that by their very nature *do things for families*, that is, Abbott's (1981) "service state." The major beneficiaries of these laws have been less advantaged families in the lower and working classes. Conservatives, on the other hand, support family laws that prescribe and proscribe certain specific behaviors. In their view, laws and policies should not *help* families *do* things economically; instead, family law should *instruct* individuals regarding what social and personal behaviors are acceptable (see Chapter 8). Moreover, unacceptable behaviors should invite punishment, not assistance. On the one hand, as Zimmerman (1978: 455) observes, conservatives favor a "hands-off" policy, as illustrated by their arguments that shelters to protect abused wives represent "interference" and "intrusion" into family privacy (see below and Chapter 8). On the other hand, however, this hands-off approach does not include rescinding traditional laws regarding definitions of legal marriage, sexuality, and so forth, nor does it entail freedom of choice regarding abortion.

While macro-level advocates promoted "family-ameliorative" legislation, "the purpose...that family policy might serve remains unsettled'' (Zimmerman, 1979: 492). One reason it remains unsettled is the hesitancy moderates experience in ''fleshing out'' or specifying the amorphous notion that ''family policy...is concern[ed] for family functioning as it affects the well-being of individual family members and society at large'' (Zimmerman, 1979: 493). Conservatives would not disagree with this general expression of the problem of order (the well-being of society and individuals), but would contend that it is achieved specifically through implementation and support of their morphostatic image of family. Non-conservatives may demur but, as Zimmerman and many others observe, they are seemingly unable to present a reasonable alternative that balances ''personal satisfaction with societal concerns and do[es] so realistically in the light of possibilities and constraints'' (Kahn and Kamerman, 1979: 2-3).

Research and Values

Contributing to the hesitancy mentioned above are genuine concerns of most social and behavioral researchers that applied issues may (consciously or otherwise) contaminate the rigor and validity of their investigations (see Chapters 1 and 9) and that advocacy will undermine their credibility as researchers. ''The important thing,'' says Christensen (1964: 974), ''is not that the scientist be *exclusively* scientist, but rather that he keep his roles of scientist and citizen separate, so that neither is spoiled by the other and so that the public will always know from which position he speaks.'' Lest one assume that conviction is out of vogue, Nye and McDonald (1979: 480) argue that ''the family policy researcher...must *attempt* to maintain a rigorous scientific objectivity throughout the research endeavor.... Whereas questions of the 'goodness' or 'badness' of policy for families lie outside the domain of family policy research, such questions are of central concern to the family policy advocate.''

However, Nye and McDonald acknowledge the ''potential dilemma'' of the researcher being called on to advocate policy based on his or her own research or expertise. Part of that dilemma, they observe, stems from the presence of conflicting interest group or "audience" goals, discussed in prior chapters. While Nye and McDonald (1979: 480) believe that it is important for the researcher to share his or her expertise, they also hold that the researcher must "guard against generalization beyond the data." Alternatively, they propose that researchers develop "cost-reward balance sheets" for policymakers, who can then make decisions as to what to do for families and children based on their awareness of the positive and negative consequences. However, Kahn and Kamerman (1979: 5) question the extent to which policy and research interests can, in fact, be kept distinct; they comment that even sound research will not significantly influence family policy "unless there is greater readiness to face and deal with the question of [the often conflicting] value perspectives from which the results are assessed and responded to."

An illustration of Kahn and Kamerman's point is the reaction of conservatives to research that, according to Nye and McDonald (1979: 479), "disproves" that the "paid employment of mothers led to neglect of children, poor health for mothers and marital conflict." Scholars such as Bronfenbrenner are presumably well aware of this body of research (see Clarke-Stewart, 1977), nevertheless, they are not convinced that it "disproves" anything—as mentioned earlier, they continue to warn against mothers' employment.[1] As I argue below, the reason for their reaction lies with, as Kahn and Kamerman put it, the "value perspectives from which the results are assessed." In this case, the values are represented by the negative appraisal of individualism held by Bronfenbrenner and like-minded advocates.

A second example of the way family research results tend to be evaluated according to one's degree of individualism is found in reactions to the recent literature on family violence. Based on recent findings, congressional bills were introduced extablishing shelters to protect abused wives.[2] However, the bills were successfully opposed by conservatives on the grounds that shelters were "unnecessary" and that they would become "anti-family indoctrination centers" and would "encourage disintegration of the family" (Goodman, 1980). Although, so far as is known, researchers did not compute cost/benefit ledgers regarding these shelters (in the Nye and McDonald sense), conservatives and nonconservatives were each able to calculate their own and, what is even more significant, to interpret those ratios in terms of their own values. Conservatives perceived the proposed legislation as damaging to the family and social order; nonconservatives defined it as protecting women (and children) and thus indirectly benefitting the social fabric. So much for Zimmerman's (1979: 493) conclusion that "contending interest groups" have attained "equilibrium" regarding "child and spouse abuse."

The complex connections between research and values can be tied to my earlier point regarding advocates' self-interests. For example, following his detailed analysis of the research and values syndrome, Aaron (1978: 158) asserts that policy research "will be an intellectually conservative force in debates about public policy." Although he acknowledges that assertion is "paradoxical" given the "political liberalism or radicalism of many of those who produce" policy research, it is nonetheless true, he argues, because all social and behavioral research can be faulted in terms of its uncertain reliability and validity. That methodological reality is compounded by the fact that

> analysts with varying political predispositions will be drawn to the subject and will advance diverse solutions to the puzzles. The incentives of the academic world will encourage people, especially newcomers bent on promotion, to discover facts not consistent with previous theories and to devise new theories to explain them. The difficulty and cost of generating new data adequate to choose among the alternative theories will assure existing puzzles of a long life. Eventually data may be discovered or developed that permit some theories to be rejected definitively. One can be fairly confident, however, that at any

given time there will coexist several theories consistent with any given set of facts that are more or less congenial to persons with differing political or philosophical predispositions" [Aaron, 1978: 158].

The upshot for laypersons and legislators is that the "conflicting research is bound to have a conservative effect.... The prudent person will conclude that action should be deferred until the controversial issues have been settled.... [The tendency] to delay is...reinforced by the tone of certitude and detachment by those who disagree.... What is an ordinary member of the tribe to do when the witch doctors disagree?" (Aaron, 1978: 158).

Tallman's assessments of government-sponsored income-maintenance programs supply an illustration of the ambiguities of conflicting research results leading to varied interpretations and necessitating seemingly unending future research. For example, some of that research (Hannan et al., 1977, 1978; Phillips, 1981) suggests that guaranteed incomes actually increase family instability rather than decrease it as its advocates had hoped it would. But Tallman (1979: 470) indicates that, since the experiments did not have adequate measures of "family functioning," "we could argue that the evidence is not fully available to judge the usefulness of the ...experiments." He then goes on to suggest the sorts of issues that would need to be addressed by future research in order for a full understanding of the impacts of guaranteed incomes to be possible. However, during the interim, Aaron's point is made, namely, that both proponents and opponents of guaranteed-income programs can advocate their own policies, based on the same empirical research but governed by the values or preferences with which they interpret the results. Ultimately, as Aaron suggests, the fact that the proposed policies are contradictory is likely to impede future actions in the name of "prudence."

Feldman (1979: 454) reflects the "prudence" to which Aaron refers when he says, "We need to know more about families

before a simple and single [national] policy can be formulated." Nevertheless, he grips the other horn of the dilemma
by stating that "this need should be balanced by the need for
action. Nelson Rockefeller is reputed to have said, 'By the time
all the information is in, it is usually too late'" (Feldman, 1979:
454-455). While it is plainly desirable to base social action on
sound research, history reveals that many social experiments
were successfully implemented prior to the gathering of con-
clusive and overwhelming empirical evidence that they in fact
represented the correct course. Even in the other sciences
(physical, natural), many applied efforts are undertaken before
"all the information is in." The reason for this course is that *all*
the evidence is *never* in. Nonetheless, applied efforts in those
sciences, though sometimes based on skimpy understanding,
become the very vehicle that broadens and deepens that understanding.

In the face of skimpy and/or conflicting data, the question
becomes to act or not to act, and on what basis to do so. Aaron
(1978: 158) responds that action occurs "only if one feels
passionately that a problem is so urgent that some answer, even
though it may be wrong, is better than none." Since passion is
stirred by values, the willingness to risk policy based on any
social research (given its high degree of uncertain validity) must
ultimately lie with the realm of preferences or tastes (Aaron,
1978: 156). In the case of family, the preferences stretch along
the continuum of individualism-familism, the polar extremes of
which are expressed, on the one hand, by Stone's (1977:151)
definition of individualism and, on the other hand, by the sort
of familism existing in the communist countries (see Chapter
4).

Therefore, since conservatives are, to a greater or lesser
degree, oriented away from individualism, they are very likely,
for instance, to highlight the inevitable flaws in those investigations that purport to discover no negative consequences
for children of mother employment. Some conservatives may
argue that we actually do not know how damaging that
situation is; others may assert a pervasive societal decay

traceable to such situations (see, for example, Lasch, 1977, 1978). Since progressives (and moderates) tend to favor individualism, they are more persuaded by the literature on this topic showing "no effects," and thus are likely to encourage social policies making parental employment less difficult (see Bohen and Viveros-Long, 1981).

Another family situation used by conservatives in arguing that the conventional family is in "decay" is *father absence*. Whether this situation is the result of divorce or of out-of-wedlock births, conservatives allege that children in such homes suffer accordingly. However, Feldman and Feldman (1975) compared children from father-absent homes with children from father-present homes on factors such as school performance, attitudes toward school, peer relationships, self-concept, and mother-child relationships. When controlling for social class, they found no significant differences between the two categories of children. Nonconservatives use these and similar findings from other studies to conclude that departures from morphostatic twentieth-century family patterns are not necessarily negative. Consequently, they say laws and policies that seek to mandate a male presence in the home may be wrong-headed.[3] Nevertheless, conservatives identify the inevitable methodological flaws in these kinds of studies and point to other types of empirical evidence (such as clinical observations) showing opposite findings. The upshot is that they continue to promote their model of family and to attack whatever societal or policy trends they perceive as undermining that model's demands that the father be present and in authority.

In sum, it seems apparent that answers to the question "Is family possible?" cannot be derived *solely* from empirical research. Because the state of the research art makes that aim impossible, citizens wanting to support policy are inexorably moved to evaluate data based on their own preferences for individualism-familism. However, at some point during the discourse (conflict) between opposing points of view, the issue of the greater general welfare, or the problem of order, must be raised. We have seen that, by and large, nonconservative macro advocates have steered clear—for a variety of reasons—of posing a general image of family well-being. But at some stage the outlines of such an image must be developed, because the conventional alternative is so sharply out of sync with the larger society, thus presumably undercutting the greater good—the well-being of society, family and individuals. In doing so, progressives should have no illusion that analyzing and describing "order" can be done on the basis of empirical work alone, as essential as that work is (see Chapter 9). It must also involve our theoretical understandings of society and family, and ultimately our desiderata regarding the "good" society.

Micro/Problem-Solving Responses

While the response of the macro advocates to "family problems" generated by economic out of phaseness has been to concentrate on legislation aimed at rearranging economic conditions (part of the social milieu in which families exist), the response of the micro/problem-solving advocates has been to examine families themselves and the ways in which they cope with, or manage, the effects of their milieu. Many micro advocates perceive a gap (extending beyond the economic realm and including the expressive matters and child-rearing problems discussed in Chapter 4) between the demands of contemporary society and the capabilities of conventional families to grapple with those demands. It is in the particular sense of limited family coping skills that they define families as being out of phase with an often inhospitable society.

Upon surveying the literature covering these two sets of responses, one is immediately struck by the degree to which each ignores the other. Aside from passing references, especially in the micro literature, to the fact that social conditions cannot be overlooked, it almost appears as if the advocates of each perspective are not examining the same phenomenon at all, namely, modern families. Instead, it is the critics of contemporary family trends who seem most likely to target both the macro and micro dimensions. Whether the critics are conservative (for example, Lasch, 1977, 1978) or operate out of a feminist mold (Safilios-Rothschild, 1974; Lipman-Blumen and Bernard, 1979), they appear to be most aware that "solving family problems," or "making healthier families," or the like cannot realistically be accomplished unless both macro- *and* micro-type issues are pursued simultaneously and interconnectedly. And certainly from the standpoint of the larger question we are considering—the problem of order—it is essential that both macro and micro levels be analyzed and connected. For example, we learned in Chapter 4 that the conventional family's fatal flaw is the lack of synchrony between it (micro level) and the macro-level larger society. An alternative model of family would presumably supply a "fit" between the two levels.

To a large degree, the divergence in the opinions of the macro and micro advocates is based on rather different viewpoints on how best to assist families. Dumon and Aldous (1979: 500) remark that both in Western Europe and America, "there does exist a widely held belief...that governments can do something to make the lot of families better." However, while many citizens may hold that belief, Dumon and Aldous (1979: 501) flesh it out by saying that "governments seem to be best at making financial grants to people.... They can also make available family counseling services...[but] governmental programs...cannot provide direct panaceas for...the kinds of problems" related to ongoing interactions and outcomes between spouses and between parents and children. Hence, Dumon and Aldous identify a prevailing sentiment among many macro-policy advocates, namely, that the most effective and efficient way in which society can assist family is to ensure that all its members have full access to quality educational and economic opportunities. Once possessing those "tickets," they will then presumably be able to make "socially responsible" choices. "Social problems are imbedded in the social structure and...only if we can change the opportunity structure for families can we hope to seriously influence the course of these problems" (Tallman, 1979: 471). This viewpoint closely resembles Bane's position (see Chapter 3), although she is more sanguine than Dumon and Aldous about the ultimate beneficial consequences of spouses struggling with interactional equality questions. Dumon and Aldous (1979: 500) suggest that "even when countries provide the means for a change in the allocation of family roles by allowing male as well as female maternity leaves or by making available child-care facilities or defraying their cost for working mothers," there is no assurance that spousal or parent-child interaction is necessarily enhanced.

Whereas the macro perspective locates family well-being within the societal context, the micro/problem-solving perspective pinpoints well-being primarily within the family itself. By no means, however, does this imply that its representatives are unaware of the necessity of taking account of the larger milieu. At the conclusion of their review of the "family communication" literature, Raush et al. (1979: 485) observe that "the family cannot be understood without examining its interconnections with its environment." Klein and Hill (1979) make those sociological connections quite explicit in their analyses of family problem solving. Hansen and Johnson (1979) do the same in their analyses of family crises and stresses, as do other analysts. But, in contrast to the macro approach, the focus of these and other micro analysts is on *dynamics within* the household. Perhaps the sharpest distinction between the macro and micro approaches is caught most keenly by the Hansen and Johnson (1979: 588) contention that "whatever else is involved, the definitional qualities are critical." That is, no matter what the "objective" social and economic conditions in the family's milieu, its capability to react to them either "effectively" or "ineffectively" depends ultimately on its own definitions of those conditions and its perceptions of how to deal with them.

Hansen and Johnson (1979: 592) also employ the term "adaptability" to describe these same characteristics—"the family's capacity to meet obstacles and shift courses." Thus, in reviewing the "family stress" literature, they conclude that the families "best able" to cope "effectively" with *externally* induced traumas (socioeconomic trauma, physical and mental retardation, natural disasters, and so on—phenomena toward which much macro policy is often directed) are those families possessing certain *internal* dynamics. Essentially, these dynamics consist of communication and negotiation patterns that enable family members to *analyze* accurately what strategies are most appropriate in dealing with the trauma, and also how to *implement* the strategies. The authors conclude that the families least effective in responding to external stress are those that are most "rigid" or least flexible, that is, most morphostatic in the face of those challenges.

According to Raush et al. (1979: 469), "clinical work evolved within this [dynamic] context. Problems of living within a family structure came to be seen less as a matter of adjustment...to fixed circumstances and more as a matter of...how relationships evolve, stabilize, and change." Raush et al. carry further their rejection of the morphostatic notion of "fixed circumstances" by asserting that "each family must evolve its own destiny, it faces tasks not only of developing its own rules but also of defining how and by whom these rules are made and the conditions for change." And since, as they say, "cultural givens" are no longer relevant, "a massive burden is thus placed on communication. That burden increases as [conventional] definitions of marriage and of family become increasingly blurred" (Raush et al., 1979: 469). The authors then apply existing "communication theory"— although they acknowledge (p. 484) that it "is not quite a theory. It is a conglomeration of more or less related concepts, with the relations among them obscure"—to family relationships. In keeping with their discard of morphostatic notions, they define their "theory" as "a dynamic orientation in its concern with the specific forces which maintain or change relationships" (p. 484).

Klein and Hill (1979: 494) generate a similar dynamic ambience (as does Roloff, 1981) by stating that the "family-problem-solving" tradition views "families as active agents in their own problem-solving efforts." Less acceptable in their view is the notion that they perceive as endemic to what they call the "social problems" approach: the notion that "families are seen as more or less helpless groups that must turn outward for assistance" (Klein and Hill, 1979: 494). Incidentally, this assessment regarding the "helplessness" of many families—especially the less advantaged—seems to pervade macro policy perspectives, if not explicitly, at least implicitly, giving rise to Abbott's (1981) notion of the "Service State." In any event, when Klein and Hill (1975: 495) use the term "problem," they refer to a "barrier" that may or may not be overcome but, in either case, the family does not view the situation as "hopeless." By "solving," Klein and Hill (1979: 496) mean that "human behavior [is] an active, coping, achievement-oriented phenomenon rather than...passive or fatalistic.... Actors attempt to solve their problems,...some are more or less successful, and...successful behavior can be learned." Klein and Hill (1979: 515) also cite Reiss's descriptions of three ways in which families may view their environment: first, as masterable, predictable, knowable, and controllable, with family members reinforcing these definitions for one another; second, while some members may view their milieu in that fashion, they do not communicate their definitions to other members; or, finally, "the environment is viewed as threatening, chaotic, and unknowable."

If a major bias in the macro perspective has been to regard families as "helpless," an equally significant bias in the micro/problem-solving perspective has been to do research on "problem families" and then to make generalizations that give the appearance of wider applicability: "What little systematic information we have about intimate adult relationships is probably based more on what is wrong than on what is right with such relationships" (Weiss and Margolin, 1977: 556). Weiss and Margolin lament this situation and hope that clinical research will someday arrive at the point that it can offer "the World Health Organization [WHO] a listing of criteria of successful, enjoyable, mutually beneficial marriages." Aspirations to exercise influence on a policymaking organization such as WHO rarely surface in the clinical literature, but their appearance here suggests that at least some clinicians consider it desirable that links should be forged between macro and micro perspectives—between governmental policies on the one hand, and programmatic and clinical efforts on the other. Furthermore, these clinicians seem to assume that these kinds of links could be much more highly specified than those cited by Dumon and Aldous (1979).

Linking Macro and Micro Responses

These and other contrasts between macro and micro approaches to family make apparent the fact that responses to the family's out of phaseness are geared closely to how that affliction is defined. In Chapter 4, I defined out of phaseness in terms of the nonsync between nontraditional society and conventional family—Western society has moved *beyond* family. But conservatives view the family as having moved *away* from certain moorings, and thus as being out of sync with those moorings. Many macro-level policy advocates contend that family poverty indicates being out of sync with societal affluence and is the result of blocked opportunities. Consequently, they argue that simple equity and justice demand that the blocks be removed so that all families can strive for that affluence on a more or less comparable footing. An important subset of macro advocates places particular emphasis on poor children and the need to increase their economic resources in order to bring them in step with the majority of American children. An article of faith with macro advocates was cited above—the opportunity structure must be opened because "for the past 30 years we have been gathering data...[on] therapy counseling, or casework, and the evidence continues to mount that such efforts...have not had any significant effect on the social problems they purport to alleviate" (Tallman, 1979: 471). Macro advocates believe that once families are relatively tangibly advantaged, they will then develop the requisite intangible skills to deal effectively with interpersonal issues. In short, if poor people do not possess the sorts of problem-solving skills just described, it is because their deprived life experiences have led them to the conclusion that Klein and Hill (1979) say is terminal: Problems are *defined* as *hopeless*.

On the other hand, micro advocates (as well as conservatives) respond to this sort of reasoning by asserting that many relatively advantaged families experience a host of "problems" in spite of their tangible resources (Halem, 1980). Indeed, the great debates about family going on among scholars and advocates, as well as in the media and other public forums, encompass the great majority of citizens, extending far beyond the poor. Questions about "family decay," "disorganization," and so on are stimulated by phenomena such as divorce, cohabitation, working mothers, single-parent families, nonmarital sexuality, illegitimacy, midlife crises, and so forth. When most people ask, "Is family possible?" these are the kinds of issues they have in mind, even though some macropolicy planners would perhaps rather the focus be on readily identifiable and "*explicit* family policies...in which consequences for families are deliberately structured, such as adoption, foster care, family planning.... [Or on] *implicit*...policies...that have nonfamilial objectives but which nevertheless affect families,...such...as special education for handicapped children, the retirement test for social insurance beneficiaries, deinstitutionalization programs for the mentally ill and...retarded" (Zimmerman, 1979: 492).

Earlier I observed that Dumon and Aldous (1979) and Bane (1976) represent the view, held by many macro advocates, that government policy cannot effectively deal with "interpersonal" issues. And although (from the above quote) we might expect that Tallman would also share that view, he nonetheless asserts that enhanced "autonomy" and "interpersonal relations" could be goals of national family policy (Tallman, 1979: 470). Indeed, enhanced interpersonal relations (as indicated by marital stability) were implicit goals of the income-maintenance experiments discussed above. *In short, it seems artificial and virtually impossible to separate any laws and bureaucratic regulations from their actual or potential consequences on family dynamics.* This conclusion holds whether we think of traditional state marriage and abortion laws, state equal rights amendments, tax statutes, federal laws dealing with parents "kidnapping" their children from their ex-spouses in other states, the sorts of matters just cited from Zimmerman, or the emerging movement to increase the "rights of children."

But, by the same token, *it is futile to try to devise laws, policies, and regulations that are not congruent with the preferences and dynamics of families.* There are *reciprocal*, not one-way, influences between the macro and micro levels (Blalock and Wilken, 1979). For 100 years the fundamental complaint of conservatives has been precisely that citizens have ignored laws governing divorce, sexuality, abortion, illegitimacy, cohabitation, and so forth. Analogously, while mother employment was never legally prohibited, there were once powerful social pressures against it (at least in white society); citizens are increasingly ignoring such pressures, to the corresponding distress of conservatives. Hence, the question "Is family possible?" is simultaneously linked to existing laws and regulations, as well as to existing preferences and goals of family members. Phillips (1981: 175) asserts that it makes little sense for macro planners to devise "family policies" if the very thing to which the policies are supposed to apply is in flux *away* from some state fixed in the imaginations of the planners. In all fairness, however, some macro advocates are keenly aware that family is in flux and try to promote policies accordingly (for example, see Keniston et al., 1977). Nevertheless, as I said earlier, most of them do not raise fundamental theoretical and philosophical questions regarding family. Consequently, at best, they make the kinds of suggestions that tend to avoid the issue of the continued viability of the twentieth-century family.

Likewise, some micro advocates and clinicians avoid that same issue by seeking to make family members better "copers" and "problem solvers" in general, while saying little or nothing about the morphostatic patterns within which they are supposed to function "effectively." Nevertheless, that silence must be broken by recognizing that if family environments are supposed to be perceived as "masterable, predictable, knowable, and controllable," as Reiss advocates (see Klein and Hill, 1979: 515), something must be done to those environments to make them appear more malleable. That "something" is discussed in subsequent chapters, especially in Chapter 8 in connection with Weitzman's (1981) analysis of state family laws. Although the need for effective communication is as much an article of faith among micro advocates as equalized opportunity is among macro advocates, Raush et al. (1979) take the trouble to explain the micro faith. Its basis, they assert, is the gradual evaporation of traditional cultural prescriptions and proscriptions. While in that sense they recognize the growing "impossibility" of seeking to impose twentieth-century family structures, they err in failing to identify any emerging overarching cultural patterns (such as those suggested in subsequent chapters) and also in their assertion that through communication "each family evolve[s] its own destiny" in a way that appears unique from every other family. If every household were indeed to become a "law unto itself" we could hardly say that the problem of order is being effectively resolved, or reasonably deny the conservative apprehension of potential "family anomie" and the possible attempt to impose some authoritarian governmental solution.

Hence, as vital an element as family communication is, it is constrained by social and cultural realities; it would not be desirable to have it otherwise if the results turned out to be arrays of idiosyncratic families.

The 1980 White House Conference on Families

Given the importance of effectively bridging the gap between macro policies and family processes, I shall elaborate this issue throughout the following pages. However, to close this chapter, I will use the 1980 White House Conference on Families (WHCF) as a case study of the amalgam of complex ideas that have emerged in this and prior chapters. WHCF was unique in that it represented the convergence in a single, governmentally sponsored setting of the interests of conservatives, moderates (macro/policy and micro/problem-solving advocates), and progressives. This convergence, however, should not imply that each viewpoint was given equal weight—that was not the case.

In general terms, WHCF was a response to the amorphous feeling of many people that "something was wrong" with *the* American family and that government attention might alleviate the situation; or, if nothing was particularly "wrong," a feeling that there was nevertheless a great deal that "enlightened" government policy could do to benefit *the* family. The strongest push for WHCF came from that segment of macro advocates (mentioned above) who wanted to broaden the net of family policy to include the nonpoor as well as the less advantaged (Tucker, 1980). More specifically, the conference chair (Tucker) asserted that President Carter called the conference because of a perceived gap (out of phaseness) between "official America" (the government) and "family America." To close that gap, Carter charged the conference to identify current government policies that "hinder" families and to propose new policies that might "assist" them.

The earliest planning stages of the conference were marked by severe ideological struggles, but in the end "the lobbies of the far right and far left" were overwhelmed by "the majority of delegates [who] were moderates [and] anxious to avoid the labels, rigid programs and predetermined agendas of ideological activists" (Tucker, 1980: 12). WHCF was thus dominated by moderates (and like-minded persons) who preferred *not* to raise underlying theoretical and philosophical issues. As Tucker (1980: 11) says, "We did not focus on the bizarre or extreme. We did not redefine the family.... A traditional definition of a family was the only definition adopted."

In brief, WHCF chose simply to live with the conventional definition of family, and the conference was used to ponder other concerns. This policy decision represented a substantial victory for conservative forces both in and out of WHCF and stood in contrast to the prior triumph achieved by progressive forces, who, early in President Carter's administration, convinced him to shift the conference's focus from *the* American family to *families*. According to Steiner (1981: 35), the impetus for this shift came through an unsolicited memo from "the ad hoc HEW Family Impact Task Group, which urged acceptance of a 'neutral' model rather than the traditional husband-wife-children model."

Given the traditional family definition, WHCF was primarily concerned with family "helplessness" in the face of "unprecedented economic, social and even political pressures.... We've learned that people are unwilling to put up with the continued neglect and harm to our families that come from thoughtless action and misdirected policies within our major social institutions. Families are moving from apathy to anger and action. They insist on changes in unresponsive and insensitive policies" (Tucker, 1980: 9).

Hence, according to Tucker, there is nothing amiss with the structure of conventional families or with the individuals that make them up. But there is malfeasance that inhibits families, and it stems from misbegotten policies in other institutions. Indirectly, these policies leave many families "struggling and some have been overwhelmed and broken" (Tucker, 1980: 9). Note how this assessment contrasts with the usual conservative view that *individuals* have deviated from fixed moral norms, as well as with the progressive perspective that family structure itself is in need of overhaul, along with the social policies that directly inform that structure. WHCF also diverged from the micro/problem-solving approach because, although the delegates did support "programs and causes" to enhance "interpersonal relationships, communication and decision making" (Tucker, 1980: 48), the action taken was not in the context suggested by Klein and Hill (1979) or by Hansen and Johnson (1979). That is, no strong recommendation was explicitly made that since among families exposed to comparable *objective* conditions those with certain coping skills fare better than those without them, such skills ought to be an integral feature of future family programs.

Furthermore, and most important, the WHCF problem locus (institutional policies) oversimplified the enormous complexity of the total situation. Although Tucker (1980: 12) claims WHCF "proposals are based on the realities of family life today," they in fact represented only one part (albeit a vital part) of "family reality." What, for example, are some of the specific institutional impediments to family identified by WHCF? Targeted first and foremost were business and labor organizations; they were urged "to take a hard look at flexible job schedules, more sensitive leave and transfer policies, child care at the workplace and other family-oriented personnel policies" (Tucker, 1980: 9). Next, government was urged to take steps "to prevent and treat drug and alcohol abuse, a major threat to family stability" (p. 9). In addition it was recommended that matters such as social security, health policies, and care of the elderly, handicapped, and disabled, should be reexamined along with "marriage taxes" and welfare policies that discriminate against marriage and help break up families" (p. 10). Family impact analysis was also boosted. In addition, the government was urged to give "greater recognition and equity for *women* who choose to be full-time homemakers" (p. 10; emphasis added). The third realm targeted was that of the overlapping responsibilities of government, media, schools, and business/labor in such areas as television sex and violence, racism, job discrimination, programs for adolescents, family violence, child care options, family life education, and so forth.

WHCF created the image of a beleaguered majority of American families beset by insensitive forces—a "we-they" confrontation. Although the forces are not necessarily conspiratorial or sinister (as, for instance, many conservatives view progressives), WHCF posited that the "forces" (they) undermine the conventional twentieth-century family. "We" (the people) "fight back" by insisting that "when government [and other institutions] touches our families, it *helps* instead of hurts—that it *supports* instead of *undermines*" (Tucker, 1980: 11). In the view of these macro advocates, the conventional family, though solid, is nonetheless under attack. In effect, certain institutional interests are alleged to be out of sync with familial interests. In order for the family to be more habitable, or better, the forces attacking it must not merely be repelled, but must be transformed into allies. And while no one would disagree with the notion of making institutional policies more hospitable to family, Tucker commits an egregious error by assuming that the walls of "fortress family" are being breached solely from the outside. As we saw earlier, Swidler (1980), Yankelovich (1981b), Shorter (1975), and many others suggest that the walls of the conventional family are crumbling from the inside out as well as the other way around. Instead of ignoring this possibility, it would seem wiser to consider the approach suggested earlier, namely, to make changes in the milieu so that it seems more "masterable" and to make changes in families so that they are more "masterful."

Significantly, in spite of the lofty ideals and goals set by WHCF delegates and their less vocal moderate constituency, it would appear that they most often behaved in what I have been calling an *individualistic* manner. Indeed, at the very root of strongly endorsed WHCF proposals for flexi- and shared-time jobs and child care options are individualistic aspirations representing a significant, albeit unwitting, departure from the conventional family that Tucker unhesitatingly claims the conference preserved. Although WHCF moderates maintained that married women's employment is a necessary response to growing economic pressures even when husbands are present, conservatives sharply retorted that many families blindly conform to what Wandersee (1981) calls the "consumerism" begun in the 1920s—choosing to maintain or increase their standard of living, rather than selecting the option of curbing it, thus allowing women to continue as full-time mothers.

Further, and more important, careful scrutiny of the WHCF recommendations on "full employment" (Tucker, 1980: 26-30) makes it clear that the delegates did not conceive of women's employment solely in terms of the dollar contributions to their households—a purely familistic notion. For example, the individualistic idea was communicated that women have the *right* (see Scanzoni, 1978: 23) to be employed for precisely the same reasons men do—for the sake of dignity, prestige, esteem, and a feeling of usefulness, along with autonomy, independence, identity, and meaning. Failure to grasp the implications of redefining, as WHCF moderates did, the meaning of work to women indicates how firmly they had shut their eyes to sources of change *within* family. Instead, reflecting the unease of many citizens regarding family (in a 1980 national sample polled by Gallup, 45 percent reported that "family life has gotten *worse* in the last fifteen years"; 12 percent said it was the *same*; 37 percent said it had gotten *better*; 6 percent reported no opinion; Tucker, 1980: 182), they conclude that external "pressures are undermining families—racism, discrimination, insensitive institutions, economic and social stress" (Tucker, 1980: 12). Perceiving societal institutions to be out of sync with *the* family, their goal was to bring those institutions and organizations into phase with family interests.

The question is, how successful was WHCF in achieving those goals, especially in view of Carter administration sponsorship of WHCF and its pledge (Tucker, 1980: 5) to speedily implement as many of the WHCF recommendations as possible? To answer this question we turn first to the Research Forum—a pre-WHCF gathering of scholars and family advocates designed to "create a factual framework" for the 2000 WHCF delegates (Tucker, 1980: 157). At this gathering progressive perspectives were presented by Hareven (Tucker, 1980: 158) and Giele (Tucker, 1980: 151). It is interesting to note that Bronfenbrenner—mentioned earlier as representative of a conservative perspective—made a comparatively "radical" policy recommendation to the forum: "Solidify the family by placing more women in positions of power in our society, and place more men in caring roles" (Tucker, 1980: 161).

While Bronfenbrenner "stressed the need for strong support systems for families and bonds between families and major institutions" (Tucker, 1980: 160), the conservative position was unambiguously enunciated by Dobson: "The American family is disintegrating because of a breakdown in the moral structure of society. The family of today is in need of something to believe in" (Tucker, 1980: 160).[4] Besides underscoring his allegiance to the conventional model, Dobson also reinforced the conservative adherence to the sort of *selective* hands-off policy described earlier in this chapter:

> Dobson admonished policy makers in Congress and elsewhere to stop interfering in family matters and refrain from imposing itself in the marital relationship between parents and children. Dobson voiced strong objection to the Domestic Violence and Treatment Act, suggesting that the federal government cannot do anything about the husband-wife relationship [Tucker, 1980: 160].

But, as Tucker observed, WHCF delegates paid scant attention to either the conservative or the progressive orientation, and instead took the posture described above. Nevertheless, in 1981 the Reagan administration not only ignored WHCF recommendations—many of which would have required hefty increases in outlays of federal dollars—it cut deeply into already-existing family-related programs—especially those touching the poor. Furthermore, the administration and its congressional allies reaffirmed the conservative "hands off the family" position. Their administration's selectivity again became apparent through 1981 senatorial attempts to arbitrarily define the fetus as human, thus enabling state legislatures to write laws permitting prosecution for murder of those persons who engage in or abet abortion.[5] Congressional conservatives also mustered efforts to try to pass the Family Protection Act, which, among other things, states that "funds would be denied to any state or local educational agency which uses funds for the 'purchase of any educational materials, if such materials would tend to denigrate, diminish or deny the role differences between the sexes *as it has been historically understood in the United States*'" (emphasis added).[6]

Thus it is clear that while WHCF represented a large-scale national effort on the part of one set of family advocates to involve the federal government deeply in family policymaking—along with business, industry, labor, and the media—those efforts were to no practical avail—at least during the early to mid-1980s. WHCF recommendations have fallen victim to the economic policies of the Reagan administration and to the conservative ideologies of its congressional allies. Nevertheless, these two realities do not necessarily signal the "conservative backlash" regarding family behaviors alleged by certain observors. From Yankelovich's (1981a, 1981b) data and from the Connecticut Mutual (1981) study, as well as from the results of an April 1981 *New York Times*-CBS national sample, there is no evidence that citizens are becoming less supportive of ongoing fundamental changes in family behaviors.[7] The *New York Times*-CBS survey reports *no increases* over the preceding four years in opposition to abortion, a federal ERA, cohabitation among the unmarried, or married women working "even if their husbands can support them."[8]

The upshot is that while conservative ideologies heavily influenced Congress at the onset of the eighties, the majority of the population continued to do precisely what Dobson and other conservatives allege—they were continuing to ignore twentieth-century family norms and behaving in new and different ways, ways more in keeping with the demands and exigencies of the late twentieth and early twenty-first centuries.

WHCF sought to identify specific societal exigencies that might be inimical to families—a necessary and worthy endeavor. However, their major error lay in explicitly attempting to reify the conventional family even though increasing numbers of ordinary citizens were gradually but perceptibly shifting away from it—a shift which, ironically, WHCF in part inadvertently endorsed.

The WHCF strategy of asserting that "the basic structure of the family is sound; it is instead society that is amiss," was clever politically in that it diverted the attention of a wide range of interest groups and persons away from their own parochial concerns and focused it instead on a "common enemy." Who could not be in favor of opposing harmful government, business, and labor policies? WHCF was thus a necessary, but exceedingly limited, first step in responding to the perceived out of phaseness between family and society. Conservatives saw it as limited and largely ignored it because of the financial cost of its recommendations, their mistrust of additional government "interference" in family, and most fundamentally because they have a different perception than WHCF of the society-family gap. But perhaps WHCF's most significant limitations can be measured by how little impact it evidently made on the general populace. To be sure, its primary intended audience was that of legislators and institutional executives. But, so far as is known, there was hardly a groundswell of support from the populace to alert legislators and executives that WHCF recommendations ought to be implemented. There was no groundswell, even though, had a national poll been taken, the recommendations would almost certainly have received considerable verbal support.

Indeed, the Gallup survey cited earlier, taken in March 1980, prior to WHCF delegate voting, indicates precisely that kind of support. Nevertheless, in interpreting the Gallup data, we find ourselves in an Aaronian-type situation. The survey was commissioned by WHCF, and the specific questions put to respondents reflected, naturally enough, WHCF interests, concerns, and objectives. Consequently, it is not surprising that the poll's results should correspond to WHCF goals and recommendations. Not measured, by contrast, were the concerns of conservatives or progressives. Defenders of the poll can easily point to certain of its items and interpret them to discredit the validity of either the conservative or the progressive orientation. In response, conservatives might argue that their concerns were not properly measured or, more likely, repudiate the validity of simplistic Gallup-type polls to capture the subtleties and nuances of their perspective. They might also contend that the family is beyond *any* empirical techniques; its basis lies in mystical and often sacred realities. Thus, in the conservative view, to use empirical means to assess family quality is the height of folly and perhaps even arrogance.

Progressives, of course, do not share this basic mistrust of empirical procedures. However, they could contend that other kinds of survey-type questions might have revealed citizen awareness of the sorts of issues progressives are raising. Yankelovich's (1981a) survey data, for instance, paint a vastly different picture of past, present, and especially future family than those collected by Gallup. More fundamentally, progressives could also argue that empirical procedures other than the simplistic Gallup survey format would tap that awareness even more strongly.[9] For instance, the kinds of issues being raised by Swidler (1980), Jancar (1978), Lapidus (1978), Heitlinger (1979), and others do not easily lend themselves to simplistic surveys and unsophisticated Gallup-type percentage distributions and bivariate cross-classifications.

It is possible, in short, to assess family on several levels. The Gallup data and WHCF recommendations tap the uppermost and most easily accessible level. But this is the level most strongly associated with *social desirability* and, whether one is answering survey questions or voting on recommendations, it is extremely difficult not to identify with this level. Judged on this level alone, there is little doubt that "family is possible"; furthermore, the implication is that the particular family that is "possible" is the twentieth-century conventional form, with certain improvements such as acceptance of wife-mother employment. But there are also deeper and more profound levels to the assessment of family, which WHCF deliberately avoided. The clever WHCF political-unity strategy and the WHCF recommendations do not approach these levels. Thus it is possible for citizens to respond in one fashion to WHCF concerns and yet to react in quite another fashion to deeper, more profound issues. And it is these issues that trigger the question, "Is family possible?" and, what is more, make the answer less pat and clear-cut. Hence, the failure of citizens to supply a groundswell of support for WHCF recommendations, and instead to indicate merely perfunctory interest, may very well suggest that the issues that trouble them most profoundly have been conveniently—and, perhaps, from some politicians' standpoint—*necessarily* ignored.

According to Steiner (1981: 46), these types of issues were ignored because President Carter "never came to grips with the differences between 'the family' and 'the diversity of families.'" Consequently, WHCF was "star-crossed" (Steiner, 1981: 198). Moreover, Steiner (1981: 46) observes that any future federal conference on families, children, or related topics that similarly fails to recognize the diversity issue is a waste of time and resources: WHCF, he concludes, "need not be replicated."

Summary

That there is a disjunction between contemporary family and society all parties seem to agree. But they diverge considerably as to the nature of the hiatus, and thus inevitably as to its proper remedy. The common thread that unites the several viewpoints described in this chapter is that by and large they tend to address symptoms rather than root causes. For example, a substantial segment of macro-level advocates in the 1960s perceived the family's out of phaseness as basically economic. Hence their recommendations focused largely on laws, programs, and policies providing disadvantaged families with financial-type inputs. A centerpiece among Great Society programs were the income-maintenance experiments, with their hoped-for benefits for poor children and their assumed potential to reduce marital instability.

With the demise of the Great Society preoccupation with the disadvantaged, other macro advocates emerged during the 1970s arguing that working- and middle-class families ought also to be part of government concerns—at least through various assessments and evaluations known as "family impact analyses." In addition, as part of the broader perspective on the nonpoor, impacts of day care experiences on children, regardless of class or race, were also investigated. However, in spite of their varied emphases, macro advocates seldom questioned underlying twentieth-century family assumptions, although they did seem to concur that legislation cannot be monolithic in its support of one family form over another.

In contrast to the nonconservatives' ambiguities regarding the kinds of family forms most likely to be least out of sync with society, conservatives are united in their definition of out of phaseness and its cure. Family members, they allege, have forsaken sound normative moorings for "deviant" behaviors; the remedy is to *return to* family patterns of the Victorian and post-Victorian eras.

One reason some nonconservatives experience difficulty in responding to the conservatives' clarity of means and objectives is the ultimate reliance of nonconservatives on empirical research for policy guidelines. But, inevitably, serious questions can be raised regarding the reliability and validity of any social or behavioral research; hence it becomes risky to plan policy *solely* on that basis. In fact, it is fatuous to refuse to face the reality that research results geared toward family policy are ultimately interpreted in the light of values and preferences held by particular interest groups. In the case of family, the preferences stretch along the individualistic-familistic continuum—with conservatives most often choosing to interpret and apply results in terms of familistic, and nonconservatives in terms of individualistic, preferences.

Micro advocates, in contrast to macro advocates, perceive family out of phaseness primarily in terms of the family's capabilities to cope successfully and effectively with the exigencies of a modern, complex society. While very much aware that societal context (for example, class and race) influences a family's coping capabilities, micro advocates see the broader milieu, including legislative policies, as comparatively less decisive than the family's own perceptions and definitions of the stresses, strains, and challenges that surround it. In an effort to reconcile macro and micro perspectives, I have suggested that family dynamics and social context factors are inextricable and reciprocal, and ought to be analyzed accordingly.

The 1980 White House Conference on Families (WHCF) was used as a case example to show how certain macro advocates sought to define the society-family hiatus as being the result of inimical societal-institutional policies. Thus, unlike conservatives, micro advocates, and certain macro advocates who perceive the hiatus in other terms (for example, as more narrowly economic), WHCF concluded that a broad range of societal policies must be altered to adjust to basically "sound" family structures. However, as with the other perspectives discussed throughout the chapter (certain micro advocates excepted), WHCF failed to address issues fundamental to family change, and focused instead on *symptoms* of family out of phaseness. Moreover, unlike certain other advocates, WHCF rejected pluralism and instead espoused the twentieth-century conventional family. However, for a variety of reasons, WHCF has made little impact on either government or the larger society.

NOTES

1. The *Chicago Sun-Times* (October 10, 1980) reported on a conference held at the Menninger Foundation on "Work and the Family: An American Dilemma." According to the reporter, the conference concluded that "traditional family relationships have been devastated by the two-paycheck household, with powerful effects at the workplace as well as in the social order." Thomas A. Murphy, chairman of General Motors Corporation, "deplored the decline of the 'American tradition of placing the interests of the family—of children—above the interests of the parents.'"

2. S-1843 and HR-2977, 1980.

3. However, that is not to say that certain progressives do not advocate male—and female—responsibility for the support of children. Bergmann (1981: 207) says, "I would tend to argue that important interests would be served by interpreting marriage vows as a promise to contribute to the support of children born of the marriage except in exceptional circumstances." She acknowledges that "children born out of wedlock" pose special problems, but nonetheless advocates attempts to require male support even in these situations.

4. Dobson is a psychologist who is well known and highly influential in conservative religious circles.

5. See Weisstein (1981) for a discussion.

6. This legislation was introduced originally in 1980: S-1810 and HR-7445.

7. See Adam Clymer in the Greensboro (North Carolina) *Daily News*; *New York Times* News Service, May 3, 1981.

8. A Gallup survey released on August 9, 1981, showed that 63 percent of Americans who had "heard about" ERA supported it (*National NOW Times,* September 1981: 4).

9. For example, multivariate and/or qualitative techniques could be used.

PART II

WHERE WE ARE GOING

6

RETHINKING THE HARMONY
BETWEEN SOCIETY AND FAMILY

Chapter 5 considered one response to the out of phaseness of the family with society, the symptomatic response. Another response is an attempt to go to the *root* of things—to try to come to grips with what family is "all about." So far I have critiqued the twentieth-century conventional family and have suggested that, in the Socratic sense of providing advantages to its members, its future seems to be in relative doubt—whether it is "possible" or not is problematic. But what is the shape of an alternative? Answering this question is the aim of the remaining chapters; in this chapter I begin by trying to show how an alternative to the conventional family turns out to be in better sync with contemporary society.

By now it should be plain that Socrates' problem-of-order notion has both theoretical and philosophical implications. It is theoretical in the sense of supplying illumination and understanding; it is philosophical in the sense of providing guidelines for application. For example, once we *understand* some of the elements and interrelationships that make up family (much as one would seek to understand any complex equipment), then we have *ipso facto* gained some clues regarding its optimal operation. In the "pure" scientific sense,

Quote from *The Prophet,* by Kahlil Gibran, reprinted by permission. Copyright 1980, Alfred A. Knopf, Inc.

understanding may sometimes be totally devoid of any known application. But in the world of social and behavioral science that disjunction is difficult, if not impossible, to maintain (Boulding, 1976). When we examine family from a problem-of-order perspective, valid understanding should lead to meaningful applications. As was pointed out in Chapter 5, research efforts by themselves do not necessarily point the way to effective applications. Unless there is an overarching theory by which to assess and synthesize empirical results, the family policy fragmentation to which Steiner (1981) refers will continue. Furthermore, sound theoretical guidelines are likely to focus new research efforts in the kinds of specific directions that will eventually result in greater illumination and more effective applications.

The Fit Between Society and Family

Stone (1977: 424) concludes that

> the key to family change in middle- and upper-class circles is the ebb and flow of battle between competing interests and values represented by various levels of social organization, from the individual up to the nation-state. The evolution of the family...has faithfully reflected the changing positions in the tug-of-war between these various interests and the values attached to them.

In analyzing these ongoing struggles among competing interest groups to establish the predominance of their own preferred family forms, Stone explicitly follows the thinking of Max Weber, an issue I elaborate in Chapter 9. Stone (1977: 409) says also that "the basic values and organization of...Early Modern England [1500s]...were hierarchical, authoritarian and inquisitorially collectivist." Moreover, there was strong convergence between that kind of society and "a family type whose characteristics [were] psychological distance, deference [women to men, children to parents] and publicity ['there was no sense of domestic privacy']" (pp. 408-409). But by 1700, according to Stone (1977: 411), both the organization of society and family had changed: "Neither the absolute monarch nor the patriachal father was any longer necessary for the maintenance of social order." He goes on to say that by the late 1700s "the happiness of the individual, his untrammelled pursuit of ego gratifications, was being equated with the public good" (p. 424).

However, Stone (1977: 424) claims that "this was a wholly unrealistic assumption" and, as we learned in Chapter 2, that situation gave rise to the Victorian family. Reacting to the perceived chaos in the larger society and in the family, an attempt was made in both England and America by religious, political, and other interest groups to impose an explicitly hierarchical family pattern on nineteenth-century society. These ongoing struggles reiterate a point made in prior chapters (especially Chapter 4), namely, that the optimum conditions for family and social order occur when there is synchrony between societal and family organization. And in contrast to Stone's description of the authoritarianism of Early Modern England, contemporary Western societies are marked, as Lasch and many others have observed, by something utterly different. Lasch may refer to it as a "breakdown of authority," but in a more positive light one could interpret the situation as an intense desire for participatory democracy (Zartman, 1976). Political, economic, community, educational, and even religious organizations are permeated by the desires of their various subunits to take part in their governance and direction—the leadership's accountability is as important as its authority.

The *goal* of participatory democracy has been accepted unequivocally in our society and some serious efforts are being made to attain that goal, although we have by no means abolished all societal injustices or established equitable participation in institutional governance. However, our goal of participatory democracy applies to all sectors of society *except* family; thus family is out of synchrony with the rest of society.

However, the situation (as seen in Chapter 3) is complex and paradoxical. The nonsync is sharpest when we examine formal policies in the shape of state laws (Chapter 8), which unequivocally promulgate hierarchical marriage and family patterns (Sachs and Wilson, 1978). Although this particular vision of family is out of phase with contemporary society, a vocal minority strongly supports it, at the same time that increasing numbers of people are "drifting" from it. And the drift is precisely that—nonsystematic efforts on the part of some people to try to reconcile traditional and emerging conceptions of family. Although some 71 percent of Americans say that they prefer something other than the conventional family (Connecticut Mutual, 1981), additional evidence assessing employment and household behaviors suggests that severe contradictions exist between the ideal of equality and the reality of hierarchy (Aldous, 1981). To complicate matters, when certain feminists have sought to remove these contradictions and shift toward equality, they have failed to address problem-of-order issues (see Chapter 3), and their efforts have stimulated conservatives to try to reinstate a hierarchy even more rigid than that which currently exists.

Throughout the past hundred years, most conservatives perceived the "deviancy" away from the conventional family as the result of the acts of random individuals; thus conservatives had no impetus to organize in a formal manner. But with the feminist revival of the 1960s and its most concrete manifestation—the Equal Rights Amendment—conservatives, many of them heirs of the late eighteenth-century revivalists described by Stone (1977), perceived that interest groups had suddenly formed, interest groups that promoted norms and behaviors that would eventually destroy *their* family. Because of their organic view of society and family, and their religious fervor, conservatives were unable to acknowledge the legitimacy of the notion that competing interest groups can promulgate differing models of family that are beneficial for those groups, and perhaps ultimately beneficial for society as well.

Boles (1979: 45-56, 196-199) documents the coalescence and crystallization of a variety of divergent interest groups around

ERA in the early 1970s. At that time, "rapid and decisive ratification in the states was predicted" (Boles, 1979: 55). But in reaction, as further documented by Boles (1979: 61-98), a variety of interest groups formed to oppose ERA (led by the charismatic and superb grassroots organizer, Phyllis Schlafly),[1] joining forces with existing organizations opposed to "abortion, affirmative action, sex education, gay rights, busing, gun control, the Panama Canal Treaties, national health insurance, unionization of the military, and the Strategic Arms Limitations Talks (SALT)" (Boles, 1979: 189)—the agenda, in short, of the New Right. Regardless of their many diverse interests, these groups united under the banner of preserving their twentieth-century family model. Perceiving ERA as a threat to that model, they effectively overcame it.

Contrasting Images of Society and Family

The three upper boxes of Figure 6.1 illustrate the conservative view of the synchrony among society, family, and individuals. The three segments are organized in terms of fixed norms as to what behaviors are prescribed and proscribed. Note that the three boxes fit together neatly in the form of an organic whole—there is considerable congruence among them. But, according to conservatives such as Lasch, many people have "pulled out" or "pulled away from" these reliable moorings; this departure is represented by the two lower boxes in Figure 6.1—individuals' actual or "deviant" behaviors. Hence, conservatives perceive an out of phaseness between their *morphostatic* image of society-family and the way individuals actually behave. This particular lack of synchrony is seen as a grave weakness in contemporary marriage and family patterns.

The solution conservatives advocate for this nonsync is a return to those original moorings (Lasch, 1977). Use of the word "deviant" in Figure 6.1 is a throwback to Parsons and his tendency to use that term (or the expression "failure"; see

Chapter 3) to describe lack of conformity to allegedly prevailing patterns. This term has not disappeared entirely from the social science literature. G. S. Becker (1981: 24) uses the word "deviant" in a similar fashion to describe boys and girls who adopt orientations contrary to their "biological dispositions" to engage in the conventional division of household and market labor (see Chapter 2): "Children with 'normal' orientations reinforce their biology, and they become specialized to the usual sexual division of labor."

On the other side, Figure 6.2 represents the situation as viewed by progressives. The basic difference between the two views is that progressives do not define society, family, and individuals as forming the sort of organic whole implied by Figure 6.1. Instead, as indicated throughout prior chapters, progressives reason from the existence of interest groups to the formation of both family and society. Following Karl Marx, Max Weber, Georg Simmel, and, more recently, Collins (1975), the idea that family-society is an organic entity giving rise to and being "served" by individuals, institutions, or groups is disputed. Instead, "social structures...are empirically nothing more than men meeting and communicating in certain ways.... Men are continually recreating social organization. Social change is what happens when the balance of resources slips...so that the relations men negotiate over and over again come out in changed form" (Collins, 1975: 48-49).

This image of social organization is displayed, in a greatly simplified form, in Figure 6.2.[2] The upper parallel *solid* arrows represent the dealings (cross-hatched area) that conservatives and progressives have with each other (as well as with other subsets of the population). Often these dealings are of a conflict nature, such as the ERA battle, abortion laws, sex education and contraceptive delivery systems, and so on. It is out of the dynamics of these complex interrelationships that societal arrangements emerge, as depicted by the lower box in Figure 6.2. These arrangements (for example, regarding marriage or divorce laws) may be relatively more or less favorable to the family-type interests of either group. The actual degree of

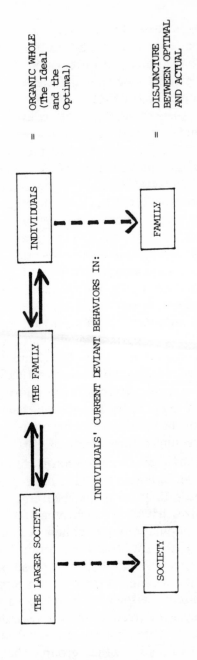

Figure 6.1 Conventional Assessment of Optimal Society-Family Model and Patterns of Deviation from It

138

favorability-unfavorability, or the impacts of these arrangements, is represented by the feedback arrows (broken lines) in Figure 6.2. Note how different the Figure 6.2 portrayal is from the general European analogue described in Chapter 3. Family unions in most European countries strive primarily to improve economic conditions and social services. Because they tend to lack the particular religiously based cleavages that exist in the United States, they have not experienced the same sorts of intense interest group clashes (see Chapter 9).

As Stone (1977: 425) puts it, "The cause of [family] change lies in an unending dialectic of competing interests and ideas." The implication of this viewpoint is that it is fallacious to view any particular set of family patterns—including those of the twentieth century—as given or necessary to family and social order. A more valid image is that those patterns exist because certain interest groups have been able to promote and enforce them effectively. However, Stone (1977: 425) observes that there is no guarantee that prevailing patterns or any proposed alternatives are "more conducive to either personal happiness or the public good than the family types which preceded" them. Nevertheless, I shall argue (as in Chapter 4) that the out of phaseness of prevailing patterns portrayed in Figure 6.1 makes it difficult for them to contribute optimally either to the public good or personal well-being.

For now, the point is that *the* twentieth-century family did not mysteriously emanate from some abstraction called "society," nor did it merely evolve out of "the interplay between 'chance' and 'necessity'" (Sprey, 1979: 133). Instead, as was shown in Chapters 2 and 3, *the* family was devised and promulgated by nineteenth-century religious (and social) conservatives—it is *their* family. These conservatives represented a powerful set of interest groups that were highly successful in achieving their goals regarding family, and family policy, in the form of state laws. Drawing from Max Weber, Collins (1975) argues that society is simply the arrangements that interest groups establish in order to achieve their ends—society is in essence a network of competing, yet interdependent, interest groups. There was, for

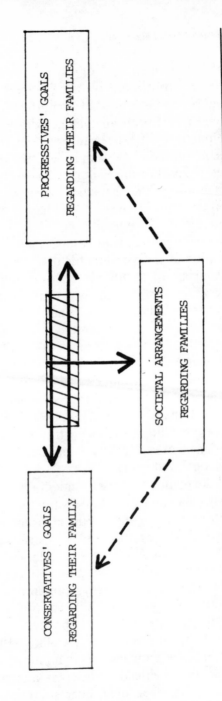

AREAS OF CONFLICT, POWER
STRUGGLES, NEGOTIATION

PROGRESSIVES' GOALS
REGARDING THEIR FAMILIES

SOCIETAL ARRANGEMENTS
REGARDING FAMILIES

CONSERVATIVES' GOALS
REGARDING THEIR FAMILY

Figure 6.2 Progressives' Assessment of Actual Links Between Society and Family

instance, no U.S. society before it was brought into being through the Declaration of Independence, the Revolution, and, especially, the Constitution.[3] In particular, the Constitution represented compromises among the varied interest groups represented at its drafting. Once U.S. society was created, other interest groups arrived on the scene (among them religious conservatives) to try their hands at shaping social arrangements (that is, society) to suit their own objectives. During the same era in England, according to Stone (1977), religious conservatives converged on already existing sets of social arrangements and sought to shape them.

One of the major means by which conservatives propogate the notion of society and family as an organic whole is to talk of "family *functions*." They use the analogy of the body, reasoning that each part of the body must perform its functions (duties) if the body is to survive, which they believe it surely must, since it (the whole) is greater than any of its parts. Thus, to assure survival, family must *produce* new members, socialize them, provide for their economic support and emotional nurture, supply affection to adults, and so on. But the conservatives' reasoning is faulty because they compare "society" to a single body. More accurately, "society" actually consists of the *arrangements* that numerous "bodies" (interest groups) establish in order to achieve their own interests. At times all the groups may share similar (as well as diverse) interests, but the result of these shared interests is the production of the tranquility necessary for the groups to pursue their own particular goals.

The conservative analogy is still less convincing when one realizes that while all human bodies require virtually the same functional requisites (for example minimum levels of calories, vitamins, and minerals, blended by identical digestive systems into similar chemical compounds absorbed by the blood uniformly in all bodies), interest groups experience far less uniformity. For example, conservatives require that *their* families reproduce and socialize children according to the particular norms and behaviors *they* prefer, but, while progressives likewise require socialized children, the contents of that socialization differ substantially. (Both groups, moreover, can and do recruit persons not born into one of "their" families, as well as "lose" some of those who were.) Actually, rather than stressing concrete contents, progressives place prime emphasis during socialization on the development of the sorts of problem-solving, decision-making, and negotiation skills described in this and subsequent chapters. The rationale for this shift from preoccupation with socialization contents to the primacy of processes is that progressives are aware, as Bell (1968: 149) puts it, that "no longer [will] any child be able to live in the same kind of world—sociologically and in-tellectually—as his parents.... For millennia...children retraced the steps of their parents...and maintained...family. Today, not only does a child face a radical rupture with the past, he must also be trained for an unknown future." Con-sequently, progressives, in contrast to most conservatives, approach the challenge of child socialization in terms described by Gibran (1980: 17):

> You may give them your love but not
> your thoughts,
> For they have their own thoughts.
> You may house their bodies but not
> their souls,
> For their souls dwell in the house of to-
> morrow, which you cannot visit, not even
> in your dreams.
> You may strive to be like them, but seek
> not to make them like you.
> For life goes not backward nor tarries
> with yesterday.

In line with this dynamic image of socialization, progressives accept the notion of a societal pluralism based on the idea of numerous "bodies" (differing interest groups) holding dif-fering family-type preferences. In contrast, since most[4] con-servatives perceive society and family as one organic body, they insist that their preferences should be held by all citizens. They are unable to tolerate pluralism because they define differing preferences not merely as "alien" to theirs, but destructive to the entire organic whole. Alternative preferences are seen as "diseases" corrupting *the* "body," and how can one negotiate and compromise with a disease?

The abortion conflict is a prime example of these differing philosophies, springing from different theories (Figure 6.1 versus Figure 6.2) of society and family (Tatalovich and Daynes, 1981: 126-127). Specifically, most progressives concur with the idea that for numerous reasons abortion is not necessarily the most desirable or ideal means of coping with unwanted pregnancies (Jaffe et al., 1981). Consequently, most of them are willing to negotiate with conservatives in order to devise public policies that might substantially reduce the currently growing frequency of abortions, particularly among unmarried adolescents (Zelnik et al., 1981). On a concrete level, progressives have urged that a totally different perspective on sexuality, along with gender roles, be promulgated by parents, teachers, churches, and community groups (Brown, 1981).[5] Progressives argue that since current prohibitions on adolescent sexuality are not working (see Zelnik et al., 1981), the emphasis must be shifted instead to *responsible* sexuality, based on males' respect for females as persons who should not be exploited (Pogrebin, 1980: 247; Brown, 1981). Integral to this notion of mutual responsibility is the proper use of the most appropriate contraceptives, access to which should be made readily available to adolescents (Steiner, 1981: 83). Since we know that over the past 20 years frequencies of unwanted pregnancies have declined among married persons owing to comparable rationales and efficient technologies,[6] there is every reason to expect the same reduction would eventually occur among unmarried adolescents. Thus teenage abortions would be likely to decline as well.

Conservatives repudiate these proposals outright, because, alongside their alleged passion for preserving developing fetuses, a second and perhaps even more fundamental reason they oppose abortion is their attitude toward "illicit" sex. Based on their analyses of several national surveys, Granberg and Denney (1982) arrive at conclusions comparable to those reported by the Connecticut Mutual (1981) study cited earlier. In particular, they found that abortion attitudes are strongly correlated with views on "personal morality." Not only did this finding appear among samples of the general population, but comparisons of NARAL (National Abortion Rights Action League) and NRLC (National Right to Life Committee) members "show some very large differences in the predicted direction. NRLC members were much more likely to take the conservative view on these matters of personal [sexual] morality than were NARAL members. If the inclination of NRLC members is to take the conservative approach to matters of personal morality, the sharply contrasting orientation of NARAL members can be described as modern, nonjudgmental, relativistic or perhaps most accurately as libertarian. In fact, abortion may be one of those issues in which the distinction between conservatism and libertarianism is especially meaningful and important" (Granberg and Denney, 1982).

In short, while conservatives view abortion as eating away at *the* body and *their* family, permissive sexual attitudes are seen as a root cause of the abortion "epidemic," and an equal if not greater threat to the organic whole.[7] But since, so far at least, it has proven difficult for them to retard the shifting sexual philosophy, they have instead chosen to attack one of its manifestations—abortion defined as a right. It is thus plain to see that a policy compromise designed to reduce abortions among the nonmarried by legitimating the *fait accompli* of altered sexual and contraceptive patterns is incomprehensible to conservatives. In the conservative view, there exists only *one* family subsystem, performing a prescribed set of vital functions for *one* larger entity, based on only one set of fixed and immutable norms—especially pertaining to sexuality.

In contrast, progressives see families as "vehicles" belonging to subsets (interest groups) of the population, not to any organic totality. As such, the vehicles differ in that the children within them are exposed to their own subset's norms and preferences, although, to be sure, there is much that these varied vehicles transmit in common. For instance, Granberg and Granberg (1980: 250) report that "those who favor and those who oppose legal abortion do not differ on 11 of 13 values ascribed to child development; but the two on which they do differ [obedience and curiosity] suggest a more authoritarian attitude toward childrearing and less emphasis on children's self-reliance among abortion opponents." For progressives, the ideas the "vehicles" hold in common provide a network of tranquility, or accommodation, called "society," in which the subgroup's particular preferences can be achieved. Consequently, the conservatives' expressed objective of domination of this network, along with their demonstrated success in frustrating the passage of ERA, influencing the 1980 White House Conference on Families (see Chapter 5), and defeating non-"moral minority" legislators, is causing progressives to take conservatives very seriously.[8]

In brief, we can describe the current situation in classic conflict-group terms (Dahrendorf, 1959; see Chapter 9). On one side is a set of interest groups possessing a coherent, though simplistic, philosophy (or ideology) and a sharply defined set of goals. One of these goals is to maintain the notion that there is an entity called *the* family, joined organically to and performing essential functions for *the* society. And, according to the results of recent national surveys (Granberg, 1981; Granberg and Granberg, 1981; Connecticut Mutual, 1981), these groups are cemented together as a result of their intense religiosity.

On the other side is an array of interest groups possessing a much less clearly coherent and lucid ideology, with wide variations in goals. Besides "Liberal, Marxist, and radical feminists" (Cott and Pleck, 1979: 14), there are other groups pressing for family changes who would not necessarily identify with any of these three factions (see Keniston et al., 1977: 213). What is the probability that a loose collection of interest groups such as progressives, with so many differences among themselves, could ever agree on a general, unifying, theoretical and philosophical approach to family? If we could explain how a model of family can address the issue of social order at the same time it recognizes the legitimate "demands" of individualism, we may be able to unify progressives as well as garner social support from the unaligned majority that is perplexed about family changes yet is currently outside progressive as well as conservative ranks.

Defining Equality

The explanation of this new model of family must begin with an examination of the thorny question of marital equality, which, while by no means a reality in the United States, is nevertheless the ideal preferred by almost two-thirds of our citizens (Connecticut Mutual, 1981: 132). When I refer to an alternative to the twentieth-century conventional family, I mean family based on marital equality—family in which the involved adults are what I have called elsewhere "equal partners" (Scanzoni, 1982). Just as conventional partners tend to be unequal over a variety of instrumental and expressive dimensions, adults within the emerging alternative family model *strive* for equality.

A common way to define equality is in terms used by Western European family advocates. According to Steiner (1981: 179), "For them the key social policy issue for the future is equality for women. And equality means not merely choice for mothers between mothering and working, but a formal recognition that all family functions except carrying a fetus and nursing an infant can be performed by either men or women." From this viewpoint, equality is defined in terms of role *interchangeability*—each spouse has access to the full responsibilities and opportunities inherent in marriage and family.

As radically different as this image of family is from Parsons's and Pitts's descriptions of the conventional family, Jancar (1978) is nonetheless dissatisfied even with the notion of interchangeability as the ultimate way of defining equality between the sexes. For her, interchangeability has certain morphostatic implications. While the focus of Jancar's study was primarily on communist societies, the relevance of her ideas for our purposes is quite evident. She asks, for example, Does equality mean "arithmetic equality"? "If a politburo has ten members, should five of these be women if women comprise 50 percent of the population?'' (Jancar, 1978: 3). As applied to our concern with households, if there are ten chores that must be done, should each spouse be responsible for five? And if a couple plans a total of two children, should the husband assume prime care responsibilities for the first child, and the wife for the second? Or if the wife moves with the husband to city A so that he can take a job, does he move with her five years later to city B so that she can take a job? And if couples perform the same numbers of chores, assume prime child care in sequence, and move in sequence, may we conclude that they have achieved "equality"?

Surely such behaviors could be used as reasonably valid indicators of equality, but Jancar (1978: 4) continues that equality may be defined not only in those arithmetic terms, but also by androgynous terms ''where both men and women can freely choose their roles and behaviors.'' This is the pattern promoted by Giele (1978) and others. However, as we observed in Chapter 4, such a blanket endorsement of individualism has no relevance for communist societies, for none ''has yet admitted the free choice of roles for anyone'' (Jancar, 1978: 4). Simultaneously, while this notion of androgyny is promulgated in Western societies, no one seriously believes that the ideal is being achieved here to any large degree.

Plainly, an arithmetic definition of equality indicates family patterns that are far less morphostatic than those in the conventional model. Moreover, Jancar's androgynous definition is even less morphostatic, and closer still to a *morphogenetic* pattern. In the jargon of systems theory, ''morphogenesis'' is the polar opposite of morphostasis, and refers to the capability of persons or groups to create and recreate new structures or arrangements continuously in response to developing preferences and goals (Buckley, 1967: 58). But if equality is defined either arithmetically or androgynously, the focus tends to rest primarily on the arrangements or structures among, say, family members. This is because with either definition equality is thought of as a goal—an outcome. As a result, Jancar (1978: 4) argues that

> instead of conceptualizing equality as a goal—arithmetic, [or] androgynous...it would seem more practical to view it as the *process* by which diverse social groups become integrated into the body politic via two fundamental political steps: (1) ability to make demands upon the government; and (2) *actual* participation in policy-making.... Equality thus is essentially a political process.

Jancar (1978: 5) goes on to say that "the key factor in my definition of equality is who makes the decisions about the distribution of goods and services in society."

Since by Jancar's definition equality is indicated primarily by processes, rather than by arrangements or structures, our focus necessarily shifts from the goals (whether of arithmetic or androgynous equality) to the notion of processes. And that, of course, is why Jancar's perspective on equality is more morphogenetic, or dynamic, than either of her two prior dimensions. By definition, processes are dynamic—they explicitly indicate flux, change, movement, shifts, ebbs, and flows. After all, it is through *processes* that morphogenesis occurs. Jancar's substantive concerns are to examine communist societies in macro terms and to explore their degree of male-female equality. However, she continually shifts from macro to micro levels, and back again. She shows, for instance, that communist women's traditional gender-role preferences, and low self-esteem, contribute to their lack of equality—a conclusion similarly valid throughout Western societies (Scanzoni and Fox, 1980).

Her macro-micro links are analogous to the connections drawn in Chapters 4 and 5 between societal type and family type: Communist countries manifest a relative degree of synchrony between society and family because both tend to be hierarchical and authoritarian. Communist regimes do not permit equality in Jancar's sense; there is virtually no conflict or competition among any types of interest groups (whether based on ideology or gender) regarding the key decisions she specifies. Similarly, available evidence (Jancar, 1978; Lapidus, 1978; Heitlinger, 1979) suggests comparable morphostasis within these societies' families as well.

As we turn to Western societies, it is apparent that, at the macro level, the *pursuit* of equality exists as Jancar defines it. Participatory democracy exists in which competing interest groups "make and support demands and...participate in policy-making" (Jancar, 1978: 4). While there are obviously laws, power (legitimate and nonlegitimate—including ample injustices) customs, arrangements, and an orderly social organization, the major focus of citizens, legislators, bureaucrats, lobbyists, and everyone else is not primarily upon those realities as fixed and certain outcomes. In elaborating Max Weber's analyses of Western societies, Collins (1975) makes it clear that parties continually engage in varied processes either to *maintain* or *extend* certain arrangements that favor them or to alter unfavorable arrangements.

Equality as Equity

These dynamic, morphogenetic processes are what Jancar means by "decision making," or what Collins calls "negotiation." However, the term *"equity"* is much more precise and useful in describing the character of these processes than is Jancar's term "equality" (Walster et al., 1978). "Equity" means that at any point during these processes of guarding, challenging, or extending existing arrangements, parties vary in the degree to which they ascribe legitimacy, justice, satisfaction with, or fairness to the existing arrangements as well as to the means (processes) used either to guard or change them. Defining equity as *satisfaction* with the perceived *justice* of the situation makes it measurable, and makes its potential to change the situation apparent. Unlike *equality*, which is exceedingly difficult to assess empirically, we can say that persons or groups are more or less satisfied with certain family-type arrangements—such arrangements are perceived and defined as relatively equitable or inequitable. It follows that, to the degree parties define the situation as equitable (fair), the less likely they will be to want to change it; parties defining the situation as inequitable are likely to try to change it. The potential for change is further accentuated by the fact that parties defining a situation as equitable at time 1 may come to perceive it as inequitable by time 2.

Stressing the links between a sense of equity and morphogenesis makes it clear that the existence of a written constitution (United States), or its absence (England), is not by itself an indication of degree of participatory democracy.[9] Sachs and Wilson (1978) and Deem (1980) show, for instance, that very little difference emerges between Britain and the United States in terms of relative male-female advantages throughout family, school, and the occupations. In the United States, continuing reinterpretations by the Supreme Court serve to bring our eighteenth-century Constitution into the twentieth-century world. What chiefly characterizes these two countries, as well as other Western democracies, is the institutionalization of decision making in Jancar's two senses: participation in both "demand making" and "policy making." Admittedly a cumbersome term, "institutionalization" was one of Parsons's favorite ways to describe his morphostatic views of society and of family. It simply meant that particular moral norms and specific behavior patterns were fixed or established (see Chapter 2). As a result, Parsons believed that the sorts of decision making Jancar (1978) describes, which he saw as inimical to society and family, could be avoided.

A New Era

Contrary to Parsons's reasoning, however, Jancar's notion of decision making is indeed intrinsic to Western societies. It is *the*

ultimate moral norm.[10] The U.S. Constitution, including the
Bill of Rights, along with congressional laws and bureaucratic
regulations, while *relatively* permanent (that is, morphostatic),
are all subject to revision and potential replacement. But what
is not replaceable is the mechanism that allows them to remain
fixed or that may modify them—the dynamic, or morphogenetic,
processes of *demand and policymaking.*

Zartman (1976: 3-4) evaluates these realities by stating that
the modern world has entered a new "age of negotiation":

> When existing systems prove inadequate for current needs,
> replacements must be devised or defined, invented or
> discovered.... Few would doubt that the current age is one of
> transition [including transitions in family patterns], although a
> transition to what is not always clear.... The situation involves a
> change from fixed rules and roles to flexible ones. If the existing
> order proves inadequate, the replacement may not be a new
> order but an absence of set systems, a...shift to a *dynamic* from
> a *static* system.... In such cases, negotiation becomes not a
> transition but *a way of life*.... The age of negotiation ex-
> tends...down into domestic life.... Wherever action was
> designated by command—in...the family...—new styles have
> added more collective and participatory ways of arriving at
> decisions. Followers, obeyers, conformers, and workers have
> become demanders, discussants, contestants and participants in
> a shift of roles and processes that clearly reflects a shift in rules
> and accepted ways and orders [emphasis added].

Zartman's subtle but critical distinction between an old order
and a new "way of life" must be grasped if we are to formulate
philosophy and policy for family adequate for the twenty-first
century. During past centuries family patterns shifted from one
set of "fixed rules and roles" to others (Stone, 1977). There
was indeed a "new order," but it was essentially as morphostatic as the old order. But as we depart the twentieth
century, what is occurring is not merely the replacement of one
fixed family order with another. Instead, the very idea of a "set
system" is becoming anachronistic, and this fundamental idea
is being discarded for a novel fundamental idea—a new "way

of life" (in harmony with the realities of modern Western societies) based on morphogenetic processes of negotiation, or ongoing decision making, linked inherently to the notion of equity as the ultimate goal. In a very real sense, this replacement is illustrated by the advent into our society of the "computer game," through which young children (the next generation of families) in their own households are grasping a mind-set totally different from, and likely to supersede, the previous board-game mind-set. The usual board game is characterized by fixed rules, finite limits of play, and win-lose outcomes. But through computer games, children learn that rules may be adjusted and limits expanded not necessarily to "beat" an "opponent," but instead to develop one's own, and often one's partner's, capabilities of *playing the game more effectively*.

In any case, neither the reality nor the significance of the extraordinary transition occurring in society and family is lost on Lasch (1977: 174), although he gives the impression that it is already a *fait accompli* rather than merely in its initial stages: "Relations within the family have come to resemble relations in the rest of society. Parents refrain from arbitrarily imposing their wishes on the child, thereby making it clear that authority deserves to be regarded as valid only insofar as it conforms to reason.... The administration of justice gives way...to *a complicated process of negotiation*" (emphasis added). In short, Lasch (1977: 184) perceives the "dissolution of authority" in the larger society, as well as the notion that "authorities no longer appeal to objective standards of right and wrong" (p. 185), as permeating and fundamentally altering *the* American family. Speaking from his conservative viewpoint, he evaluates this transition negatively and indicates his belief that it ought to be reversed.

Summary

In rethinking the synchrony between society and family, I began by critiquing the functionalist and conservative view that society and family constitute a single organic whole, in which, if the conventional family model suffers, the whole will suffer. In the progressive view, society is seen as the outcome (network) of complex negotiations between powerful interest groups. Each group maintains preferred family patterns that seek to promote the interests of that group. Given their pluralistic view of society, progressives accept the notion that alternative views of family should be allowed to "compete" in the marketplace, with nonaligned persons being allowed to gravitate toward those patterns suiting them best. But, given their organic view, conservatives cannot accept this notion.

Progressives contend that, since the essence of Western society is morphogenetic, their morphogenetic image of family is more synchronized (in harmony) with modern society than is the conventional morphostatic model. At the core of the progressives' model are the notions that involved adults should *strive* to become equal partners, and should seek to achieve *equity* among family members. Since equity rests on the dynamic processes occurring among family members, the focus of attention shifts chiefly to those processes, instead of resting primarily on particular outcomes, patterns, or goals. According to Zartman (1976), we are entering an era in which negotiation processes are becoming a *way of life* permeating family as well as all other institutions. While Lasch is aware of this development, he, unlike Zartman, perceives it in negative terms. Hence, in effect, the "bottom line" difference between the conventional and the progressive images of family is appraisal of the desirability of morphostatic patterns versus morphogenetic processes.

NOTES

1. Felsenthal (1981) presents an astute analysis of the woman and her crusades.
2. See Collins (1975) and Scanzoni and Szinovacz (1980) for an extended discussion of the dynamics inherent to such a model.

3. The existing colonies, obviously, were the foundation on which the society was built.

4. I say *most*, in reference to spokespersons who have recently been most vocal. However, conservative Senator Barry Goldwater publicly attacked the "Moral Majority" and the "New Right" precisely because of their unwillingness to tolerate societal pluralism: "The uncompromising position of these groups is a divisive element that could tear apart the very spirit of our representative system if they gain sufficient strength" (quoted by Judith Miller, in Greensboro [North Carolina] *Daily News, New York Times* News Service, September 16, 1981).

5. Compare the discussion of Scales's research in Chapter 8.

6. There are, of course, many differences in fertility control matters among married compared to unmarried persons (Scanzoni, 1975).

7. As one of their spokespersons says, "The Rockefeller Commission ... recommended not only abortion, but sex education and contraceptives for teenagers without parental consent, subsidized family planning services for all, widespread sterilization of males and females, and government subsidized child care centers for all families wishing to make use of them. Is this very far from Hitler's Germany?" (Koop, 1980: 92). Koop was nominated in 1981 by the Reagan administration to be surgeon general of the United States.

8. They must be taken seriously, because, as one of their number recently wrote, "A resort to power politics is the only answer," with reference to keeping homosexuals (and other practitioners of nonconventional sexual lifestyles) from teaching in the public schools (Case Hoogendoorn, *Eternity* magazine, June 1981: 42). Weisstein (1981) argues that they must be taken seriously with regard to their efforts to reimpose earlier abortion statutes.

9. In subsequent chapters, I draw on Sachs and Wilson (1978) to make the point that, by itself, ERA possessed no *automatic* guarantees of greater female participation in society.

10. See Ellis (1971) for the definition of "moral norm"; see also Chapters 3 and 7.

7

SOME IMPLICATIONS OF
THE EMERGING FAMILY

Using the terms "conservative" and "progressive" as I have
throughout prior chapters could give the unwarranted impression that these categories are discrete entities with no
degree of overlap. In fact, they are end points on a continuum
with many shades of differences in between. My frequent
references to the "unaligned majority" should help clarify the
notion that persons may lean toward either polar position or
find themselves somewhere in between (see Chapter 9).
Nevertheless, the evidence in prior chapters suggests that
differences between the two major perspectives (or "ideal
types") are very real and quite significant. Since Chapter 6
delineated the fundamental characteristic of the progressive
model (that is, morphogenesis), the purpose of this chapter is to
elaborate or "flesh out" some of the implications of this
emerging image of family.

To help in this task, I shall put three questions to
progressives and conservatives alike: (1) What do they as individuals want from marriage and family? (2) What are they
prepared to give to family? (3) What do they perceive family
can do for the larger society? One can readily see that in answering these questions, we are grappling with Socrates'
conception of the problem of order. Furthermore, assembling
responses from the conservative perspective is considerably less
difficult than gathering them from the progressive standpoint,

largely because progressives do not have as lengthy a history and tradition on which they can draw. Also, progressives are not organized in the same ways conservatives are, nor are they as equally unified in terms of their philosophies, goals, and objectives.

Conservative Responses

Asking what conservative men and women want from marriage highlights the matter of hierarchy (nonequal-partner marriage) and the differential status and power of the sexes. Traditional women, for instance, want nurture (including sexual satisfactions) and emotional support from their husbands; but they also expect husbands to be the ultimate financial mainstay of the household. Likewise, traditional men want nurture and support from wives; in addition, they expect wives to be ultimately responsible for household duties and child care. This fixed difference in responsibilities and opportunities is, in large measure, what locks women into subordinate status within the household and, if they venture forth, within the larger society as well—not only in capitalist but also in communist societies. Moreover (although it may vary somewhat by social class), traditional women and men expect their spouses to subordinate all other friendships to the marital relationship. Friendships in which couples socialize as pairs are deemed most desirable; having same-gender friendships in which the spouse is not central is less desirable but is at least acceptable; extraordinarily suspect are opposite-gender friendships.

A third facet of what conservatives want from marriage (besides economic and household arrangements and companionship patterns) pertains to children. Marriage and family are thought to be inseparable—the anticipated gratifications of children make unthinkable the idea of voluntary childlessness

(Polonko and Scanzoni, 1981). Moreover, the woman is the prime parent—the outcome of which is ordered according to the conventional scripts described in prior chapters. What is primarily expected from children is that they should conform to the same basic scripts in the same ways as their parents.

The response of conservatives to the second key question, regarding what to *give* to marriage/family, is equally apparent. Conservatives are prepared to *conform* to the received scripts and to give *commitment* to their spouses, children, and parents. Commitment is defined in terms of the unswerving loyalty (permanence for its own sake) described by Swidler (1980; see Chapter 4).

Finally, what do conservatives perceive family doing for the larger whole? Since to them there is only *one* family and *one* society, they see family contributing (through conformity and commitment of both adults and children) to a whole in which their preferences are carried out in its religious, educational, political, and economic realms.

In pondering these three sets of responses, we conclude that the conservative vision of family is a morphostatic one because order (defined as maintenance of the status quo) is achieved through conformity and (the conservative view of) commitment, obedience and obligation. Yet, precisely because this ideal is morphostatic, it makes no realistic allowance for several kinds of potentially disruptive elements. One that is becoming increasingly (and painfully) apparent to a great many ordinary citizens is that it constitutes a financial "straightjacket"—it takes more money to maintain than most people have. Fundamental to this ideal is a husband who earns enough dollars to support his family in all sorts of contingencies—thus freeing the mother from the necessity of paid employment. Intrinsic to this monetary ideal are the following notions: (1) that all husbands are highly motivated achievers who strongly wish to perform occupationally to the full extent of their capacities; (2) that all husbands have access to at least adequate educational and occupational opportunities—a notion quite indefensible in the case of many blacks and some whites; and (3) that husbands and wives will live together for five or six decades, and wives will not need to face the possibility of having to provide for themselves (and their children) through marketplace activity.

Second, and related, the conservative model assumes that contingencies such as mental and physical impairments can somehow always be "managed" by means of the family's own tangible and intangible resources. However, it is clear that, beginning with the Social Security Act and extending through welfare, Medicare, and more recent programs directed toward families with impaired persons, enormous government effort has been expended to assist families lacking necessary levels of those resources.

Third, and also related, this vision of family assumes a two-parent household; it further assumes that both parents place high premiums on the overall development of their children. However, death, divorce, and out-of-wedlock births are producing growing numbers of single-parent households, which subvert this assumption of "intactness"; the growing need for foster care programs and an increasing awareness of parental indifference and neglect, as well as actual child abuse, also subvert the assumption of universal parental solicitude.

To be sure, conservatives are aware of these three kinds of negative elements, but they do not interpret them as casting doubt on the workability of their model—their vision. As Parsons (1965) argued, people simply need to be more strongly committed to conventional moral norms in order to reduce the frequency of these sorts of disruptions (see Chapter 3). But progressives wonder if these disruptive elements do not instead constitute more evidence of the nonsynchrony of the twentieth-century family with modern Western society. After all, progressives ask, how viable can a model of family possibly be for the late twentieth century that stems primarily from the nineteenth century? Consequently, if we put the three critical questions to progressives, we get very different responses.

Progressive Responses

The prime reason we get different responses from progressives is that their vision of family is primarily morphogenetic. To be sure, the progressive vision includes order, but the order is not maintenance of the status quo. Instead, order emerges out of the ongoing development of satisfactory equity (see Chapter 6) as well as intimacy: Creativity replaces conformity and flexibility supersedes fixed duties. Moreover, the progressive vision or model necessitates the elimination of fixed gender-specific structures. Instead, progressives' attention fixes on the twin dimensions (or interests) that constitute marriage. Freud (Swidler, 1980) argues that adults require meaningful work and meaningful love relationships. As one of Ibsen's (1970a) characters puts it, "Yes, the joy of life.... That—and the joy of work. Yes, they're really the same thing, basically." And this is what progressives want from marriage—they want it to be the *context* that facilitates optimal attainment of both goals for both spouses. Thus, rather than conceiving of marriage in terms of roles—husbands do certain things, wives do other things—progressives see marriage as a context for the facilitation of interests held by both spouses. Consequently, one does not enter marriage in order to carry out *predictable* duties so that one can ultimately get certain *prescribed* sex-typed benefits; one marries because marriage provides a malleable setting from which *mutual* (but not necessarily rigidly prescribed) benefits can be extracted. It takes on the possibility of being shaped to fit the interests of the participants, rather than (as in the conservative model) the participants "shaping up" to fit unremitting marital demands. This is the working definition of the equal-partner marriage.

Bear in mind that conservatives *expect* certain fixed-role performances from each spouse. Progressives hold no specific expectations of this type. However, what is requisite for each spouse and what each spouse must be prepared to *give* to the arrangement (the second critical issue above) is genuinely wholehearted attention to equitable, fair, and just decision making regarding any and all matters. Recall that Jancar (1978) defined equality between the sexes (which I redefined as equity) in terms of full participation in the processes of what she labeled "demand making" and "policy-making." In other words, equality/equity stems from comparable involvement in marital/familial decision-making dynamics; in turn that involvement gives rise to a shared sense (consensus) of satisfaction with jointly fashioned outcomes (Scanzoni and Szinovacz, 1980). I share Jancar's thesis that no fixed structural pattern can ever be said to represent gender (or any other type of) equity adequately, either in or out of the family. The genius of the formal governmental arrangements of the United States or of the parliamentary democracies is not just that they *decree* equality to any political party or category of citizens, but that they provide a context in which equity among parties and citizens (satisfaction, perceived justice) may be negotiated. Similarly, in marriage, the context for equitable decision making begins by ignoring fixed role structures and, instead, giving ascendance and prime significance to the two mutually shared and overriding interests of love and work. Once acknowledging the desirability of the equal-partner ideal, the task incumbent on the couple is to participate effectively (that is, equitably, justly) in the necessarily complicated processes of demand and policymaking covering both love and work. (This is not to say that family does not require some objective "constraints," which are "out there," analogous to a political constitution; but more of this in Chapter 8, when I discuss Weitzman's [1981] "contract" notions.)

Take, for instance, the issue of love, or intimacy, as analyzed in Chapter 4. The practice of the four previously predominant dimensions of love (commitment [permanence for its own sake], attachment, self-sacrifice, and libidinal restraint) was orchestrated by conventional scripts mandating that men and women behave in predictable ways, requiring relatively little negotiation. Furthermore, in his analysis of intimacy since the Colonial era, Gadlin (1977: 40) makes the illuminating point that in the presence of "a clear hierarchical organization, social status serves as a mold within which the contents of intimacy are shaped. Social status therefore provides limits to the meaning of intimacy, assuring that all relations reproduce authority relations. In such a manner the equalizing potential of caring can be contained." I have indicated that traditional marriage arrangements tend to perpetuate a gender hierarchy. Moreover, within that sort of hierarchy, according to Gadlin, intimacy becomes restrained. People in a superior-subordinate relationship rarely become as deeply intimate as genuine peers or equal partners. Hence, in conventional marriage, the basic dimensions of intimacy were not only seldom negotiated, they were also intrinsically limited—owing to status differences partners could go only so far in exploring these dimensions. the role scripts mandated both the status differences and "proper" intimate behavior, concomitantly making it "improper" or "deviant" or at least difficult to negotiate, for instance, enlarging the boundaries of "acceptable" intimacy with one's partner or with others.

In contrast, Gadlin (1977: 70) expresses the progressive vision, or model, of marriage when he states: "Clearly, a social structure does not guarantee the actualization of persons. Certainly the elimination of economic and sexual inequality...[is] not the same as satisfying, passionate and loving relations. But I cannot believe that such relations are possible between people who are not free to be equals." Within the progressive vision, the emerging dimensions of love (choice, rebellion, self-realization, and libidinal expression) are sought by women and men who are able to participate equitably in decision-making (demand and policymaking) processes regarding those dimensions. And, following Gadlin, the underlying assumption is that the quality of these four love dimensions is enhanced (and thus greater intimacy is experienced) precisely because of this equity in demand and in policymaking.

However, conservatives and other critics of the equal-partner model are fearful of its individualistic implications. As noted in Chapter 4, if each spouse enters marriage asking how he or she can maximize the four emerging dimensions of love, how can any sort of bonding take place? Does marriage simply degenerate to the level of spouses selfishly plucking from each other what they can, and then exiting when they have gotten all they want? To make the model seem even less desirable, critics allege that demand and policymaking processes simply do not jibe, and indeed are totally inconsonant, with what intimacy is basically all about (Leik and Leik, 1977).

Taking the latter criticism first, it is quite true that the progressives' morphogenetic decision-making model is inappropriate for morphostatic, conservative marriages in which the four *traditional* conceptions of intimacy are predominant. As long as the basic affectional ties that bound partners were founded in commitment (as defined above), attachment, self-sacrifice, and libidinal restraint, demand and policymaking (decision-making) equity may have seemed quite irrelevant. But if Swidler and other analysts are correct, increasing numbers of persons are foresaking these four particular facets of intimacy. Furthermore, Swidler (1980: 137) contends that their four emerging counterparts *require* decision-making processes if they are to be viable. In short, these kinds of processes are as necessary for the achievement of optimum intimacy within the progressives' vision of marriage as they are unnecessary within the conservatives' vision. And if one asks why people are forsaking the four traditional facets of intimacy, part of the answer lies with Gadlin's analysis: These traditional facets were intrinsically linked with a set of gender relations that favored men over women, and thus proved costly to both sexes in terms of restrained intimacy.

As to the criticism regarding selfish pursuit of the four emerging facets, followed by "abandonment" of the other party—this sort of exploitation is, of course, always possible. But exploitation is just as possible within conventional arrangements—perhaps it is even more likely, because women find themselves at a disadvantage to men both in terms of tangible and intangible resources. Indeed, even if no exploitation occurs under the emerging model, Swidler's observation is correct that permanence for its own sake and stability do not carry the same *overriding* significance in the progressives' vision as they do in the conservatives'. But facing up to the reality of potential flux does not assume selfishness and irresponsibility. Quite the contrary is true—Swidler's assertion that the modern intimate relationship requires as much energy, attention, and careful thought as does the modern career means that one ignores, neglects, overlooks, or takes relationship matters for granted at one's own peril if one values continuity. Given that reality, one could say (and Yankelovich, 1981b, does) that the emerging model engenders a greater degree of selflessness and responsibility than is often the case under the conservatives' model.

There is considerable literature (Lewis and Pleck, 1979; Pleck and Pleck, 1980) suggesting that many women do not feel that their husbands are making adequate levels of inputs into intimacy and nurture, into child care and household chores, or into appreciation for their autonomy strivings. However, given that these women tend to be in conventional marriages, there is often little they can do to alter what they perceive as male irresponsibility and selfishness. Appeals can be made by women and counselors, and through self-help books, but the fact of greater male status and privilege means that ultimately changes in conventional marriages are largely a matter of male good will.[1] Consequently, at least the *potential* for male selfishness is greater under the conservatives' model because women are at an inherent disadvantage.

By way of contrast, no gender disadvantage *inheres* in the progressives' morphogenetic equal-partner model. Ideally and potentially, women and men with comparable levels of tangible and intangible resources form relationships in order that both might pursue the twin goals of optimum love (expressive) and work (instrumental) well-being. Nevertheless, owing to the basic notion that each partner is ultimately resource independent and thus autonomous (see Chapter 4), each is more able to ensure that the other's irresponsibility or selfishness is kept in check during those periods of perceived inequity when the mutuality of the preceding ideals is overlooked. Since, in particular, the woman is not ultimately dependent on the male for economic support or identity, he is less likely to be able to "take her for granted." Because he does not "possess" her (he cannot say, "She is mine," in the same sense that his father could speak of his mother), he must be alert to the very real possibility that she may eventually terminate the relationship if he does not continue to contribute inputs that will satisfy her. And, of course, the woman in such a relationship must exercise the same vigilance, since she does not have her mother's security of "belonging" to someone. The realization of the absolute necessity of continuing to make worthwhile inputs is a major distinguishing feature of the progressives' model; it is this realization that tends to militate against (but does not guarantee the absence of) selfishness and irresponsibility in pursuing the four emerging facets of love and intimacy.

In an exceedingly prescient 1968 essay regarding twenty-first-century gender relationships, Carl Rogers (1968: 271) asserted, "It is becoming increasingly clear that a man-woman relationship will have *permanence* only in the degree in which it satisfies the emotional, intellectual, and physical needs of the partners. This means that the *permanent* marriage of the future will be even better than marriage in the present, because the ideals and goals for that marriage will be of a higher order. The partners will be demanding more of the relationship than they do today." Some empirical verification of Rogers's thesis comes from a longitudinal study of white married couples from 16 U.S. urban areas. In 1974 Udry (1981) measured the perceptions of the husbands and wives in his study as to "how much better or worse off they would be without their present spouse, and how easily that spouse could be replaced with one of comparable quality." Udry (1981: 896) reports that within 3 to 4 years, "couples in which both spouses are high in marital alternatives have several times the disruption rate of couples in which both spouses are low in marital alternatives." In short, rather than viewing permanence *for its own sake* as the highest good, it would appear that at least some Americans maintain their marriages primarily because they perceive that the benefits outweigh the costs, as well as outweigh *alternative* sets of benefits.

However, lest it be surmised that the partners' basic autonomy and their resulting vigilance generate continual anxiety and insecurity, and make any sense of bonding or interdependence tenuous at best, we need to consider an additional orientation intrinsic to the progressives' vision. To combat atomistic individualism on the one hand and suspicious insecurity on the other, equal-partner couples endeavor to maintain what Kelley and Schenitzki (1972) call "maximum joint profit," or MJP. It might also be described as a sense of equitable reciprocity. Thus, during demand and policymaking (decision-making) processes pertinent to intimacy issues, for example, couples communicate, discuss, and negotiate with each other in a spirit of mutual cooperation, with the best interests of each party kept in full view (see Scanzoni and Szinovacz, 1980). Neither subordinates his or her interests *merely* on the basis of gender tradition—such as the woman being willing to settle for less than desired sexual pleasure or equitable task sharing, or either partner automatically avoiding close cross-gender friendships. But, at the same time, each partner realizes that compromises and concessions must inevitably occur if the other is to be satisfied and the relationship maintained. Moreover, each realizes that, after all, their relationship is the source of their current gratifications. As long as these types of gratifications are deemed worthwhile, it would be counterproductive to jeopardize the relationship by behaving in a selfish or irresponsible manner. Development of a sense of MJP takes time, of course, and is closely related to trust (Scanzoni, 1979). But the gradual nurturance of MJP and trust do serve, over time, to bond the relationship, generate interdependence, and reduce suspicion and insecurity.

Yankelovich (1981b: 250) identifies these same phenomena as elements of an emerging *ethic of commitment,* defined specifically as "a social ethic better equipped to achieve the goals of self-fulfillment than either self-denial *or* duty to self." New types of "giving and getting compacts," in which partners may make *mutual* sacrifices in order to gain greater good for themselves and for their relationship simultaneously, is how Yankelovich (1981b: 260) describes what I have called decision making aimed at maximum joint profit. Recall that in Chapter 4, I was critical of Swidler for focusing too narrowly on "duty to self." Her arguments match those of Farber (1964) and McCall (1966), in that they state that in order to repudiate traditional notions of self-denial (in which women did most of the sacrificing; Scanzoni, 1978), some contemporary people tend to embrace a kind of self-indulgence. Yankelovich criticizes this tendency (what Lasch calls "narcissism"), yet contends that since we can never go back to an ethic of self-sacrifice, the elusive goal of self-fulfillment is best achieved through his new *ethic of commitment.*

However, given that the cultivation of MJP, trust, and commitment require *time,* a problem arises in view of Swidler's observation that time is precisely what contemporary partners are becoming increasingly unsure of. That is, within the conventional model, the assumption was that since the relationship was unquestionably permanent, one could and should invest in it the totality of one's tangible and intangible resources (including energy and effort, and so forth). It was thought that such investments were sure to pay off in the long run. But, if no long run is assured, why make the sorts of investments necessary to establish MJP and to nurture trust? The fact is, of course, that many conventional marriages have not been permanent; nevertheless, people made great investments in them, based on their faith and trust that they would be permanent. Since conventional marriages (in which permanence is valued for its own sake) do not *guarantee* an atmosphere conducive to the growth of trust, the question becomes, what does? In actuality, there is no guarantee whatsoever that whenever parties make themselves vulnerable to and make investments in each other that the investments will be worthwhile or that the vulnerability will not be exploited.

But the only alternative to trusting is not trusting; the only option aside from investment is the withholding of significant inputs. And clearly, at both the micro and macro levels, it is demonstrably true that the risk involved in vulnerability and trust can be far more satisfying and desirable than not risking.[2] One only need compare U.S.-Canada relations with U.S.-Soviet relations to validate this conclusion in its starkest terms. Given that there is no alternative to risk, the fundamental issue becomes, are the risks greater and potentially more damaging when one naively dismisses or overlooks the possibility of risk (as in the conventional model), or are its potentially negative effects minimized when the risks are faced and one takes appropriate steps to manage them as effectively as possible? If we assume that the latter option is relatively less punishing than the former, and thus more desirable, then increasing numbers of persons are likely to favor the emerging *process* model of equal-partner marriage. Doing so in no way relinquishes the vital notions of trust and commitment. Instead, the possibilities of achieving them appear just as great, if not greater, than was the case under the conventional model. Not that exploitation and injustice could not emerge in a morphogenetic context, but to the degree such a context encourages people to become more fully aware of both the potential rewards and risks in trusting, trust will become more wisely placed than it often tends to be within the conventional context.

I concurred above with Swidler's (1980) observation that conservatives and progressives view permanence and stability (and thus divorce) in very different ways. Conservatives see stability as the goal of every legal marriage—it becomes a highly prized end in itself (Stein, 1981: 192). Progressives see no virtue in permanence *for its own sake*. Permanence, as Rogers (1968) suggests, has significance only insofar as it is the outgrowth or indicator of a satisfactory relationship; or, in the absence of that, permanence may have meaning if it could be shown that a certain period of stability might in certain cases enhance rather than hinder particular interests, especially of involved children and also perhaps of adults. Obviously, therefore, progressives do not consider divorce a "failure," nor is a stable marriage necessarily "successful."

Halem (1980: 285), for instance, criticizes earlier "shifts in thinking on divorce...[because they fell short of] a complete transformation—a replacement of the old with something entirely new." According to Steiner (1981: 192), that "replacement" has already occurred in Sweden, where enhancing marital stability is no longer a public policy goal. The replacement begins with the repudiation of the notion of divorce as "failure." Instead, divorce could be viewed primarily as the termination of a relationship because one or both parties are unable and/or unwilling to engage in the kind of decision making that results in MJP. Rather than something to be ashamed of, a blow to one's self-esteem, termination of such a relationship can be considered positive in the sense that it ends an unsatisfactory and thus, presumably, punishing situation. The preceding, of course, assumes that both parties perceive the wisdom of termination. If one party does not, then the potential pain reduction for the one seeking termination becomes the source of pain increase for the other.

According to Swidler (1980: 130), the crux of the matter is accepting the notion that "the greatest sin a lover can commit is not betrayal, reneging on the commitment, but obstruction, trying to thwart, hamper, or limit another's freedom to grow.... We are [sometimes] asked to feel that the relationship between two lovers must end because staying in the relationship would mean stagnation, while the end of the relationship forces valuable if painful growth.'' While Swidler is probably correct in asserting that defining love in those terms represents a significant break with tradition, recall from Chapter 4 that Ibsen accurately previews it by describing the agony Wangel experiences before finally coming to the place where he can ''allow'' his wife to ''choose [her] own path...because I love you so much.''

In short, progressives argue that redefining marriage so as to eliminate the idea of permanence as an end in itself (while simultaneously making people, older as well as younger, aware of the reality of the increasing likelihood of marital impermanence—assuming that mid-1970s divorce rates remain constant, Weed [1980] estimates that within 40 years, virtually half of those mid-1970s marriages will have been legally terminated) would go a long way toward reducing guilt, anxiety, lowered self-esteem, and other forms of painful termination reactions. These individual benefits would be in addition to the prime social consideration that once the high probability of impermanence is grasped, some people may take the sorts of steps described above to guard against it. Progressives wish to guard against it because, although they reject permanence for its own sake, they strongly value ''continuity with stimulation.'' The distinction can be illustrated by contrasting a placid, ripple-free lake with a mountain stream. The lake presents a picture of quiet, orderly, predictable, safe *stability* and tranquility. But the stream, while continuous, is moving, shifting, changing—and, if there are rapids, it can be hazardous to travel. The image it projects is continuity balanced with stimulation and challenge.

Consequently, the fundamental issue is not, as conservatives claim, ''responsibility versus irresponsibility,'' but, instead, which image or vision of marriage/family is preferred. For example, in reflecting on his wife's divorcing him because "she needs freedom, independence, out from under what she felt was a smothering relationship," Martin (1976: 383) observes, "I don't feel this way but I am left with a crumbled view of a marital world which doesn't have much popularity anymore." He goes on to suggest that his wife was irresponsible for behaving as she did and for repudiating a lifestyle in which their four boys played in the woods behind their "large comfortable house in Connecticut.... Across the street [is] a lake where the whole family goes swimming and boating" (p. 384). During the winter they play ice hockey on the lake, and "snug" before "the big fireplace in [their] living room." While no one could or would object to these activities in themselves, the whole tenor of Martin's essay is that these activities are the essence or core of marriage and family life. The ideal is to arrive at a pleasant, warm, comforting equilibrium in which "you found someone who was the 'other half'...and you put them [complementary qualities] together and marched in lockstep through marital happiness." Martin feels that is a *responsible* lifestyle, in contrast to his wife's repudiation of "notions like commitment [permanence for its own sake], responsibility and an even more discredited concept, suffering" (p. 384).

While those are Martin's preferences and opinions, it is not the case that the progressive perspective is "irresponsible," or that "suffering" is repudiated. Yankelovich (1981b), for instance, argues that mutual sacrifices are often required to achieve the "new ethic of commitment" that he sees developing in contemporary American society. In any case, since the term "divorce" still maintains some opprobrium, it might be well to eventually discard its use in the same ways we seek to avoid the use of such terms as "Negro," "queer," "illegitimate," "broad," and so forth. The increasing popularity of expressions such as "formerly married" suggests that the time is ripe for more concerted efforts to describe marriages as having been "dissolved," "terminated," or merely "ended."

CONTRIBUTIONS TO SOCIETY

It seems appropriate that a consideration of marriage termination leads us to the *third* of the critical questions being put to progressives: What can their model of marriage/family do for the larger whole—for the *society* of which they are a part? The juxtaposition of termination with this issue is apropos because I began this book with the observation that when nineteenth-century conservatives first began to herald the downfall of *their* family, they reasoned that the downfall was because of divorce, which in turn would result in the downfall of society owing to its supposed negative impacts on children.

However, if one rejects the functionalist and conservative organic view of society and family, and reasons instead from an interest group perspective, the conservatives' chain of reasoning (that is, divorce undermining society through its negative consequences for children) has no relevance. Conservatives are obviously free to continue dealing with their children as they wish, no matter what nonconservatives do, in spite of the increasing reality (see Chapter 4) that their own conventional socialization is out of sync with other aspects of the larger society. However, that reality no doubt contributes to a growing awareness on the part of some conservatives that it is exceedingly difficult to socialize their children in conventional ways; and that, consequently, their interest groups are ultimately being weakened and their vitality eroded. But it is fallacious and ludicrous to transfer this erosion to the remainder of "society." By identifying themselves with a nonexistent larger organic whole, conservatives create the illusion (which some—perhaps most—of them believe) that what is happening to them is also happening to that whole.

Since society is not an organic whole, what each subset of citizens does with its own children affects them primarily, and affects its relations with other subsets of citizens secondarily. To be sure, certain subsets of society can impinge on any other, thus making the task of the impinged upon group more difficult. Impingement is now occurring to conservatives and has for some time been affecting lower-class blacks—through impingement of a different sort. Because of a long history of white discrimination, many lower-class black adults have been unable to socialize their children to participate effectively in the American opportunity structure, even though that has been their goal (Scanzoni, 1977). The result is large numbers of deprived citizens who, in one way or another, make demands for greater privileges on advantaged whites (and blacks).

The progressives' idea of what they contribute to the larger whole is tied to their view of society as an intricate network of competing interest groups—not an organic whole. The key factor uniting these numerous groups into the network called "society" is what Zartman (1976: 3-4) calls "negotiation," or what Jancar (1978) calls "demand and policymaking," or what others simply label as participatory democracy, that is, ongoing processes of competition, power, conflict, cooperation, and accommodation. Those macro-level processes are morphogenetic, as are the micro-level decision-making processes between spouses just examined. The most profound distinction between family processes and those occurring outside the family is the centrality of intimacy to family. But aside from that particular focus, the "nuts and bolts" of the process notions themselves are generalizable inside and outside family.[3]

What is the essential difference, for example, between Gordon's (1976) Parent Effectiveness Training (PET), in which the goal is to carry out parent-child conflicts where "no one loses," and the consummate politician, Lyndon B. Johnson, bringing conflicting interest group leaders into his office and saying, "Let us reason together"? In spite of many less pivotal distinctions, the essential, ultimate, "bottom line" goal in both situations is to make all concerned parties as satisfied as possible with what they get, and also to reduce as much as possible their disaffection over what they must give up or do not receive (Fisher and Ury, 1981). These kinds of goals are considered "good politics" at federal, state, and local levels; they are "good business" and they are also "sound principles" for management of intrabureaucratic decision making. They are "good" and "sound" not merely because they promote individual short-term interests, but equally because they enhance cooperativeness (MJP) and trust on which long-term, mutually beneficial relationships can be built. But conservatives never did, nor do they now, consider those process-type goals crucial to family. Instead, as we have seen, their family goals center in script conformity for both adults and children. Progressives, on the other hand, consider effective and equitable decision making regarding intimacy, as well as instrumental matters, *the* prime goal of equal-partner relationships. Furthermore, they simultaneously (along with the 250,000 parents who have taken and the 8,000 professionals who have taught Gordon's course "in every state"; see Gordon, 1976: i) hold these same kinds of goals to be the prime objectives of parent-child relationships.

It is in this fashion that progressives see their vision of family contributing significantly to the larger whole. If "healthy" government, business, education, communities, churches, and so on are achieved through effective participatory democracy and decision making, then progressives believe it is critical that younger citizens be prepared as fully as possible to behave in the requisite manner. Those behaviors are clearly antithetical to rigid conformity to prearranged scripts, but involve instead creative and innovative capacities, or at the least the willingness to entertain the innovative and not immediately be threatened by it. Thus as a subset of citizens (still a minority, to be sure, when compared to conservatives), progressives view this kind of process-based, or "problem-solving" type of socialization to be in their own best interests because presumably it produces children who tend to promulgate their own goals and interests throughout other realms of the larger society.

At the same time, progressives believe that this type of socialization benefits the larger whole because, in their view, it makes for "healthier" families (the assumption is that family "health" is indicated by equitable and satisfactory decision-making processes) both in this and in the next generation, and also because they see themselves preparing citizens to function as optimally as possible in a morphogenetic society. In effect, their assumption is that children who develop in morphogenetic environments *will contribute more significantly* to the irrevocably twenty-first-century morphogenetic milieu into which they are passing (Yankelovich, 1981b; Toffler, 1980; Ferguson, 1980) than children who develop in morphostatic families. For this reason, progressives perceive their model of equal-partner marriage (spouse-spouse) and family (parent-child) to be much more in sync with and beneficial to con-temporary and emerging Western society than is the con-servative model.

Yankelovich (1981b) contends that with the alleged recent tendency toward self-indulgence, people have seldom con-sciously thought about their own and their families' con-tributions to the larger society. Therefore, he urges that "people must [become very self-conscious about] form[ing] commitments that advance the well-being of society as well as themselves" (Yankelovich, 1981b: 259). Drawing on Hannah Arendt, he argues that the "meaning of human fulfillment...is to find and safeguard the lost heritage of freedom" (p. 222). Defining freedom as participation in the shaping of one's own (and society's) destiny, Yankelovich's conclusion is that op-timum human fulfillment and optimal societal well-being are necessarily correlated—not mutually exclusive. It is therefore plain where family fits into this reasoning. Yankelovich would urge adults wanting both fulfillment *and* the *good* society to develop intimate relationships with other adults, and with children, that are fundamentally *participatory* in nature. Note that Yankelovich's definition of freedom is synonymous with Jancar's (1978) description of equality or *equity*: participation in the (decision-making) processes of demand and policymaking. Therefore the conclusion is that family can enhance societal freedom if it is indeed structured in terms of participation, freedom, and equity. Freedom, like equity, is not a steady state; it is instead Jancar's (1978) participation (decision-making) processes. Organizing family within those morphogenetic assumptions is thus likely to contribute much more significantly to societal well-being than is maintaining its current morphostatic image and arrangements.

Incidentally, the model of children learning and participating in effective decision-making processes in no way precludes long-standing policy concerns with the *psychological* and emotional well-being of children (Shure and Spivak, 1978). In fact, a strong logical and empirical case could be made for the argument that a positive relationship exists between learning and executing effective decision-making behaviors and childrens' cognitive and emotional development (White et al., 1979). Opportunities to participate meaningfully in the decisions that affect children's lives must be preceded by the sort of parental training designed to enhance children's self-esteem and feelings of confidence. In turn, as a consequence of *both* the enhanced self-esteem and decision-making participation, children's sense of overall well-being is likely to be further enhanced, along with the realization that there actually is a payoff in seeking to develop one's own capacities and talents to the fullest extent possible. Thus, over time, there are very likely to be ongoing positive feedback effects between the psychological well-being of children (intrapersonal development) and their sociological well-being, that is, their capabilities to participate effectively and meaningfully in the shaping of their short- and long-term existence.

This is not to say that conventional parents, dealing with their children in a morphostatic fashion, are unconcerned about their children's psychological development. The overwhelming majority of such parents are deeply concerned about their children, but most of them assume that conformity to the conventional scripts is what produces individual as well as social well-being. However, they fail to realize that although there may be a short-range lack of tidiness in child rearing when they set aside the scripts and instead actively involve their children's creative participation in decision making, their children's long-range interests are thereby likely to be enhanced.[4]

Progressives and Order

Reflecting on progressives' responses regarding what they want from family, what they are prepared to give, and what contributions their model makes to society, we can see how their responses speak to Socrates' formulation of the problem of (family) order. The *first* part of his formulation—"how can social organization be made highly advantageous to persons"—is met in that persons participate in the shaping of that organization, or the arrangements that order their own lives and relationships. Since they participate, they naturally seek to arrive at arrangements that are as advantageous to them as possible, within the constraints, of course, imposed by the requirements of equity and MJP. Those requirements constrain them to seek arrangements that are beneficial not only to themselves, but to other involved parties as well.

By comparison with the conservative model, less is arbitrarily *imposed* on those parties from the "outside"—that is, from "they," or "society," or "people." And the fact that less is imposed speaks to the *second* aspect of Socrates' formulation—"persons being made aware of advantages." Since they seek mutually advantageous arrangements, they are likely very much aware of the relative costs and benefits that they ultimately negotiate. There is less need for external spokespersons to admonish them on the "goodness" of their specific family arrangements, as is routinely the case in conservative circles, where the conventional norms must be and are indeed continually being reaffirmed. Finally, Socrates' *third* facet—"always acting socially"—also flows from participation as well as awareness of relative advantages. This third facet subsumes motivation and actual behavior—having negotiated some type of presumably equitable social arrangements, the parties are more likely to actually carry out their agreements, thus behaving in a manner that is responsible and responsive to interests beyond their own.

Another way to describe the Socratic sense of order, and its attainment through morphogenetic processes, is to use, but redefine, the term "commitment." Parson's view of commitment was unswerving loyalty to specific conventional norms. A more dynamic approach is to conceive of commitment as "feelings of solidarity and cohesion" (Scanzoni, 1979: 87), which is analogous to Yankelovich's (1981b: 250) view of the emerging "ethic of commitment" and its link to self-fulfillment. The sense of solidarity is generated through participation in arrangements that are mutually advantageous. As long as the arrangements continue to be perceived as advantageous, there is a sense of solidarity, or commitment (compare Rogers, 1968). But commitment is not a fixed, static state—solidarity and thus commitment can and do fluctuate—it can grow or decline.

For example, let us assume that at some point a couple manages to achieve the sort of "negotiated [family] order" to which Strauss (1978) and others refer. Having achieved this, however, in no way implies that equal-partner couples inevitably maintain equity, justice, and consensus, or that nonlegitimate power (sometimes including violence) and coercion may not sometimes erupt.[5] If and when they do, these *processes* of coercion, nonlegitimate power, and inequity tend to undermine the couple's sense of cohesion or solidarity, and thus commitment. From our earlier treatment of marital termination, as well as from Swidler's (1980) analysis of the notion of permanence, it is plain that equal-partner couples (whether legally or informally joined) can and do experience certain levels of separation and dissolution. Proportionately, perhaps, the levels may, currently at least, even be greater than among conventional marriages—especially when one spouse who used to be conventional begins to change and starts seeking negotiated equity, while the other prefers to hold on to script conformity (Bowen, 1981; Martin, 1976).

However, such "breakups" are not a threat to social order, or predictability, in the same way that divorce is perceived to be threatening by the conservative subset of the population. To conservatives, if the conventional patterns are disturbed (such as gender-linked behaviors based on permanency), then aspersions are being cast on the "rightness" of their family norms. What is comparable across thousands of conservative families are those specific patterns. But to progressives, what is comparable across families is not males, females, and children acting rigidly in prearranged or scripted ways. Instead what welds equal-partner marriages/families together as a coherent and discernible subset are identifiable patterns of negotiation and decision making pertaining to both task-oriented and intimacy issues. These are the fundamental similarities of behavior that they share.

DISTINCTIVE MORAL NORMS

Underlying these particular behavior patterns, equal-partner households also share at least four *moral norms* in the sense that "moral" is defined by Ellis (1971: 696)—prescriptions that are beyond and greater than one's own narrow self-interests and that are also beyond the realm of participatory decision making. These four norms sharply distinguish the emerging egalitarian from the conventional model. Supplying structure, shape, form, and uniqueness to the equal-partner model, they also demonstrate how it achieves Yankelovich's notion of "social responsibility." One of these is the norm that "everything should be negotiable except the idea that everything is negotiable." This norm is the ultimate and inviolate principle of every genuine democracy. The absence of this moral norm makes a nation, as well as family, something less than fully democratic. Of course, everything cannot always be negotiated satisfactorily, nor is power necessarily consistently symmetrical. But apart from this norm, parties have little *moral* compulsion to seek either mutually satisfactory negotiations or symmetrical power.

A second moral norm that is shared in common by and thus aids in identifying equal-partner households is that demand and policymaking processes themselves, as well as the arrangements to which they give rise, should be characterized by justice and equity, that is, the absence of exploitation. These notions have been discussed elsewhere in this and the prior chapter, but they deserve reiteration at this juncture because they, like the first moral norm, do indeed help us distinguish progressive from conventional households. And although I discuss violence later in this chapter, it is well to note here that one of the axioms of this second moral norm is that adults should not physically assault each other. It would seem that a precondition for achieving optimum family justice is a remote probability of violence.

A third moral norm, besides "Thou shalt never place anything above negotiation" and "Thou shalt always strive for equity," was also alluded to in Chapters 4 and 6, namely, behavioral interchangeability: "Thou shalt always be prepared to work either in the home or in the marketplace." As discussed in Chapter 6, this norm in no way imposes a fixed rigidity regarding household chores, child care, or paid employment. Since it is tempered by the first norm, neither partner need feel constrained, for example, to be "locked in" to continuous full-time year-round employment. Either may wish to reduce (or increase) his or her occupational efforts at particular times in response to certain circumstances. Of course, a partner's reduction in effort will probably mean that he or she has fewer economic resources, which could very well influence the symmetry of negotiating power in the relationship (Scanzoni and Szinovacz, 1980). In any case, the same flexibility applies to child care and household duties. The pivotal issue here is *capability* to function effectively in any and all of the three cited spheres, depending on the couple's definition of their maximum joint profit at any particular time.

A fourth moral norm flows from the prior discussion of children, namely, that the prime objective of child socialization should be to actively involve children in age-specific participatory decision making based on the three preceding norms—a socialization that results in positive self-image and sense of control of one's own destiny.

These four moral norms, along with the actual behaviors inherent in genuine demand and policymaking, are what identify equal-partner households and enable us to recognize them as both comparable with each other and distinctive from conventionals. For example, as we contrast the two sets of households, recall that in terms of the first of the four dimensions the conventionals' ultimate concern is the maintenance of order and predictability (see Martin, 1976). When order is viewed as the prime objective, then everything (work, household, intimacy patterns, and so on) is clearly *not* negotiable. (Incidentally, to say that everything *should be* negotiable does not mean that *anything* is possible or desirable. It simply indicates that nothing is *ipso facto* outside the realm of discussion and *possible*—not necessarily actual—change.)

Regarding the second norm, the contrast inheres in the reality that within conventional households, issues of equity and justice often find themselves subordinated to tradition and custom, that is, the "normal," "right," "ordinary," "usual," "common," "accepted"—*legitimate* ways of doing things.

In terms of the third issue, interchangeability, nothing is potentially less tidy than both partners seeking flexibility with regard to paid employment, household chores, and child care. Consequently, within conventional households the norm is that gender should shape the sphere in which the person is expected to function most consistently and effectively. After listening to a male expound the conventional view of male/female role specialization, Bolette (in Ibsen, 1970c) tests the idea of interchangeability: "Has it ever occurred to you that perhaps a man could also be absorbed that way, over into his wife?" "A man?" he responds, "No, I never thought of that." "But why couldn't it work as well one way as the other?" queries Bolette. "No, because a man has his vocation to live for. And that's the thing that makes a man strong and stable, Miss Wangel. He has a calling in life, you see."

Finally, with regard to the fourth dimension, the chief task of conventional socialization tends to lie with the transmission of contents, rather than with creative problem solving.

In sum, it is not that certain conventional families do not recognize ideals of equity and participatory decision making, but that they tend to do so within certain prescribed boundaries. Thus it would appear that conventional families tend a priori to set more stringent constraints on the possibilities of innovation, consequently limiting opportunities for morphogenetic activity. The upshot is that the contrast between the concept of a static and predictable order and the image of a negotiated order sharply distinguishes the two generic kinds of households. And just as the conventional family has been the predominant and most readily recognizable form throughout this century, we can expect that equal-partner households will gradually gain that same sort of recognition and ascendance throughout the next.

Recalling that we entered this discussion of comparability among equal-partner households (and contrasts with conventional households) via the context of marital permanence, it must be noted that if during the course of a couple's demand and policymaking processes they are unable and/or unwilling to arrive at mutual definitions of equity, a potential (though almost always painful) outcome may be to terminate the relationship. But since whatever specific behavior patterns the couple may have negotiated are not considered sacrosanct, and would perhaps have been renegotiated and replaced eventually anyway even had the couple stayed together, the termination of the relationship would in no way threaten the *Socratic* sense of order. On the other hand, what could threaten that particular sense of order is the maintenance of relationships in which participatory decision-making processes themselves are abused—a violation of the progressives' fundamental moral norms. Thus, contrary to the conservative vision, stability may indeed turn out to be more vice than virtue, an idea proposed by no less than John Milton (1963) during the seventeenth century.

For example, when one partner uses coercion or nonlegitimate power to achieve his or her (selfish) ends at the expense of the other (maximum individual profit), then the other loses the sense that the arrangement is "highly advantageous." As long as the other can correct the disadvantage either through renegotiation or, if that falters, through termination, the morphogenetic participatory processes themselves are being validated in the sense that they are being used to attain justice and equity. But if one party succeeds in imposing *and maintaining* coercive and unsatisfactory arrangements, then to that degree morphogenetic ideals and moral norms are being ignored, and social order is accordingly being diminished. Order is being diminished in the sense that coerced persons perceive few or no advantages in their arrangements but nonetheless participate in them, often to avoid the perceived costs of not doing so. Their commitment is low, yet their behavior is mandatory. The likely outcome of this type of situation is a "convulsive explosion" of one sort of another—hardly conducive to orderly change.

The classic case of this sort of coercion emerges from the conventional family model. According to Straus (1980: 229), one of the prime explanations for husband-wife violence in American society is the different social statuses of, and thus tangible and intangible resources possessed by, men and women: " 'Wife-beating' is largely a reflection of the nature of the society, its family system, and its typing of sex roles and male/female personality traits." Since the conventional family model places men in a position of fixed advantage, some tend to abuse that power by resorting to the extremes of violent behavior. Some conventional women leave their husbands for this reason, but others do not largely because they possess neither the tangible nor intangible resources requisite for such a move, and also because there is often only a limited (or no) social network into which they can fit while they are attempting the transition from their former life to another. Consequently, many battered women perceive it as mandatory to continue in a disadvantageous and punishing situation, even though they sense little or no commitment (as redefined above) to it. "Women struggle...against cultural ideals that still require a woman to submit to almost any form of treatment that her husband considers appropriate and against the policies and responses of various social agencies which often demonstrate direct or indirect support for the husband's authority and his use of violence" (Dobash and Dobash, 1979: iv).

While violence may sometimes erupt within marriages organized along morphogenetic lines, it is highly unlikely that it could ever become a fixed feature as it has among a certain proportion of conventional marriages. By definition, violence is the extreme form of coercion; it subverts all canons (moral norms) of equitable demand and policymaking. The majority of men, and probably all women, who are eager for equal-partner marriages are simply unwilling to tolerate ongoing violence; moreover, women in such marriages are almost always able to fend for themselves should they choose to leave. The relative incapacity of either partner in an egalitarian marriage to be perpetually coercive (even in a nonviolent fashion)—owing to the presumed parity of tangible and intangible resources—is perhaps the major reason that it would be comparatively rare to discover among them instances of low commitment combined with "mandatory" stability.

By this point in our discussion, it should be plain that conservatives grossly misunderstand the progressives' vision of family when they accuse progressives of being infected by the sort of narcissistic individualism described in earlier chapters. The progressive vision of equity and justice is fundamentally incompatible with the diminishment of order and commitment as defined above. Consequently, progressives ideally are highly motivated to negotiate for equity, thus enhancing commitment and order, but they do not deem martial terminations in and of themselves to represent "failure" or disorder. That is because of their "faith" (Rogers, 1968) that over the long term (into the twenty-first century) their ideals and norms will result in a greater proportion of marriages than at present achieving greater "health," as well as facilitating greater individual well-being. Moreover, they believe that their ideals and norms will result in greater "societal health" in the sense that adults, and their children who later become adults, will be better able to participate effectively in and contribute to society's morphogenetic dynamics.

Thus Parsons (1965) was correct when he perceived family as a laboratory or training ground for society; but he misjudged the nature of the requisite training (see Chapter 3). Expanding the notion presented in Chapter 4 of "out of phaseness," we can be explicit in concluding that preoccupation with script conformity and stability as indicators of order is probably harmful both to individuals and society. At the very least, individuals growing up morphostatically are likely to experience greater difficulty in adapting morphogenetically (Kohn, 1978); at worst, they may participate in and foster situations (both in and out of family) involving coercion, exploitation, and perhaps violence. From a macro standpoint, "societal harm" or diminished societal well-being accrues on account of both omission and commission: When participation in morphogenetic process is omitted from their family experience, persons cannot carry these processes over into society and thus contribute through them; moreover, when authoritarianism and/or coersiveness have been central to people's family experiences, they may tend to carry those over into the larger society, with very likely negative societal consequences.

The question of the relative advantages and disadvantages of growing up in a morphostatic versus a morphogenetic home can be connected to the meaning attached to marital termination, as noted above. A central facet of conservatives' opposition to divorce has been its alleged negative impacts on children's development, although, as was shown above, there is no clear evidence to support that charge. On the contrary, a widely accepted conclusion (Feldman and Feldman, 1975) is that (among conventional marriages) there are no significant differences between children from intact and dissolved marriages over a variety of measures of children's well-being, *when controlling for social class.* Furthermore, numerous analysts have contended that children are probably harmed less by parental separation than they are by continued exposure to a "stable" marriage characterized by acrimony, hostility, and coercive conflicts.

However, given the relative lack of progressives' emphasis on permanence *for its own sake,* the question arises, does that climate breed insecurity among children? Is children's development negatively affected by an ambience in which they cannot be "certain" of permanence? A response must take cognizance of the current reality, which is (even in a climate in which permanence continues to be valued for its own sake) that many of today's children do not in fact experience such permanence (see the discussion, above, of Weed's 1980 findings). The more fundamental issue becomes, is children's cognitive, emotional, and social development best served by a morphostatic climate, in which permanence for its own sake is maintained as an ideal but is increasingly difficult to attain, or is it best served instead by a morphogenetic model, in which continuity is always a viable possibility yet is contingent on the capabilities and willingness of the parents to achieve equitable arrangements? If parental candor and straightforwardness are related to children's well-being, then it would seem that the latter model is more desirable. Furthermore, children in morphogenetic, egalitarian homes appear more likely to develop the skills that will enable them as adults to achieve continuity based on equity (continuity with stimulation), instead of merely maintaining stability as an ideal masking what Goode (1963) and others label "empty shell" arrangements. In brief, there is no compelling argument that children who develop in families that do not adhere to the ideal of stability for its own sake are necessarily harmed compared to those who are raised in conventional families. On the contrary, a case can be made that developing in situations in which continuity is not merely a static ideal can actually be beneficial to children's development, both over the short and the long term.

Family Pluralism

Thus far in analyzing the progressive "vision" we have focused almost exclusively on heterosexual couples with their children. However, the model is in no way limited to that sort of household composition. Unlike the conservative model, which posits that particular composition as the *summum bonum,* a morphogenetic model, by definition, cannot do so (see Ward, 1981). Not only is it theoretically impossible for a morphogenetic model to be limited to that composition, but the composition itself is becoming increasingly less universal. Throughout these pages, I have repeatedly made the point that, in spite of conservatives' protestations, ordinary citizens (the unaligned majority) have gradually been drifting away from the conventional model for over a century. Recent census data compiled by Masnick and Bane (1980) underscore this point quite dramatically at the level of the total society. For example, in 1960, legally married couples made up 75 percent of all American households.[6] By 1975, that figure had declined to 65 percent; and by 1990, these same analysts project (based on continuation of current trends) that the figure will drop another 10 points, to 55 percent (Masnick and Bane, 1980: 49).

Alongside these trends, Cherlin (1981: 12) observes that during the 1970s, "many [couples]...began to live...in a decidedly untraditional way—sharing a household without marrying.... Between 1970 and 1979, the number of cohabiting couples more than doubled, to 1,346,000." And although the Census Bureau classified cohabitors as being in households with two—and only two—unrelated adults of the opposite sex, they did not determine what proportions were actually lovers or merely housemates. However, Cherlin (1981: 13) asserts that "most of these persons undoubtedly were involved in an intimate relationship with their housemates."

Moreover, while the proportion of legal unions was dropping and the proportion of informal unions was increasing, the proportion of male-headed households (children present, but no female adult) increased from 8 percent to 11 percent between 1960 and 1975, and is projected to grow to 16 percent by 1990 (Masnick and Bane, 1980: 49). Correspondingly, the proportion of female-headed households (children present, but no male adult) grew from 17 percent (1960) to 24 percent (1975); and they are projected to reach 29 percent of all households by 1990. Furthermore, growing numbers of men and women are living alone, and Masnick and Bane (1980: 19) comment: "The increase in the number of one-person households is a dramatic departure from most of our historical experience; traditionally, adults have lived in households with other adults." They go on to say that "the most striking change that has taken place in the overall [composition] of American households is the decline in the share [proportion] headed by a married couple" (p. 21). For instance, between 1975 and 1979, 6 million new households were formed in America. These "new households" may have been formed in many ways: couples become legally married and start living together; people who had formerly been in the military, married, or living at college, with parents, or with housemates start living alone; people start living with their children but with no other adult; or people start living with an unrelated adult or adults. Masnick and Bane found that between 1975 and 1979 only 12 percent of the 6 million newly formed households were headed by married couples, whereas 69 percent of these households were headed by a man *or* a woman (who may or may not have children living with them or who might be living with unrelated adults). What does this array of numbers seem to imply? "The once typical household—two parents and children, with a husband-breadwinner and a wife-homemaker—has faded in prominence" (Masnick and Bane, 1980: 95).

In line with Swidler's (1980) analysis, Masnick and Bane (1980: 113-114) say that "unmarried individuals [single, widowed, divorced] live in more 'fluid' living arrangements than married couples...with more rapid turnover of household members.... How long do people stay in single-person households? What is the average number of partners or roommates people live with before they get married? How many different individuals does this involve? How long do children [actually] live in single-parent households?" In addition, how many single persons maintain their own households, yet regularly spend days and nights with their partners.[7] Surely the census classification "living alone" carries a vastly different meaning for them and for our understanding of marriage and marriage-like arrangements than the term "living alone" held during the 1940s and 1950s.

What is particularly fascinating about these kinds of questions is not that they have not been researched, but that they are now being asked for the first time. As recently as a decade ago, few researchers would have thought to raise these questions, chiefly because the actual incidence of such behaviors was believed to be very small. But now these questions become vital since we may expect continuing increases in transfers between and among varied kinds of living arrangements and lifestyles. Hence, morphogenesis not only characterizes *intra*household behaviors, but *inter*household patterns as well. This realization makes it all the more imperative that children and adults develop an awareness of the resources and skills requisite to effective demand and policymaking (that is, decision making—see Chapter 8). Modern life is "relentless," as Swidler (1980) puts it, in placing decision-making demands on people who are outside, as well as those who are inside, of dual-partner heterosexual (as well as homosexual) households.

In sum, an additional strength of the emerging morphogenetic model is that it can subsume the growing numbers of cohabiting, single-person, and single-parent households. Similar to Masnick and Bane (1980: 113), Stein (1981: 15) suggests the notion of "life-spiral" (replacing the predictably sequential "life cycle") to capture the reality that contemporary persons may over time experience considerable flux in and among the various statuses (relationships) of singleness, cohabitation, marriage, divorce, single-parenthood, and so forth (see Scanzoni and Szinovacz, 1980: 258). Hence, in proposing the equal-partner model, progressives are able to suggest that the four moral norms by which it is structured provide a general basis for persons to make orderly transitions among those several life-spiral statuses, or types of relationships. By shifting our image of what marriage/family ultimately is from a set of gender-specialized behaviors to a set of interlocking moral norms governing all these types of relationships, it can be said that persons in these various sorts of households constitute "families," a convention in fact recently adopted by the Bureau of the Census. The prime point is that even though there may not be another adult (or child) living in the household at any given time, each actor deals with friends, housemates, lovers, and potential partners in terms of these norms, so that the constant norms operate as the persistent structure governing the ever-present possibility of behavioral expansion into a two-adult (plus one or more children) household. Should a multiperson household eventuate, these same norms would continue to govern it, as well as any future developments toward the one-adult household.

Paid Work and Housework

Throughout most of this chapter, I have focused primarily on the nontask-oriented implications of a process approach to family. A basic inference has been that a morphogenetic model is much more likely than the morphostatic to result in relationships that simultaneously possess *both* continuity and stimulation. In shifting to task-oriented implications, it follows that both paid work and housework would also be addressed in morphogenetic fashion, thus supplying a broad range of *work options* (that is, greater "freedoms" as defined above) for both sexes. Women, for example, increase the possibilities of their social and economic contributions to the larger society as well as their meaningful participation in the forces that shape their own destinies (Giele, 1978; Andre, 1981). Meanwhile, men gain possibilities of more meaningful participation in nurturant relationships with women and children, and with other men (Pleck and Pleck, 1980), as well as greater flexibility regarding their own participation in the paid labor force.

While some observers have suggested that recent increases in married women's employment are merely the result of a fad, and will eventually be replaced by a return to "hearth and home," Smith (1979: 72), on the strength of his analyses, concludes, "There is absolutely no basis for anticipating that the growth in the female [labor force] participation rate is about to end. No matter how the projection is made...the conclusion is...that the participation rate of women in the year 1990 will be significantly larger than it was in 1977." He estimates that "about 52 million women will be in the labor force in 1990—an increase of about one million per year." Moreover, most of these added workers will be in the 25-54-year-old range, married, and will have minor children (Smith, 1979: v). Masnick and Bane (1980: 71) concur with Smith regarding increased *participation,* but also go an important step beyond him by concluding that "the data point to a picture of gradually increasing *attachment* to the labor force among women" (emphasis added). By "attachment" they mean working full time, year-round, and also continuity. Continuity means consistency and refers, for example, to the total number of months out of the past five years, or ten years, that a woman or man has been employed (Maret-Havens, 1977; Scanzoni, 1978).

As female work participation and attachment increase, the issue arises regarding corresponding changes in male domestic participation. Bernard (1981a: 45) argues that

> to be a man one had to be not only a provider but a *good* provider.... A man who was successful in the good-provider role might be freed from other obligations to the family. But the flipside of this dispensation was that he could not make up for poor performance by excellence in other family roles. Since everything depended on his success as provider ["The husband is the earner of the income on which rests the whole structure of family life"; Seeley et al., 1956: 176], everything was at stake. The good provider played an all-or-nothing game.

While this has been the morphostatic image since the 1830s (Bernard, 1981a: 2), Pleck's (1982) analyses of national data suggest that certain profound changes are taking place. First, he says, "Husbands' and wives' levels of time expenditure in family roles are converging." Since the mid-1960s, time-use research reveals that women have been spending less time on "family work" (routine chores and child care), while men have begun to spend increasingly more time on such work.

Second, Pleck maintains that "employed wives no longer experience 'role overload' relative to their husbands, on the average." Based on a 1975-1976 study of time use, he found that "husbands and wives in two-earner couples now spend almost exactly the same total time per day in the combination of their paid work and family roles." Significantly, he adds that even husbands of nonemployed wives are becoming more involved in family work than ever before.

Third, says Pleck, "Social sentiment that husbands should perform more housework and childcare continues to increase." To demonstrate this claim, he cites trend data showing that wives want greater contributions from their husbands to family work, whether wives are employed or not.

Finally, "employed wives' [marital] adjustment is affected far more strongly by their satisfaction with their husbands' level of housework and childcare than by their own or their husbands' actual levels of family work and paid work." Pleck says that how much family work the husband actually does is not as important a predictor of an employed wife's marital adjustment as "wanting her husband to do more housework and childcare." Apparently what I earlier called a "sense of equity" is operating here—the actual level of male behavior is less significant than how *fair* the wife judges it to be.

Hence, alongside (and undoubtedly connected to) the profound changes in the nature of intimacy described above (and in Chapter 8), an increasing body of evidence reveals that the task-oriented dimension of marriage is likewise undergoing significant alterations. And, as Smith (1979: 72) observes, these changes of necessity generate critically "important policy issues." Nevertheless, it should be plain by now that in the context of morphogenetic society, the key to shaping these sorts of policy issues does not lie with rigidly enforced "solutions" or ready-made formulae. Neither individuals nor society are best served by the mere replacement of the conventional morphostasis with an unconventional morphostasis. For instance, as vital as it is for employers, unions, and government to begin experimenting with "flexi-time" (flexible work schedules; Bohen and Viveros-Long, 1981), expanded child care facilities, shared jobs, and so forth, what must be kept uppermost is that the "genius" of the morphogenetic egalitarian model is that specific task behaviors, as well as nurturant issues, are continually approached from a fresh, creative, and innovative mentality. To the degree that this sort of mentality becomes the overriding concern of persons in "relationships," both task and nurturant-type issues become more likely to be rewarding rather than punishing to the involved participants. This is not to overlook the vital importance of public policy in reinforcing this mentality—the issue to which I turn in Chapter 8.

Summary

Progressives differ significantly from conservatives in what they want from marriage and family, what they expect to give to these relationships, and how they expect marriage and family to contribute to the larger society. These substantial differences emerge from the contrasting morphostatic and morphogenetic images of society and family held by conservatives and progressives, respectively. Progressives want an equal-partner model of marriage/family to contribute to their interests and goals in particular ways; they expect to invest in marriage and family through equitable demand and policymaking; and they expect family to contribute to a morphogenetic society by effectively training children in the dynamics of equitable decision making.

At the same time, a process approach addresses the problem of family and social order because the participants themselves are attempting to fashion the arrangements that affect both themselves and the larger whole of which they are a part. Charges of narcissism and irresponsible individualism lose their credibility when we recognize that goals such as trust, maximum joint profit, and commitment can be attained just as effectively, if not more effectively, in a morphogenetic context compared with a morphostatic context. In addition, progressives differ from conventionals in providing cogent reasoning as to why marriage termination is not viewed as "failure" or as necessarily harmful either to children or to society. Finally, not only does a process approach provide potentially greater benefits to individuals (children and adults) and society, it also far more effectively subsumes the growing numbers of households composed of other than the conventional makeup of two legally joined heterosexual adults and children.

NOTES

1. In a recent analysis of contemporary housework, Andre (1981: 103-104) suggests that women who want their husbands to participate more fully in household chores should request it, simply resign from housework, or "design a work-sharing system" among household members. She goes on (pp. 131-140) to discuss family *power* relationships, but fails to make sufficiently explicit and specific the logical connections between the two topics (getting husbands to do housework and family power).

2. In a recent classroom discussion of these matters, one student observed that she would prefer to marry and take the risk of marital dissolution in order to enjoy what she sees as marriage benefits, rather than not marry, thus avoiding the possibility of divorce, and forgo marital gratifications.

3. See Fisher and Ury (1981) for this same argument; see also Scanzoni and Szinovacz (1980).

4. Compare similar arguments in Chapters 4 and 8.

5. See additional discussion on violence later in this chapter.

6. The Census Bureau defines "household" in terms of persons' primary dwelling unit, usually including plumbing and/or kitchen facilities.

7. See Scanzoni and Scanzoni (1981: 221) for "a continuum of relationships between the single state and the married state."

8

SUGGESTIONS FOR SOCIAL POLICY

Critique of Federal Family Policy

In Chapter 5, I referred to President Carter's attempt to make family policy a central pillar of his administration. Steiner (1981: 203-204) comments that, unfortunately,

> family was unveiled as a major policy area without a theory to explain and guide public intervention.... In contrast with the approaches to poverty, civil rights, or welfare, no tentative explanation of just how government action would effect change accompanied [President Carter's] call for family policy.... Policymaking depends on at least an implicit theory. Without one, politicians who call for government action are guilty of bad planning.... If Carter began with an implicit theory of the nuclear family as the norm, he undermined it by shifting to an acceptance of the diversity and pluralism of families.... Family policy in the form of a reasonably well developed approach to a perceived national problem has not been rejected nor has it been tried and found wanting. It does not exist. Those who raised the issue had no ideas or plans.

While the knowledgeable persons cited in prior chapters concur that no national family policy exists in Steiner's sense, it is equally apparent that at the state level an implicit theory or philosophy does exist, and that it tends to be based on the conventional family model (Sachs and Wilson, 1978). Moreover, at the national level, while Carter himself may have waffled on whether to endorse the conventional model versus some sort of pluralism, we learned in Chapter 5 that the White House Conference on Families organizers left no ambiguity as to which model they were promulgating. There seems little doubt that at the formal policy level, the most widely recognized and coherent philosophy of family in the United States is the conventional one. In contrast, although what Steiner (1981: 18) calls "liberals" (his term subsumes a somewhat narrower spectrum than what I have been calling "progressives") may, at the ideological level, agree that the "national government [should supply] aid and services to the family as a way to redress old wrongs to blacks, to the poor, and to women," their alliances tend to fragment when, as must eventually be the case, specific issues are addressed. Family policy, says Steiner (1981: 215), must be more than the equivalent of "peace, justice, equality, and freedom.... When the details are confronted, family policy splits into innumerable components."

Steiner (1981: 200) illustrates his assertion of "liberal fragmentation" by raising the much-discussed and concrete matter of child care facilities. Assume that certain progressives propose that such facilities should be available on demand, at nominal cost. That, claims Steiner, is often the extent of some progressives' vision of "family policy." However, he says, such a program will either be opposed or ignored by other progressives who have equally narrow but divergent views of what family policy is supposed to be. For example, progressives who believe that family policy should maximize in-home child care will oppose such a program; those who think that above all family policy should mean depopulating institutions and putting children in permanent family situations will give such a program "only casual support." Finally, Steiner (1981: 200) concludes that progressives who advocate family policy in the form of three-generational housing arrangements "will simply be indifferent to child care."

According to Steiner (1981: 200), this programmatic fragmentation among progressives results because "the clear self-interest necessary to develop enough group support to transform a dream into a public issue—or to suppress it—does not attach to family policy." Since progressives have been unable to conjure a vision of family comparable in scope, coherence, and persuasiveness to that of the conservative vision, they have accordingly been stymied in establishing "a set of specific priorities" (Steiner, 1981: 212). Since progressives lack both a unifying vision, or model of family, and specific priorities, conservatives have effectively put nonconservatives on the defensive by accusing them of favoring programs that smack of "indolence, promiscuity, easy abortion, casual attitudes toward marriage and divorce, [and] maternal indifference to child-caring responsibilities" (Steiner, 1981: 17). The conservatives point to their own vision and their well-tested priorities and contend that the liberals want to use "national resources to legitimize behavior not consistent with behavior of the typical American family. Right-minded national policy [say conservatives] should reinforce traditional American patterns, not abide deviations that smack of irresponsibility" (p. 17).

And there we have it—the conventional-progressive split we have been following since Chapter 1. Conservatives are seeking to maintain long-standing traditions at the same time that many Americans are quietly ignoring them (Steiner, 1981: 7). But in drifting slowly from the old, Americans have not yet fashioned the new—there is no coherent and recognizable vision of a twenty-first-century family that compares to the coherence, logical appeal, and powerful sentiments attached to the old. It is this absence of alternative possibilities and ideologies rivaling the old in legitimacy and attractiveness that must be addressed if progressives are ever to join forces on specific programs and convince the majority of nonaligned citizens of the reasonableness of their viewpoints. To be sure, increasing numbers of citizens are, by trial and error, carving out novel behavior patterns, but they tend to do so apart from the collective wisdom of a supportive network.

The resulting drift, uncertainty, guilt, and social costs accumulate and become subsumed under what Steiner (1981: 202) calls "the many [family] problems...that do not vanish. If those problems affect a large or growing segment of the population, anxiety about them can be expected to increase." Although many progressives are becoming increasingly aware of this anxiety, most of them have not been able to escape preoccupation with parochial interests in favor of devising an all-encompassing model of family that could not only cement their own constituencies, but also eventually appeal to the broad range of average citizens. As Steiner (1981: 202) puts it, "The choice is not between pollyannaism and alarmism. The family can be both here to stay and in trouble." Furthermore, he makes a distinction between "a workable family form" and the "best." But while conservatives can state decisively what is "best," progressives have been unable to do so. Consequently, in order for progressives to weld their constituencies and attract broader support, a progressive model of the "most desirable" is essential. It is also essential because it will make possible the specification of issues around which progressive groups can coalesce, and for which they can seek particular changes both in laws and social customs.

The Need for Fresh Thinking

In recent years, there has been much discussion of the resurgence of conservative political, social, and economic ideas, and the corresponding bankruptcy of liberal or progressive thinking in these realms. We hear that the New Deal, the Fair Deal, and the Great Society have become relics. Liberals, we are told, must come up with fresh ways to cope with both domestic and foreign policy issues. If they are to effectively lead the country and not merely react to conservatives, liberals must begin to look ahead rather than backwards to their former ascendancy. As I observed in the Preface, humorist Russell Baker (1981) claims that liberals currently "gat no heat," that is, no "ideas" or "philosophies worth sacrificing for." Baker continues that "the American people...are still most likely to be stirred by political visions firmly pronounced and firmly pursued, and Carter had none." This vacuum included family issues, as Steiner has noted (see above). One editorial writer looks hopefully ahead to the next "wave of public innovation" and "social construction," which, "we hope, will be less 'pragmatic' and more structural, less palliative and more truly radical" (New Republic, 1981: 6). On the threshhold of the twenty-first century, progressive thinking requires revitalization in virtually every area of domestic and foreign concerns.

Family is no exception. In recent years, progressives' approach to family has been what the above writer terms "programmatic." Accepting the conventionals' family model (in spite of Yankelovich's [1981a: 58] claim that national surveys over the past 30 years reveal substantial, even "dramatic" changes in persons' norms and behaviors regarding family), progressives have attempted to "tinker" with it to try to make it "work better." As we saw in Chapter 3, for example, progressives were the prime architects of a host of federal programs aimed at ameliorating the needs of (mostly disadvantaged) children and adults. Nevertheless, more recently, certain policy advocates have shifted their attention to "family impact analyses" involving comparatively advantaged citizens. Bohen and Viveros-Long (1981), for instance, examined and evaluated links between flexi-time work schedules and family patterns among federal workers. However, in spite of this necessary trend away from looking exclusively at the economically disadvantaged, most of the attempts to explore fresh ground continue to have that "programmatic" and "palliative" flavor rather than being characterized by what the *New Republic* editorial writer labeled "structural" or "radical" change. Using the word "radical" immediately raises a red flag, but if we define it as we did earlier—as going to the *root* of the things—its frightening aspects are replaced by positive connotations. All that "radical" or "structural" mean here is that progressives should accept the full implications of the model depicted in Figure 6.2 (see Chapter 6), including its conflict basis, and explicitly converge around the morphogenetic, equal-partner framework as the model or image of family best suited for the twenty-first century (see Chapters 6 and 7). Once this model is adopted, it should be promulgated by every means possible, and federal and state legislation, along with community programs and clinical efforts, should be specifically geared into or meshed with that model.

This "radical" move would provide an umbrella or alternative ideology to that of the conventionals. Currently, conservatives are on the "offensive," so to speak, in that they possess a coherent ideology that enables them to transcend the mere "programmatic" and capture the allegiance (the minds and hearts) of a certain proportion of citizens. Moreover, the fact of their overarching ideology congeals them and enables them to set priorities regarding specific customs and laws they wish to change, retain, or eliminate, and what programs are or are not most desirable. Conservatives possess what Steiner (1981: 200) calls a sense of "clear self-interest" regarding what is optimum for family and society. Alongside that, they clearly perceive what Steiner calls "a national problem," and they know what their reaction to it should be. Consequently, progressives have at least two options regarding family:

OPTION 1

The first option for progressives is to remain on the "defensive" and avoid explicitly adopting and vigorously promulgating an alternative image of family. In this case, they would tacitly maintain the legitimacy of the conventional model at the same time that they search for legislation, programs, and clinical efforts to ease the difficulties inherent in the sorts of behavioral changes documented by Masnick and Bane (1980) and for solutions to related difficulties pertaining to child welfare, socioeconomic disadvantage, and so forth. During these searches, they find themselves continually fending off suspicions, criticisms, and attacks from conservatives. Their defensive and beleaguered posture is illustrated by the ERA ratification struggle (Boles, 1979). Because ERA proponents never considered it particularly imperative to tie this particular matter to some larger, coherent vision of society and family, they were stung by the severity and effectiveness of the conservatives' onslaughts. They had no politically effective response to charges that ERA would result in men and women using the same public restrooms, that homosexual marriages could be legalized, that child-support and alimony rights would be lost, that working women would be forced into physical tasks too great for them, or, most devastating of all, that men and women would no longer have any sense of responsibility toward children and family, which would lead to societal decay.

ERA proponents were continually reduced to refuting these inane allegations; they spent their energies denying all of the "bad" things ERA would supposedly do. Unfortunately, they were never able to transcend the negative by accentuating the positive things that ERA could do for most ordinary citizens. In any case, according to Sachs and Wilson (1978: 221), there would have been no instantaneous effects from ERA even if it had passed, since the amendment did not make any old laws automatically obsolete nor any new ones *ipso facto* incumbent. As with any other constitutional amendment, it simply provided a touchstone against which the legislative branch could measure the discrimination implications of any laws it might pass; the same touchstone would then be used by the judicial branch to assess charges of discrimination.

But immediate legal effects aside, the conservatives intuited something about ERA that progressives seemingly did not, namely, its *symbolic* impact. Conservatives understood that the passage of ERA would be one more sign of the conventional family's demise—a family model based squarely on women's dependence and assumed need for protection. They grasped that meaning in the same way that they grasped the significance of building federally funded shelters around the country for the purpose of housing abused women and children. On the grounds these shelters would become "anti-[conventional] family indoctrination centers" (Goodman, 1980), congressional conservatives successfully opposed a 1980 bill that would have provided funds to build them. To conservatives it was apparent that the shelters would supply additional symbolic evidence in hundreds of local communities around the nation of the undermining of the husband's traditional authority, and thus would further subvert *their* family. This sort of grassroots demonstration of the anomaly of the conventional family was intolerable. It is apparent that conservatives can rally considerable emotional and political support against specific proposals, such as ERA and community shelters, because they can point to a shared vision—a model, an ideal that those specifics do in fact threaten.

In reaction, many progressives simply denied that ERA was a threat (which convinced no one); and, at the same time, they failed to promulgate an alternative family vision. Thus they had the worst of both worlds: By playing according to the rules of the conservatives' game they lost and by not having their own game they lost again—their objectives were not attained in either world. Progressives lack the "clear self-interest" that conservatives possess; they also lack a perception of a "national problem" and its "solution" that sufficiently distinguishes them from conventionals.

One option progressives have is to continue in this essentially defensive and, thus far, not very productive posture. They can continue to be "programmatic" and "palliative" (in the sense cited above) by developing strategies to alleviate strains on the conventional family. In and of themselves the strategies are first class (for example, the "family impact analysis" notion tested by Bohen and Viveros-Long, 1981); but the basic issue is, how effective can they ultimately be in the absence of a clearly defined formal alternative to the conventional model?

OPTION 2

A second option progressives have is to cease being defensive and instead "go on the offensive," as conservatives have done. That is, they can try to develop a sense of their own self-interest (analogous to what the Marxists call "class-consciousness"; see Chapter 9) and promulgate their own solution to a perceived national problem, by first of all seeking to create a sense of "deprivation" on the part of ordinary citizens (for example, if they are not in some way participating in the equal-partner model). Second, they could create a felt *need* on the part of the public to adopt progressives' perspectives to relieve that deprivation. But the question is, how can progressives make their appeal regarding what they believe to be the superiority (stemming from greater society-family harmony) of their image of family? Recall that Kamerman and Kahn (1978) observed that children have been the major focus of most family policy, although they detect a shift away from that long-standing emphasis. Steiner (1981: 90) remarks that "through most of the 1970s, both conservatives who opposed it and liberals who favored it understood child care legislation to be the sine qua non of family policy." Steiner (1981: 179) also observes that most European family advocates are "numbed by the size of the American research investment in child development." In spite of that reaction, most American politicians and advocates have concurred with the logic of Keniston (1977) and the Carnegie Council on Children that children are the "innocent victims" of the adult pursuit of individualism and the societal changes facilitating it. Consequently, they felt that children should be assisted, not merely because they may be in need, but because *they represent the future of society itself*. To damage children is presumably to undercut the greater good of the larger whole.

Steiner (1981: 6) continues that "according to the [Carnegie] Council responsible parents must become advocates for their children's interests." While no one could disagree with this lofty ideal, two basic questions arise immediately: (1) What is the best way to be that sort of advocate? (2) Who will advocate parents' interests? Rapoport et al. (1977) argue cogently that parents without resources (intangible as well as tangible) have little left over to pass on to their children. Failure to recognize this social law is a serious chink (perhaps even a fatal flaw) in the conservatives' armor. To combat the child socialization dilemmas described in Chapter 4, conservatives merely exhort parents to "carry on" and "do their duty" through instilling the conventional scripts in their children. Conservatives, in short, rarely advocate parents' interests—nor do they consider that to be the prime issue. Consequently, progressives can capitalize on the sociological reality that appeals for concerted action are heeded most strongly if self-interest is at least somewhere in view. Thus when we add the notion that progressives can advocate effectively for parents' interests to the complementary notion that they are actually better advocates than conservatives for children's interests, we have the beginnings of an ideology that might eventually appeal to the broad range of citizens, convincing them of the greater desirability of the progressive vision.

Analyses of both dimensions—children's interests and parents' (adults') interests—appeared in Chapters 4, 6, and 7. Since we are moving inexorably into an era of even greater societal flux, change, and morphogenesis than we have yet known, we do our children no favors by training them in the traditional scripts. At the same time, adults do themselves no favors by insisting on the conventional scripts either for their children or for themselves. Within the egalitarian model of family, adults and children are advocates for each other and for themselves simultaneously.

In Chapter 7, I cited Yankelovich's notion that in dealing with each other adults must self-consciously try to foster *mutual* well-being, rather than self-sacrifice or self-indulgence. In that same vein, the conventional notion of parents "living for their children" may have once appeared to be altruistic (prosocial), but in reality may have masked subtle efforts of parents to control their children's destinies covertly. In any case, while offspring do require considerable parental sacrifices for some years, the emerging goal is to move them as expeditiously as possible from dependent child status to peer status (Scanzoni and Szinovacz, 1980: 210). As peers, they are able to act as advocates for each other's interests more effectively. But this advocacy must begin among adults who grasp how difficult it is to parent "in a society such as ours, with its conflicting and rapidly changing directives.... Neither traditional sources nor the experts provide satisfactory guides" (Rapoport et al., 1977: 364).

In rejecting both traditionalism and an "expertism" that fails to question the conventional family fundamentally, progressives assert that "neither is it acceptable that parents should simply do as they feel; the vulnerabilities and difficulties of such a course are too great.... What is required...is a cultivation of the capacity to work with and resolve problems of living as parents in today's society" (Rapoport et al., 1977: 364). This "capacity"—being morphogenetic in a morphogenetic milieu—is the core of the progressive vision of egalitarian marriage and family. Therefore, to convey the progressive model is to convey the proposition that children

developing within it will be better off than they would be
otherwise; moreover, the society they eventually help to
develop will also be better off. How can one advocate more
strongly, elegantly, or eloquently for children's interests?

Although several observers (Aldous and Dumon, 1980;
Masnick and Bane, 1980) comment that the number of children
in families and households is likely to continue to decline into
the twenty-first century, any implication that children should
therefore be less central to family advocates is unwarranted. On
the contrary, since there will be fewer of them, it becomes more
imperative for societal well-being than it was previously to
concentrate on the *quality* of children's lives. We will be less
able to leave the matter of children's development pretty much
to chance, as we have under the conventional model. However,
I am not suggesting that we place an overlay of "experts" or
government regulations onto conventional forms—schemes
that Berger and Callahan (1979) and Rapoport et al. (1977)
show are fatuous. Such schemes are actually superfluous to a
progressive model since egalitarian parents are exceedingly self-
conscious about the difficulties and opportunities of trans-
mitting egalitarian gender roles and participatory decision-
making styles to children. By comparison, conventional parents
are more likely to take for granted the task of training children
by the same scripts through which they were fashioned. Any
difficulties they perceive in their child socialization tasks stem
from a hostile and incompatible milieu—for instance, consider
the 1980 WHCF mentality. But they perceive no particularly
unusual difficulties inherent within the task itself. However,
since egalitarian parents do grasp how difficult their task is *in
and of itself,* they take nothing for granted, and leave as little as
possible to chance.

By the same token, adults who seek these types of emerging
interests for children must also certainly be seeking the benefits
of a morphogenetic equal-partner model for themselves. Indeed, if they cannot execute the model in their own situations, it

will be exceedingly difficult for them to transmit it either explicitly or implicitly to their children. *Thus there is balance between their own self-interests and their concern for their children's interests.* These dual sets of mutually reinforcing and reciprocal interests are what could make the progressive model inherently appealing to increasing numbers of people. To further increase the appeal, progressives can argue that part of their "self-interest" is to create "new children for a new society." The upshot of this ideology is that self-interest blends with the interest of the whole. The perceived problem that progressives must convey to the public is that under the present scheme of things many individuals and families suffer because they are unable to operate in a morphogenetic fashion. And the progressives' solution to the sense of deprivation created by this realization must be to encourage the adoption of their family image, along with specific proposals that may be derived from it (see below).

Social Engineering?

One of the charges that is sure to be lodged against progressives if they become vocal and assertive regarding a morphogenetic family is that they are merely "social engineers." By using this term of contempt, conservatives imply that "liberals" are "tinkering" with a single fixed family structure while trying to impose their *avante-garde* notions on people that are essentially satisfied with it. As was shown in Chapter 6, however, the analogy of merely one "machine" is fallacious. Recall from Chapter 2 how the conservatives once effectively "engineered" their own particular machine into predominance. During the 1960s, certain progressives did indeed try to tinker with family structure, primarily because it was not working efficiently for disadvantaged (lower-class) people. However, the fact that this sort of tinkering is no longer possible, along with the fact that increasing numbers of more advantaged (working- and middle-class) people are simply ignoring the "machine," leads present-day progressives to suggest a new "machine" or model. Actually, "engineers" and "machines" are totally inappropriate analogies; more accurate is the "competing interest group" notion cited in prior chapters. When the situation is viewed from this perspective, the pejorative "social engineering" charge becomes meaningless.

Nevertheless, Steiner (1981: 190) applies this label to certain Swedish family advocates wanting to expand and enlarge what they call "parental insurance" benefits. This program first allowed women (and later men) to "draw social insurance in lieu of earned income after the birth of a child" for 9 months. However, 5 years after the program was expanded to cover men, only 10 to 12 percent of eligible fathers participated. According to Steiner, the present language of the law encourages disproportionate use of benefits by women, and some Swedish advocates have complained that this pattern reflects a "backward drift both in thinking about equality and in government action." In contrast, Steiner (1981: 190) says that perhaps Swedish hesitancy to expand the law "suggests...that the real preferences of the Swedish people are different from those espoused by social engineers." However, in all fairness to Steiner, he immediately forsakes that analogy in favor of the interest group notion to account for the situation. The political party that most strongly espoused expanding the parental insurance program lost seats in the Swedish parliament to parties less in favor of it and to some who outright opposed it.

Steiner's comparison of the overall Swedish family policy situation, as well as that of other European nations, with the situation in the United States is highly instructive. The U.S. situation is "muddled," he says, because issues of child development, day care for children of mothers who *must* work, and other kinds of *survival* matters for less advantaged children and adults are confounded with *individualistic* (defined in Chapter 2) matters such as "day care for children of mothers who want an alternative to uninterrupted child care...changes in family structure...escalating divorce and remarriage figures...cohabitation...abortion...implications of the women's movement for family life" (Steiner, 1981: 191). In contrast to this confounding, European policy is much more sharply focused, according to Steiner. Since "equality of men and women is accepted in most [European] countries as a fundamental principle" (Kjellin, 1980: 144), most Europeans have been focusing on the protection of children. "For example, cohabitation, divorce, and marital questions are not part of Swedish family policy, which has as its goal the protection of children, not the stability of marriages" (Steiner, 1981: 192), nor are sexuality (adolescent or adult), abortion, and single parent-hood considered burning issues, as they are in the United States.

The sharp divergence between the European and U.S. situations can in large part be attributed to the types of historic religious influences discussed in prior chapters. The present-day heirs to these influences, the "moral minority," flatly reject the assumption that it is legitimate for women to be equal to men in all spheres of life or that the goals of socialization are participatory decision making and a gradual transition from child to peer status (Fallwell, 1981). Thus it is they who make political issues out of the individualistic matters cited above. Since the European nations never experienced the moral fervor of this particular religious tradition, it has been relatively simpler for them to move to the sharp focus that Steiner describes.

However, de Bie (1980: 17) observes that the Europeans are not without their divergences, since some interest groups in certain nations lean toward values that he calls "traditional and conservative.... Their values...lead them to favor some family types—such as a large family...an authoritarian, male-headed family...and, perhaps, a family with both parents present."

Not surprisingly, "it is chiefly in the Scandinavian countries that...new values in family policies appear.... Sweden is most advanced in the development of a family policy that is reflective of new values" (de Bie, 1980: 19-20). In an effort to deal with conflicts between the old and the new, the Europeans have established a "Council of Europe, aimed at harmonizing and reforming European family law.... The value of differences based on old traditions is more and more in doubt. Rules and habits reflecting the agricultural society of old have no part in a modern and efficient law.... In this context, the long experience of the Nordic countries in harmonizing discrepancies in the law can be of some value" (Kjellin, 1980: 145).

In contrast to the emerging European effort to develop uniform policies and laws reflecting the twenty-first century, the U.S. situation is extraordinarily muddied and confused by the contrast between the formal level of laws, pronouncements, and exhortations and the actual behaviors of ordinary citizens. From these behaviors one could infer a kind of informal, tacit acceptance of the European aim of somehow trying to blend women's (and men's) interests with those of children. As Kamerman and Kahn (1981: 2) put it after their study of child and family policies in several European nations, "The problem of caring for the very young child [is]...the central question...: can adults manage productive roles in the labor force at the same time as they fulfill productive roles within the family—at home?" Implicitly, at least, some (mostly younger) Americans seem to be emulating Europeans in expending less energy on maintaining conventional family scripts and more on trying to find ways to blend adult and child interests effectively.

This is not to say that many Western European nations have necessarily made great strides in this direction—any more than have the communist societies discussed in Chapter 4, and for much the same reasons. Some (not all; see Lory, 1980) Western advocates promoting equality at home and in the work place continue to think in the arithmetic terms described by Jancar

(1978; see Chapter 6). Although such innovative strategies as affirmative action, flexi-time, shared jobs, parental insurance, work-site child care, and round-the-clock community child care facilities are important, they all fall into the category described by the *New Republic* (1981; see above) editorial writer as "programmatic." They are all essentially efforts to alter the work place and upgrade the quality of family life without going to the root of things—without first addressing the image of family to which these strategies can be attached. Most assuredly, it would be much simpler if the strategy of tinkering with the conventional family would "work" in the sense that it would stimulate women to feel free to pursue occupational goals with whatever intensity and vigor they desire while, at the same time, it would supply incentives for men to participate fully in mutual nurturing with their partners and their children. Unfortunately, the record of this strategy has not been glowing—the difficulties of imposing these programmatic overlays on the conventional model are enormous.

A "Gentle Revolution"?

In her study of the decline of American feminism between World Wars I and II, Wandersee (1981: 122) argues that a major reason for that decline was the fact that "the great majority of women remained committed to family life." But, in spite of that commitment, S. D. Becker (1981: 264) observes, feminists of the 1920s and 1930s "never attempted to develop an ideology which would help women integrate work outside the home with marriage and children. Their interest in the social and psychological effects of inequality was always peripheral to their main concern—civil equality which would bring in its wake the all-important economic equality for women." Today, says Wandersee (1981: 122), "the issue of women and the family remains a critical one for the modern feminist movement."

Although feminists may argue that the family is "the final oppressor of women" (Wandersee, 1981: 121), most women and men do not feel that way, and the situation is not changed merely by blaming "false consciousness." As long as adults remain committed to the conventional family at the formal level, attempts to encourage arithmetic equality will be perceived as "foreign" even though adults may in fact be drifting from the conventional model. This paradox by itself could be considered a "national problem" in terms of its potential consequences for adults, children, and eventually the larger society.

If tinkering with the conventional family does little good, Wandersee (1981: 122) wonders if it may be "necessary for family life to be revolutionized, if women are to gain full equality. But women's [and men's] historical commitment to the family indicates that the revolution will have to be gentle if it is to have a broad base of support." But does acceptance of the egalitarian model presented in Figure 6.2 (see Chapter 6) constitute a "gentle revolution"? Indeed, it is "revolutionary," not merely because it seeks to replace the conventional model presented in Figure 6.1, but because it goes beyond common definitions of equality, and instead redefines it as *equity,* in Jancar's demand-making and policymaking senses. The "revolution" lies with the nature of male-female relations, *and shifts the primary focus from arithmetic-type outcomes to decision-making processes.* Hence, to the degree the sexes gradually learn to be comfortable in dealing with each other on these dynamic terms throughout a variety of contexts— including friendship, dating, and sexuality, along with parenting and family itself—female-male equity (equality) will be possible throughout other aspects (political, economic, religious, educational) of the larger society.

Put more strongly, it is difficult to see how there can be anything approaching gender equity "out there" until there is gender equity "in there." This is not to say that we should ignore the sorts of social programs being pioneered in Europe; in reality those programs can and do contribute to the development of the "gentle revolution." However, a major problem currently facing U.S. programmatic advocates is that the programs often tend to generate relatively little enthusiasm from the broad citizen base to which Wandersee refers. One reason for this reaction is the incongruence most citizens perceive in grafting those programs onto conventional family assumptions. Consequently, in spite of the fact that it would be enormously simpler merely to tinker, that course is not likely to achieve much more than what we see around us right now. Progressives, in short, must consider how to promulgate the "gentle revolution" in order to provide an alternative coherent philosophy, or family ideology, into which those types of specific programs can be pegged, thus making greater sense of them to citizens and generating support for them in the resulting struggles with conventional advocates.

Focusing on State Laws

When pondering the "revolution," an issue that would be easier left ignored (but that must be faced) is the impact of state legislation on family. In stark contrast to the European nations, where family statutes are generally centralized, the United States has 50 jurisdictions, all able to legislate family matters pretty much as they please, except where federal courts intervene "largely through complex interpretations of the constitutional right of privacy and due process" (Sachs and Wilson, 1978: 149), for example, as in the abortion issue. As has been pointed out previously, these state laws—reflecting nineteenth-century conventional family perspectives— "continue to determine the roles and rights of married people" (Sachs and Wilson, 1978: 149). Hence, for both symbolic and pragmatic reasons, progressives must face up to the unpleasant and formidable task of addressing state family laws.[1]

Pragmatically, the very essence of the laws is morphostatic "because [the patterns] are not allowed to specify through *negotiation* what their legal relationships will or will not be.... A marriage 'contract,' therefore, is a legal fiction...because the...roles of both parties have already been determined by law, custom, or religion" (Sachs and Wilson, 1978: 149; emphasis added). Moreover, law, custom, and religion converge in bestowing higher status and greater rights and privileges to men than to women.

Consequently, even when equal partners might morphogenetically negotiate written or unwritten agreements regarding their relationships, those agreements have no ultimate binding legal or moral force in the eyes of the community. Law and custom override them. For example, since every state prescribes that the male is ultimately responsible for the family's economic well-being, a couple may negotiate that he not work at all, but their agreement has no legal or pragmatic binding effect: "Most American courts simply will not recognize or enforce...any kind of marriage contract between men and women that either alters the essential elements of the marital relationship, namely, 'the husband's duty to support his wife and the wife's duty to serve the husband,' or is made to facilitate divorce" (Sachs and Wilson, 1978: 150). As Weitzman (1981: xvii) puts it, "They are *not* free to write a contract to structure their marriage as they choose."

Perhaps even more crucial than the pragmatic consequences are the *symbolic* effects of challenging state laws mandating morphostatic scripts. It is utterly incongruous for progressives to propose a new image of family for the twenty-first century and yet have its ultimate governance lie with nineteenth-century statutes—wholly outside the dynamic processes of demand and policymaking by its own members. Kanowitz (1969: 4) observes that "as long as...[the law] continue[s] to differentiate sharply...between men and women...the likelihood...[of their] coming to regard one another primarily as fellow human beings...will continue to be remote."

To be sure, some may argue that confrontations of this sort with (highly traditional) state legislatures sap energy and resources that could better be used elsewhere—especially since increasing numbers of persons negotiate their own lifestyles regardless of archaic statutes. In the short run, this may be a valid argument, but it also reveals the current progressive penchant for overlooking the importance of the symbolic element in social change. Tufte and Myerhoff (1979: 9) underscore the significance of the symbolic by showing that an "image," such as the egalitarian model or vision depicted in Figure 6.2 is a particular type of symbol because it "appeal[s] primarily to our senses, and present[s] information through them, [thus] reaching us.... Their sensory nature gives images great potential power to convince and manipulate." In any case, if it is true, as many observers (such as Steiner) say, that efforts to fashion *federal* family policy will continue to be fruitless for some time to come, it makes sense to turn to the states, where the policies are established that, formally at least, affect most aspects of most people's family lives.

Failure to ratify ERA at the state level reveals a grave weakness of progressives—lack of organized grassroot support for its objectives (Boles, 1979). But, as I said above, ERA's immediate benefits were nebulous and its proponents were continually on the defensive. Working for the removal of archaic domestic laws and the promotion of new laws giving equal partners *freedom* to negotiate flexible marital arrangements are ways in which progressives can "take the offensive." If this "offensive" is based squarely on something akin to the theoretical and philosophical rationales of prior chapters, conservatives are likely to discover themselves on the defensive, arguing "against freedom"—freedom to arrange marriage/family so as to bring it into greater harmony with society, thus benefitting both individuals and society as a whole. Meanwhile, throughout this scenario, progressives find themselves on the side of a symbolic *coup*—greater individual freedom combined with greater social well-being.

THE INTIMATE CONTRACT

Weitzman (1981:351-352) reports that in the absence of state laws permitting "intimate contracts," the courts have nonetheless begun to move in the direction of saying that "marital partners entering into agreements should have the same assurance as other contractors that the courts will enforce the terms of their agreements." Additional court modifications include allowing certain "antenuptial agreements that contemplate divorce." However, Weitzman (1981: 2) asserts that "no court has yet upheld a husband's attempt to contract away his obligation for support *during marriage.*" The traditional marriage contract, she says, contains four provisions: The husband is the "head of the household" and "responsible for [wife and child] support"; the wife is "responsible for domestic services" and for "child care." These four provisions are, of course, tantamount to what I have been calling the "conventional" model.

Furthermore, Weitzman (1981: xxii) delineates the assumptions from which these provisions stem, and these assumptions are also inherent in the conventional model: a "first marriage; life-long commitment [permanence for its own sake]; separate roles for husbands and wives; the white, middle-class family; and the monogamous heterosexual norm." She concurs with the argument made in Chapter 4 that these assumptions are out of sync with modern society by saying they are "outmoded...[and] contradicted by the reality of [people's] own experience" (p. xvii). Weitzman (1981: xx) continues: "While new societal and individual needs require more flexibility and options in family forms, the rigid obligations imposed by traditional legal marriage appear increasingly anachronistic." According to Weitzman, proponents of the conventional contract argue that it is requisite in order "to preserve the traditional family," precisely what advocates of the Family Protection Act assert. But given the drift away from the conventional contract, as well as its basic out of phaseness, she wonders how much sense that "preservation logic" makes.

To those who point out that many people are informally establishing their own marriage/family patterns apart from state laws, and thus progressives should not dissipate resources in challenging those laws, Weitzman (1981: xvii) responds that "only when persons begin to disagree about their respective obligations or to make arrangements for their responsibilities after divorce [do] they discover...to what extent their freedom to decide their own fate is restricted by the terms of the state-dictated marriage contract that is codified in family law." To further support her contention that progressives ignore state marriage laws at their own peril, Weitzman (1981: xx) identifies three fundamental objections to the traditional marriage contract: (1) it "creates an unconstitutional invasion of marital privacy"; (2) "it discriminates on the basis of gender by assigning one set of rights and obligations to husbands and another to wives"; and (3) "the law denies...diversity and heterogeneity in our pluralistic society."

Weitzman proposes that current domestic laws be replaced by state legitimation of legal and enforceable contracts negotiated by the parties themselves. Such contracts "would facilitate the freedom of married and unmarried couples [she includes homosexuals] to order their personal relationships as they wish and to devise a structure appropriate for their individual needs and values" (p. xxi). In short, Weitzman's "intimate contract" would have two prime benefits: (1) It would likely make marriages "healthier"[2] from the outset because it would be incumbent upon persons to self-consciously participate together in deciding those specific matters that shape their intertwined destinies; (2) among marriages that terminate, there would not be the sudden emergence of dictated constraints imposed upon them without their foreknowledge. These imposed constraints may add additional levels of mutual hostility and bitterness to whatever levels may have existed prior to their unforseen imposition. The constraints may also contribute to a sense of bitterness toward, and disrespect for, the rule of (the apparently inequitable) law. Such consequences are hardly beneficial for individuals, family, or society.

The first benefit Weitzman notes (healthier families) is extraordinarily significant in view of the discussion in Chapter 5 concerning the conclusion from the micro-communication literature that families that perceive their environments as "masterable" are more adequate "copers" and "problem solvers." In that discussion, I suggested that one way to give marriages/families a greater sense of this "mastery" and "control" would be to provide them with the opportunity and the legal right—the responsibility—to shape their domestic relationships from the outset in ways they deem to be mutually equitable. People would become aware that from the initiation of their marriages, the arrangements they negotiate (and renegotiate) bear the force of law. Thus the macro legal system would be utilized by individuals to support and serve their own micro arrangements.

This bridging of the macro and micro levels fosters a sense of control of "domestic destiny," and it is also intrinsically tied to the discussion in Chapter 7 regarding Socrates' formulation of societal order. The essence of Socrates' argument is that the more fully persons participate in organizing the conditions that affect their destiny, the more likely they are to behave in accordance with those conditions, thus promoting order (Weitzman, 1981: 239). The legal right and responsibility to shape one's own marriage/family would, unlike the current imposed situation, permit a greater sense of participation and thus would presumably enhance the public order.

Recall that in Chapter 6 I made the point that one of the central features of modern societies is the *institutionalization* of participation in demand and policymaking. How better to institutionalize this feature into domestic life than by altering state family laws so as to make the partners ultimately totally responsible, in a full legal as well as moral sense, for their marital/familial arrangements? Under these new policies people would be free, of course, to establish arrangements as conventional or even more conventional than those currently imposed on them. No one already married under the current system would be required to adopt the new policies, although they would be free to do so. The point is that the current situation of macro and micro family advocates often talking past each other might be partially mitigated through Weitzman's suggested innovations. Micro advocates argue that families require a "new sense of themselves" in order to cope with their societal milieu, but often say little about effectively changing that milieu. Macro advocates want to change the milieu but are often at a loss as to how best to do so even for poor—to say nothing of nonpoor—families. Weitzman's innovations would be a "radical" (as defined above) means both to change the milieu significantly and to give a very different and very new sense of what it means to be "legally married." Unlike the provisions and assumptions, cited above from Weitzman, that currently undergird the conventional model, the "new" provisions would flow from the kinds of assumptions intrinsic to the four moral norms described in Chapter 7.

Sachs and Wilson (1978: 149) warn that because of the "unequal socialization of women in American society it is unlikely that most women could negotiate a fair contract (see Weitzman, 1981: 246). However, a prime effect of these proposed changes in state laws would be to make women (as well as men) keenly aware that it is *incumbent* on them to "work out" their own arrangements with partners. Such changes would serve to impress upon them that they can no longer take anything for granted in marriage/family matters. Especially precluded would be the currently prevailing idea that conventional marriage laws are intrinsically benevolent toward individuals and beneficial for society. Legal changes such as those proposed by Weitzman are likely to force individuals to become more effective decision makers. Furthermore, while current "family life education" programs for adolescents and singles are generally a charade,[3] some formal means would clearly have to be established to train persons in effective demand and policymaking techniques pertinent to gender equity. Moreover, it is imperative that such training make persons aware of how context factors (tangible and intangible resources and so on) impinge on decision-making processes.[4] These kinds of training programs would obviously have wider applicability than family (for example, in any work or other nonwork setting), and thus progressives could argue that as we enter Zartman's (1976) new "era of negotiation," Toffler's (1980) "future wave" society, and Yankelovich's (1981b) time of "new rules," in which participatory decision making will be central, progressives possess a *positive* approach, with beneficial consequences ranging far beyond family. In reaction, conservatives would be operating against what progressives could term the inexorable "wave of the future."

FAMILY MEDIATION POLICY

Significantly, we do not have to rely solely on training programs to assist people in enacting Weitzman's proposals. In recent years, there has emerged what Vroom et al. (1981: 8) call "a new kind of professional: a family mediator." Up to now, the mediator has been most active in divorce-related issues: "Several states have passed laws providing for mediation as an alternative to the court system. Most notably, California now mandates mediation in all child custody disputes" (Vroom et al., 1981: 9). The role of mediator is defined as neither attorney nor counselor-therapist. Instead, the mediator has two chief functions: facilitator and trainer. When a mediator is utilized, the immediate objective is to enable persons to negotiate issues currently facing them, but the long-range objective is that as a result of undergoing their current experience, persons learn how to engage more effectively in future demand and policymaking processes without outside assistance.

Girdner (1982: 6) cites Gulliver's (1979) and her own anthropological research on mediation in asserting that "contrary to the strong American cultural belief, the mediator is not a neutral party or simply a catalyst.... The mediator 'facilitates and, to some degree, influences, even controls, the exchange of information, the concomitant learning, and the consequent readjustment of perception, preferences, and choices.'" Importantly, the modern mediator's aims and ideals are remarkably similar to those intrinsic to the emerging family forms outlined in prior chapters: to get "the couple in mediation [to] work cooperatively to form their own solution to their own conflict. The result [ideally] is a new, workable relationship in which both parties are winners, and the family continues transformed" (Vroom et al., 1981: 8).

Furthermore, Vroom et al. (1981: 10-11) argue that mediation and the mediator can be useful at all stages of the life cycle "in both traditional and nontraditional family situations." These situations are found in many areas, including those involving "premarital mediation, teenagers and parents, teenage pregnancy, disabled and handicapped, runaways, homosexuals, rolocation, unmarried cohabitants, domestic violence, separation and divorce, property settlements and support payments, retirement, custody and visitation, wills and estate planning, the elderly vs. their middle-aged children."

According to Vroom et al., family mediation appears to be "an idea whose time has come": "Mediation represents a fundamental change in the way Americans are looking at their institutions of justice, the family, and the resolution of personal problems." In addition, Vroom et al. report that in 1980 Congress passed the Dispute Resolution Act, which, though never funded, "called for the establishment of alternative dispute resolution mechanisms nationwide to be administered by the Justice Department." There is also a fledgling Family Mediation Association, headed by Coogler (1978), a pioneer in the area.

In short, the notion of the use of mediation in family matters seems to be very closely allied with Weitzman's concept of an "intimate contract." Mediators and mediation provide a potentially concrete policy mechanism to which Weitzman's proposals can be pegged. If state laws were altered so that marriage/family would be based on negotiated contracts, presumably the new laws would include proposals for enhancing the role and significance of the mediator. (Such proposals would very likely also take into account a reactivation of the federal interest noted above.) In any case, the notion of mediation—in terms of both facilitation and training—helps add legitimation and significance to Weitzman's proposals. By making them appear more feasible and practicable than would otherwise be the case, the idea of mediation helps "sell" Weitzman's proposals to the unaligned majority.

Currently, there is much discussion among family policy researchers regarding "support networks." Gulliver (1979) and other anthropologists have shown that in traditional societies one of the major functions of kin and community is to mediate nuclear family disputes. In the emerging twenty-first-century society, it could be argued that the mediator will become a most critical element in family support. If morphogenetic processes, and one expression of them in legal contracts, increasingly become the foundation of family, then it would not be too far afield to expect that mediators could eventually come to function as a type of twenty-first-century "quasi-kin."

My elaboration of Weitzman's (1981) proposals is not aimed at an exhaustive critique of their numerous pros and cons. She herself does not supply such a critique, although she does attempt to at least identify the full range of major problems and concerns. More importantly, her proposals vividly illustrate the discussion in Chapter 5 regarding the linkages among research, values (preferences), and family policy. As described further in Chapter 9, apart from actual changes in state laws, it is very difficult to investigate (for example, through the use of impact analyses) the potentially far-reaching effects of such proposals.

Consequently, arguments for and against enacting such significant changes must come from whatever theory and research are available and from the logical arguments presented by both proponents and opponents of change. Ultimately, as Aaron (1978: 158) concludes, such changes will come about only if (1) progressives feel "passionately that a problem is so urgent that some answer, even though it may be wrong, is better than none"; and (2) progressives are able to wield enough political power at the grassroots level to convince the unaligned majority that such profound changes are worth at least a "trial run" of some sort.

In this vein of progressive grassroots power, *New York Times* conservative columnist William Safire (a former Nixon speech writer who also apparently has entre to the councils of Ronald Reagan) reports that President Reagan will support a constitutional amendment that would return abortion legislation to the states[5] (see also Tatalovich and Daynes, 1981: 183-196). If progressives are unable to prevent congressional passage of such an amendment, which has great political appeal to national politicians since, according to Safire, it is "the democratic way out," they would be *forced* to confront legislatures—first, to try (presumably) to oppose ratification; and second, if that fails, to influence the actual abortion legislation. As I said earlier, being progressive and being feminist are not necessarily equivalent; nevertheless, progressives and feminists are natural allies. According to Weisstein (1981) feminists would strongly oppose rescinding current abortion rights at both federal and state levels, and most progressives would presumably join them, though perhaps progressives may wish to expand the discourse to focus as much attention on the negative consequences for society and children of being an "unwanted child" as on the issue of women's individualistic rights.[6] In any case, if such an amendment ever reached the state level, its defeat would require more effective use of grassroots power than was demonstrated in the fight to pass ERA. Thus conservatives' abortion efforts could conceivably someday serve as a catalyst, uniting progressives and feminists not only to achieve an immediate goal, but bonding them in long-range efforts to completely overhaul state family legislation in a morphogenetic direction.

Regardless of the course of this proposed abortion amendment, it is well to keep in mind, as we reflect on the broader shift of attention from federal to state legislation, that conservatives seek to place increasing amounts of social, economic, and political responsibility at the state and local levels. Whether they will succeed or not in this endeavor is currently unclear, but progressives will apparently face many sorts of confrontations at these levels, including confrontations concerning family. For example, Safire reports that the Reagan administration wants to "focus on 'mediating structures.'"[7] He says that the administration's policy will be to develop "reliance on school, union, church, business, and *above all family,* to undertake more responsibility for liaison between individual and society" (emphasis added). What precisely is meant by this statement is not certain, but one could infer that the administration's aims are not too dissimilar from Jimmy Carter's (as analyzed by Steiner, 1981): Strengthen *the* family so that it can make better citizens and society, thus relieving federal, state, and local governments from numerous burdens.

Throughout most of this century, social scientists and practitioners alike have viewed the (conventional) family as beleagured by the forces of urbanism and industrialization. In this sense, the 1980 White House Conference on Families (see Chapter 5) reinforced a venerated belief. To a large extent, the conventional-type family is indeed helpless vis-à-vis external forces (such as economic forces or the impingements on socialization described in Chapter 4), primarily because it is morphostatic in nature and thus often unable to generate the adaptability and coping skills necessary for survival (see Chapter 5). Thus the contemporary conservative aim of making family less passive and more active in shaping both its own and society's destiny represents a departure from prevailing twentieth-century wisdom regarding family's inevitable "receptive" or passive role vis-à-vis the larger society. This aim is unlikely to succeed if conservatives continue to assume the conventional family model, however. Consequently, progressives have a unique opportunity to connect with what is very likely to be an increasingly popular cause. And while making this connection they can point up the sharp contradictions inherent in requesting a morphostatic entity to engage in creative, morphogenetic shaping.

The Reagan administration has been fond of saying that in the political and economic realms we should "forsake old ideas and forge new, bold, and imaginative ones." That the administration would be willing, however, to apply this formula to family is not probable. Nevertheless, the slogan is enormously appealing, and progressives can build on it to argue that it is they who have the "new" and "bold" ideas. Moreover, these are the very ideas that have the greatest likelihood of *eventually* (there is no "quick fix") accomplishing the common goal of actually giving family greater responsibilities and capabilities in order that it may positively influence its own destiny and that of society. Progressives, in contrast to conservatives, urge society both to face up to and accept the movement from morphostasis to morphogenesis that is already occurring in family, and to develop it systematically.

The Meso Level

As implied by the preceding pages, the center of the development from morphostasis to morphogenesis is likely to occur, if it does at all, at the *meso* level, or at the level of what Safire calls "mediating structures"—the sorts of groups and organizations found midway between the macro and micro levels described in Chapter 5. These include community groups, agencies, and organizations, churches,[8] and local chapters of national organizations such as NOW, ACLU, Planned Parenthood, Family Service Association, unions, political action groups, local political party groups, and so forth. Furthermore, in spite of the problems endemic to empirical research (see Chapter 5), there is no substitute for it; hence these groups will need all of the scientific as well as clinical information they can possibly get. Therefore researchers and clinicians will presumably join forces with them, both in terms of their scholarly and professional activities, as well as in education and social action. This conglomeration of progressives would carry out these two related aims of education (consciousness raising) and social/political action.

Through whatever community forums possible (churches, public meetings, organizations such as YWCA and YMCA, and so on), serious discussions, analyses, and critiques of competing family forms could be offered. Citizens could be made aware that there are options—that whatever dissatisfactions and uncertainties they sense in trying to make the static, conventional family "work" in the midst of a dynamic milieu can at least be explained and understood. The continuing drift from the conventional model can be set forth plainly, and the alternative ideology presented as a means to develop a coherent and consistent view of family as we enter the next century—a view suggesting the potential for benefits greater than those offered by the conventional model to adults, children, families, and society.

Alongside the consciousness-raising aim is social/political action. Not only state domestic laws, but local statutes as well become targets for reform. The issue of how to establish and fund programs of "decision-making training" has both local and statewide ramifications. For example, should local schools or other entities be responsible for such programs? What is the minimum age at which such programs should begin? Scale's (1981) empirical studies of the efforts of 23 American communities to establish school-based sex education programs are instructive regarding the larger matter of attempting to influence the full range of family-related policies. He reports that in virtually all the communities studied, most (80 percent) of the citizens, as well as most school officials, support sex education programs, a finding validated by national Gallup (1978) surveys. Nevertheless, support for these programs is usually tacit; supporters are not organized as a pro-sex education "interest group." On the other side, Scales reports that opponents of such programs, a surprisingly tiny minority (1-2 percent), were extremely vocal and well organized, and thus successful in their political efforts to stymie the proposed programs. Most important, Scales found that program proponents were never able to garner the whole hearted support of the majority of citizens; they were never able to allay the understandable fears regarding sensitive aspects of the sex education issue. Not only that, but proponents failed to convince the unaligned majority that concerted political activity on this issue was in the majority's best interests.

The lessons from Scales's research are quite obvious. In spite of majority citizen support for matters such as sex education, abortion, ERA, and so forth, and in spite of apparent growing disenchantment with the conventional family in general, progressives have not been able to communicate effectively an image of a viable (egalitarian) alternative, or to achieve specific sociopolitical goals. Until they are able to do both at the state and local levels, it is unlikely that they will ever be able to make much impact on federal family policy. The implicit assumption of 1960s and 1970s liberals that family policy could be fashioned at the federal level and then it would "filter down" to the masses is, as Steiner (1981) shows, untenable. For a wide range of reasons—not least of which is the fact that conservatives are well organized at the state level and thus are choosing to make that the battleground of the 1980s and 1990s for numerous issues—it appears that progressive efforts must first take root among the unaligned majority at the state level if these results are ever to "surface" at the federal level.

Prospects for Progressive Programs

That the political struggles ahead will be long and arduous is obvious because they concern " 'way of life' issues, and as a result they easily arouse the most intense political passions" (Smith, 1975: 90). However, Smith refers specifically to "single-issue" matters, in which groups are identified as being *solely* for or against abortion, sex education, and so forth. He also excludes economic and civil rights considerations. In contrast, the conflict I have been describing is not a single-issue conflict, nor does it exclude economic and civil rights matters. To be sure, conventionals (such as the New Right, and the "moral minority") have been much more effective than progressives in uniting diverse interests into a workable coalition because they have a clear vision of *their* family. By comparison, progressives remain much more splintered and "visionless."

Nevertheless, time, economics, and civil rights issues are on the side of progressives. As far as time is concerned, Masnick and Bane (1980) document the continuing drift away from conventionalism that we may expect at least until 1990 and probably beyond. As for economics, although Novak (1977), Skerry (1978), and others argue that working-class people feel more threatened than middle-class people by challenges to traditional family patterns and traditional roles for the sexes, the Connecticut Mutual (1981) survey demonstrates something more subtle than mere class differences. Although it may appear that this is a situation in which the great masses of "average-educated" citizens are resisting significant family changes on ideological grounds, that survey shows that religious commitment is a more critical factor than social class in predicting orientations toward family change. Given this conclusion, and considering the potentially beneficial economic options of the emerging patterns, one can argue that women especially, but also men, within the lower-middle and working classes are not beyond recruitment into the progressives' camp (see Chapter 9).

The civil rights matter is, of course, connected to the notions of freedom, equity, and human fulfillment discussed throughout prior chapters. It is on this fundamental level that the progressive vision is perhaps most compelling; it offers the greatest potential for uniting diverse interest groups. As Weitzman (1981) contends, the conventional model intrudes on the civil rights of both women and men, at the same time that it is incapable of optimally performing its morphogenetic socialization function for society. Thus is would seem that over an extended period of time, as progressives become more skillful in communicating their vision of freedom and equity, along with this vision's inherent social responsibility, they will be likely to gradually achieve their aim of developing synchrony among people's actual behaviors, formal family policy, and the larger society.

Disadvantaged and Disabled Families: The Issue of Economics

Earlier, I cited the growing feeling among certain family advocates (such as Rapoport et al., 1977) that family policy must be directed to nonpoor as well as poor people. In her study, Halem (1980) repeatedly makes the point that apprehension over family has moved from the lower and working classes into the middle classes. But in our concern to develop an alternative approach to the conventional model, are we neglecting the poor (especially blacks) as well as the physically and mentally disabled? As noted earlier, during the 1960s and early 1970s, the prime assumption of many Great Society planners was that if households could somehow gain economic resources, resident adults would be in much better positions to begin to fulfill their material and emotional needs as well as those of their children. Nothing has occurred during the intervening years to invalidate the basic reasonableness of this proposition.

Halem (1980: 292) comments that there is "a general agreement that economic supports and alterations in work and work-related patterns and options are probably the first order of priority in any major effort which favors the extension of equality and individual freedom." She asserts (correctly) that poor people need supports and that working- and middle-class people need work alterations such as the options of shared jobs and flexi-time. However, in their study of federal government employees' flexi-time programs, Bohen and Viveros-Long (1981: 201) conclude that as *necessary* as these kinds of programs are, they are not *sufficient*: "They will not alleviate work-family conflicts unless they are accompanied by shifts in values about the appropriate connections between work and family life." They conclude, in effect, that alongside those work programs there must be a whole new philosophy of family—one that is morphogenetic enough to supply dynamic frameworks that can accommodate the potentially ever-changing work and family preferences of household members.

Just as the egalitarian philosophy and theory underlying the model of family depicted in Figure 6.2 (see Chapter 6) are totally compatible with work-alternation schemes, they are also congruent with, indeed they *assume,* at least minimal household economic well-being. The rationale for this assumption returns us to Socrates' prescription for social order: Make the milieu advantageous to persons, and then make them "aware" of it so that they will "act socially."

We learned earlier that when people participate in the shaping of their own milieu they will try to make it advantageous and thus will be motivated to conform to its constraints. But "acting socially" in this fashion requires that people have a stake in their milieu. On September 3, 1981, *CBS Reports* presented a profile of the increasingly widespread use of guns (and subsequent murders) by mostly poor and deprived adolescent males. While teenage gangs have always had "rumbles" to settle turf disputes or to revenge a member's humiliation, fistfights and the use of knives have gradually been replaced by the use of firearms. The major conclusion of the report was essentially a reversal of Socrates' dictum: These people have no stake in their milieu because they did not participate in its shaping and it is not advantageous to them; thus, rather than behaving "socially," they seize the only response they perceive as open to them—the totally individualistic option of imitating the "heroic" cowboy by "packing" a gun and being ready to use it, because, as one boy put it, "If I don't get him first, he'll get me."

While we cannot make the mistake of "blaming" poor families for these sorts of behaviors, as did the Moynihan (1965) report in connection with related problems, we must realize that the sense of having no stake in the larger society is linked with the economic deprivation lower-class children experience very early in their development—although most of them, of course, do not subsequently engage in the kinds of violent acts just described. It is clear that fresh thinking is needed regarding what new policies must be established at local, state, and federal levels to deal with the issue of poverty among American families. It is to be hoped that the aim of these socioeconomic policies will be to make families economically self-sufficient, at the same time they assume the morphogenetic character of the Figure 6.2 model. A basic premise in the design of these policies should be that *maintaining* economic independence (from social service bureaucracies) is likely to be very difficult for low- to moderate-income families unless they can learn to generate (and regenerate) creative ways to organize their households. This point is illustrated by one of Ibsen's (1970b) characters, who says, "I come from a poor family...and I've had ample opportunity to observe what the most pressing need is among the lower classes.... It's to play some part in directing our public life. That's the thing that develops skills and knowledge and self-respect." Failure of Great Society planners to recognize this issue (along with their implicit adherence to the conventional model of family) was one reason for the demise of many of their schemes (Abbott, 1981).

BLACK AMERICANS AND EMERGING FAMILY FORMS

The issue of what family forms blacks might choose for themselves—in contrast to those chosen by whites—has been with us at least since the early 1960s (see Chapter 5). European family advocates have long observed that the relative racial homogeneity of their countries stands in sharp contrast to the economic and cultural differences between black and white Americans; thus, presumably, U.S. family policy is more difficult to construct (Aldous and Dumon, 1980). In 1971, I concluded that while sharp black-white economic differences did exist in the United States (owing to white discrimination), there was no evidence of unique cultural differences in family preferences—instead, many black Americans seemed to prefer the sorts of family patterns prevalent throughout the larger society (Scanzoni, 1977). This is not to say that blacks wished merely to imitate whites; they simply wanted access to the economic resources requisite for the fulfillment of whatever family-type options they might adopt. A major distinction between black families and white conventional families of that era was that "the option of market work versus home work and/or leisure is a luxury that few black married women have enjoyed. Overwhelming economic reasons [for example, white discrimination against black men] for supporting and sustaining the family have kept them in the work force" (Wallace et al., 1980: 3-4).

In 1971, I suggested that "the realm of female employment represents perhaps the one area where white patterns are moving in the direction of black family patterns" (Scanzoni, 1977: 231). More recently, Wallace et al. (1980: 101) conclude that "well-educated black women have learned how to balance the demands of the work environment, where they experience racial and sex discrimination, and the demands of their home.... With the increased labor force participation of married white women, is there anything that they might learn from the experience of well-educated black women who have combined several roles? We think so."

If Wallace et al. are correct, one might conclude that not only is there nothing antithetical to black interests within emerging morphogenetic family patterns, but also that well-educated blacks constitute part of the vanguard of those patterns. Furthermore, over the years numerous studies have reported greater levels of egalitarian gender-role preferences and of egalitarian decision making among black than among white families (McAdoo, 1981). Recent works by Rodgers-Rose (1980), Gary (1981), and Staples (1981) support the notion of basic compatibility between black interests and emerging patterns. Hence, there would appear to be no reason that black interest groups could not join with other progressive groups in promoting those sorts of patterns. The idea of joining forces with progressives could be particularly appealing to black Americans given that the majority of blacks continue to experience economic hardships, and also given the fact that for the Figure 6.2 model to be accepted throughout all strata of society, there must be greater levels of economic opportunity for all citizens.

Promoting Intimacy

In Chapter 4, I discussed the connection that Swidler (1980: 133) draws between work as a quest and intimacy as a quest. The "American Dream," which black as well as white parents presumably still hold for their children, is essentially a quest— anticipated movement from lesser to more advantaged status. How realistic this dream now is for families of any race or social class level remains to be seen, but what seems vital is that no pocket of the population be exposed to the sorts of debilitating circumstances currently faced by poor families and their children so that they consistently and systematically view the dream more pessimistically than others. For instance, in comparing middle- and working-class parents, Kohn (1978) found that the former are more likely to teach their children to "think for themselves" and to be autonomous persons, whereas working-class parents are more likely to instill conformity in their children. Thus less advantaged children not only have the handicap of fewer economic resources, they tend to lack the vital intangible resource of freedom from rigid conformity and the capability of "figuring out" how to act upon, rather than be acted upon by, their milieu. It is only a small step from there to infer that middle-class children are more skilled than less advantaged children in effective demand and policymaking techniques. It therefore follows that policies meant to enhance the economic well-being of disadvantaged children (including their social mobility) cannot afford to overlook the development of this critical intangible resource.

Reasoning from Swidler (1980; and also from Weitzman, 1981), people at all social class levels who are able to view both work and intimacy in morphogenetic, or dynamic, terms should, during the twenty-first century, be able to generate more meaningful (intimate) family experiences both for themselves and for their children. In thinking of significant applications that clinicians and counselors (the micro approach discussed in Chapter 5) can make during the coming years, one would hope that the sorts of ideas and strategies suggested by Raush et al. (1979; see Chapter 5) would continue to expand. That is, alongside establishing programs to train people in effective demand and policy making techniques, there will be increasing need for the sorts of counseling efforts that explicitly adhere to a morphogenetic model of family, supporting persons at all social-class levels in their struggles to achieve and maintain that model.

As Gadlin (1977) observed, intimacy cannot be guaranteed, much less legislated, by any family model. But he also asserts that a morphogenetic image, in which egalitarianism and the related moral norms discussed in Chapter 7 are pivotal, is likely to be the most conducive cradle for the development of intimacy. Pleck and Pleck (1980) argue that the greatest hindrances to intimacy in the past have been conventional male scripts. Discarding these scripts, as illustrated in Figure 6.2, should at least open the door to greater levels of cross-gender intimacy. It seems curious that in spite of the fact that most women and many men form relationships wanting intimacy as a prime outcome, family policymakers, whether progressive or conventional, have had very little to say on the subject until recently.[9] There are probably many reasons for this omission—not least of which is the fear of government trespassing into "family privacy." Perhaps another reason is that, since most of the advocates had been "socialized male," intimacy never seemed to be a priority for discussion.

In any case, Swidler's (1980) penetrating analysis and presumed changes in male orientations make intimacy a topic that can no longer be left to artists, writers, and poets, much less to "pop culture" and "self-help" books. The work of social historians in unearthing diaries exploring the nature of intimacy decades ago as well as recent research into its contemporary manifestations make us aware of how complex a phenomenon it has been and is increasingly becoming. As Swidler (1980) tells us, the simplistic images created by the romantic films of the 1940s and 1950s, in which the hero and heroine inevitably married and "lived happily ever after" have become anachronistic. According to Swidler, new images of intimacy for a new era are developing; intimacy is coming to be seen as enormously complex and risky as well as potentially rewarding. These notions, along with all other aspects of the Figure 6.2 egalitarian model, must be discussed openly and presented frankly to the men and women—black and white— who are establishing and will establish twenty-first-century families. These notions involve "a search for models of self and models of love that are compatible with continuing growth and change, that permeate with moral significance the ups and downs of daily life, the struggle to live well, rather than giving moral meaning only to the dramatic moment of the shift from youth to adulthood" (Swidler, 1980: 144).

Summary

According to Steiner (1981) federal family policy in the United States has been confused and muddled in comparison to that of Western European nations. In a variety of areas, progressives are being summoned to generate fresh ideas to meet the distinctive challenges of a new century. With regard to family, progressives have the option of remaining on the "defensive" or going on the "offensive" by actively promoting some variation on the theme of the morphogenetic model illustrated in Figure 6.2. In taking the latter route, they can continue to make children's well-being the centerpiece of their appeal to the "unaligned majority"; in addition, they can transmit the message that they are equally concerned with adults' interests. The progressive vision or image of family represents a "gentle revolution"; it is linked with the premise that only to the degree that gender equity is realized in family can it be realized throughout the larger society.

Since state and local legislation, as opposed to federal legislation, most directly affects family, and since most of this legislation tends to reinforce the conventional family, it becomes a potential target for progressive reforms. By undertaking such sociopolitical reforms, progressives can build grassroots organizations at state and local levels. These "meso-level" entities (existing midway between the macro and micro levels) could serve as a mechanism for applying and negotiating matters of specific interest to progressives, such as the establishment of programs to train people in demand and policymaking skills, and related context issues. Also, means of extricating families from the cycle of poverty must be developed; these means must be consonant with a morphogenetic approach to family.

Finally, the curious discrepancy between the populace's overriding concern with intimacy as a prime marital goal and prior family advocates' failure to address this issue should be remedied. Intimacy must be publicly examined in the light of Swidler's (1980) analysis of its changing character, as well as in terms of the related question of which model of family is optimally suited to the attainment of intimacy throughout the twenty-first century.

NOTES

1. According to William Safire (Greensboro [North Carolina] *Daily News; New York Times* News Service, August 22, 1981), conservatives intend to make the states the arena for many of their envisioned long-range policies, including those concerning family.

2. The definition of marital/family "health" is much debated in the research and clinical literatures; as used here, it refers to the kinds of matters described throughout Chapter 7. "Health" can be said to be a sense of well-being and satisfaction that flows from patterns of morphogenetically achieved equity.

3. These classes may be categorized as such because they often ignore contemporary realities under pressure from a minority of conservatives.

4. Context factors such as education, income, self-esteem, gender-role preferences, decision-making history with present partner, and negotiating experience in general are critical to current decision making (see Scanzoni and Szinovacz, 1980; Hill and Scanzoni, 1982).

5. See note 1.

6. For example, the fate of the unwanted child has been a long-standing concern of Planned Parenthood.

7. See note 1.

8. If the Connecticut Mutual (1981) data are valid, most citizens involved in churches are *not* part of the "moral minority" (see Chapter 3).

9. The Aldous and Dumon (1980) volume is an exception.

9

DIRECTIONS FOR
THEORY AND RESEARCH

It is traditional for books on family studies to close with a chapter on policy implications after having presented empirical findings and theoretical analysis. But since the bulk of this book was devoted to policy issues, I take the liberty of reversing revered custom, and close with a chapter on research and theory implications.

Ever since Hill and Hansen (1960) published their ground-breaking piece on conceptual frameworks for studying family, analysts have attempted to identify the most useful approaches for understanding, explaining, and predicting family phenomena. Since accounts of those efforts are readily available, there is no need to review them here. Holman and Burr (1980) make the point that no one framework, approach, or "theory" currently overshadows any other in making sense of family. They imply that during the years ahead family studies will likely be characterized by an eclectic spirit in which insights are drawn from a variety of frameworks in response to a particular research question or substantive issue.

In his assessment of 1970s family research, Berardo (1981) observes that perhaps the most significant development was the surge of interest in the changing roles of women and men. Significantly, this surge of theoretical and empirical interest did not spring from an intellectual agenda; there was little or nothing in the 1960s body of research and theory (in family or any other substantive area) that would have stimulated analysts to move in this direction. Instead, the move was stimulated by happenings in the "real world"—in particular the revival of feminism and the growing impact of inflation on women's employment. The incapacity of family theory in the 1960s to anticipate (much less account for) the marked shifts that have occurred in family behaviors is indicative of the apparent irrelevance of that theory. It would not be inappropriate to say that for the past 15 years the "real world" has been the "tail wagging the dog" of family theory and research. This is not to say that the reaction of scholarship to contemporary events has been a negative development. Quite the contrary—this reaction has contributed substantially to the relevance and significance of family scholarship.

However, since it has been almost twenty years since the first stirrings of renewed feminism, one wonders whether family scholarship needs to remain in this essentially reactive posture. For instance, can family scholarship ruminate on the policy issues described in prior chapters in order to develop the beginnings of an eclectic approach to family that can provide theoretical understanding and also make use of that understanding to inform policy? Is it possible to work toward reciprocal feedbacks between theory and policy so that each guides the other? Rather than merely reacting to practical demands of the real world, can theory and research anticipate what some of those demands might be in order to fashion policy accordingly? Positive responses to these sorts of questions would lead to an extraordinarily ambitious agenda. As one small step toward grappling with this agenda, let us consider some of the theoretical issues and research questions implied by the discussion in the preceding chapters.

A Macro Perspective

As far apart as Safilios-Rothschild (1976) and Bell and Vogel (1968) are in most respects, they share a common concern that family sociology has been preoccupied with micro-level issues. To its own detriment, they say, family sociology has neglected macro matters. As a way of correcting this shortcoming, Bell and Vogel (1968: 17) advocate the usual functionalist approach to the larger global picture of family and society: Examine the functions (consequences) of the nuclear family for, say, the economy (labor, family assets) and, reciprocally, consider the economy's functions for the family (goods, wages). For example, earlier chapters used this approach in considering the family's function for society in socializing children. It became clear from this use of the functionalist approach that although there is nothing necessarily wrong with describing the global picture in functional terms, functionalism tends to "freeze" socialization contents. The fact is that macro-level analysis of family and society is too complex for the limited scope of functionalist assumptions; hence, we must look for other means to conduct such analyses.

Attempts to grapple with this complexity are found in Safilios-Rothschild's (1976) analysis of family and a stratification system based on dual rather than single earners. Osmond (1980) expands this theme and integrates it with a wide body of cross-national research on women and family. Elder's (1981) exhaustive summary of the recent family history literature also reveals enormous complexities in the interplay between historical sociodemographic forces and family. He approaches the current era through what he calls the "study of the life-course," an adaption of the classic Thomas and Znaniecki study.

Prior chapters also suggested other ways to grasp the macro or larger picture of society and family. One is the Marxist approach, in which family in capitalist society is seen as a creature of the ruling class. The Marxist thesis is that the foundations of the conventional family arose, and have been preserved, by males who wished to use women to maintain their wealth, power, and privilege. Socialists in Russia or in Israeli kibbutzim, wishing to modify the conventional family, abolished a capitalist class and attempted to shift the family's ultimate control to the political system. Chapter 4 demonstrated that in spite of socialist aspirations for gender equality, this goal commands much less priority than economic development and hence little actual effort is expended to achieve it. Nevertheless, the point remains that socialists (whether in Russia, China, or Israeli kibbutzim) view family as an entity they can shape to serve the needs of the state. Rather than being a creature of the ruling class, family must, in their view (until the state "withers away"), be a creature of the Communist Party.[1]

Another, more complex, version of this particular macro approach is seen in Stone's (1977) work (described in Chapters 2, 3, and 6). Significantly, Stone (1977: 22) acknowledges his debt to Max Weber, because implicit in Weber is a notion that Stone makes explicit: Family is a creature of prevailing interest groups. In the periods of English history studied by Stone, and in the period of German history analyzed by Weber (Bendix, 1962), social classes operated as the interest groups promoting particular family lifestyles:

> Attitudes and customs which were normal for one class or social stratum were often quite different from those which were normal in another. Such changes as took place sometimes affected one class but not others; for example, the rising rates of premarital pregnancy... [and] the drift toward a more child-oriented attitude.... Patterns of behaviour found in the leading sectors of value-change, the professional and gentry classes, do not necessarily apply to the [other classes since]... there is a plurality of family styles and values [Stone, 1977: 23-24].

Stone's (1977: 414) observation that, historically, England experienced "a growing diversity of family types, a widening pool of cultural alternatives" carries a very contemporary ring. Furthermore, his conclusion that "the cause of [family] change lies in an unending dialectic of competing interests and ideas" (p. 425) is, of course, pure vintage Weber (Bendix, 1962).

Perhaps the most critical distinction between the *Marxist* approach (not only in the classical sense, but also as promulgated by contemporary Marxist feminists such as Sokoloff, 1980) and the *Weberian* approach is that Marxists identify the central conflict as patriarchy (men) versus women. (Some radical Marxist-feminists have attempted to blend economic and gender issues by contrasting capitalism and patriarchy with socialism and equality.) Conversely, Weberians view the contemporary scene as best apprehended not primarily as a male-female (or socialist-capitalist) struggle, but as struggle between the sorts of interest groups identified in prior chapters. Empirically, there is some support for the latter view: The Connecticut Mutual (1981) survey described in Chapter 3 discovered that religious commitment was a far stronger predictor of conventional family preferences than gender. In short, there are men and women *together* on one side of the issue of family change, and there are men and women *together* on the other. But, respond Marxist-feminists, women on the conventional side are afflicted with "false consciousness," and women on the progressive side are not radical enough. And men on both sides are, to one degree or another, said to be self-serving.

In contrast to these interpretations, a Weberian approach to the macro study of family seems to hold considerable promise for generating exciting research efforts and, through those efforts, obtaining a better understanding of contemporary trends and expected future patterns. It turns out that some research has already been carried out based on this general notion of "clashing family lifestyles." Scales's (1981) research on community forces for and against sex education was cited in Chapter 8; Tatalovich and Daynes's (1981) work on community conflict over abortion was discussed in Chapter 6. Granberg's (1981; Granberg and Granberg, 1980, 1981; Granberg and Denney, 1982) studies on abortion follow this same approach of lifestyle clashes (see Chapter 6), as does the research of Zurcher and Kirkpatrick (1976) on "antipornography crusades for status defense." Zurcher and Kirkpatrick (1976: 306-307) conclude that "antipornography crusades...express and attempt to resolve strains concerning the stability of traditional social institutions [such as]...family...[and] concerning the rewards [persons] receive from enacting roles in those institutions.... Pornography...[is] perceived to represent the alternative life styles and changes and would be labeled dramatically and specifically as the source of evil." Boles's (1979) account of the ERA struggles presents a similar picture of community conflict over lifestyle and family values. (See also Tax, 1980; Wandersee, 1981; S. D. Becker, 1981.) Finally, one of the prime conclusions of the Connecticut Mutual (1981) study is that a substantial minority of the population views a whole set of behaviors as supportive of their conventional family (and in their judgment those behaviors and their family are being threatened), while other people view family lifestyle in somewhat different terms.

Because of these perceived threats the conventionals in American society have formed what Dahrendorf (1959: 180-181) calls actual interest groups: "They are the real agents of group conflict. They have a structure, a form of organization, a program or goal, and a personnel [roster] of members...[who] are in contact with each other...by virtue of their membership or by way of their elected representatives." These people are engaged in what Zurcher and Kirkpatrick (1976) call "status-defense"; they are trying to guard a particular kind of lifestyle, with their family at its center. On the other hand, progressives have tended to form what might be labeled "quasi-groups" (Dahrendorf, 1959: 180). These are "aggregates or portions of the community which have no recognizable structure, but whose members have certain interests or modes of behavior [lifestyle] in common, which may at any time lead them to form themselves into definite [interest] groups."[2]

Let us say that there are at least two broad categories of citizens who fall into the "quasi-group" category. The first and largest is what I have called the unaligned majority—people who are simply drifting away very gradually from the conventional model, neither explicitly questioning it very much nor explicitly reasoning about potential alternatives. These people increasingly share common lifestyles regarding sexuality, marriage, employment, household chores, decision making, children, divorce, and so forth. Nevertheless, they possess little if any motivation to form interest groups to enhance their lifestyles, even though, as Yankelovich (1981c) indicates, they sense a great deal of incongruity among the family lifestyles of their parents, their own lifestyles, and how best to socialize their children. This unaligned aggregate includes adolescent boys such as those interviewed by Levine (1976: 157). They know, he says, that the world will be different for their female peers, but for themselves "somehow it didn't look much different from the present." Levine calls this a "failure of imagination."

The second and smaller quasi-group is made up of people who are more explicitly self-conscious in their comparisons and critiques of traditional and emerging lifestyles. Occasionally, in addition to their verbalizations, they may participate in actual interest group activities focusing on particular issues, such as gay rights, sex education, abortion, or marriage and divorce law reform. However, in comparison to conventional interest groups, there are fewer and probably less powerful progressive interest groups. More important, as I said in prior chapters, they lack the cohesive vision (set of common values and interests) possessed by conventional interest groups.

It is clear that a pivotal research question for the 1980s and 1990s concerns what Dahrendorf (1959: 182) calls the "empirical conditions" under which progressive interest groups form (or do not form) and thrive (or languish), and the sorts of conflicts they do (or do not) have with conventional interest groups. Dahrendorf (1959: 158-187) lists three conditions that influence whether quasi-groups evolve into active interest groups. The first of these he calls the "technical conditions of organization," by which he means personnel, especially a cadre—"certain persons who make this organization their business, who carry it out practically and take the lead." Another technical condition is an "ideology," such as the egalitarian model (cohesive vision) suggested in prior chapters. A second general condition is political. According to Dahrendorf, in a totalitarian society competing interest groups are not allowed to form (we saw empirical evidence of this in Chapter 4). Dahrendorf's third general condition is *social*, by which he means the physical contacts between members of the aggregates that make it possible for them to discover and share common concerns and objectives. Dahrendorf also stresses the importance of "recruitment" of quasi-group persons by the cadre into their interest group. For example, Boles (1979) and Felsenthal (1981) show how extremely successful the anti-ERA cadre was in recruiting citizens to oppose ERA.

A researcher might try to identify actual situations in which it would be appropriate to measure the existence (or lack) of these three kinds of conditions. For example, let us say that an interest group forms in a certain state to achieve the sorts of marriage/family law changes described in Chapter 8. The alert researcher would first document the *technical* conditions, namely, the existence of a cadre and an ideology. Since the second (or political) condition is a given, the researcher next would try to identify the social conditions used (including the use of mass media) to promulgate the ideology, increase physical contacts (such as public meetings), and enhance recruitment from among the aggregates. Finally, the researcher would trace the actual struggles and their outcomes between the progressives bent on change and the conventional interest groups, which would presumably emerge in that particular situation to resist change. Over a longer period of time the researcher might try to determine the degree of influence, if any, of these struggles on the family norms and behaviors of individuals who remain in the aggregate. That is, even if laws, policies, and programs are not changed, does the agitation on the part of progressives itself tend to increase the degree of drift on the part of aggregate persons? Or, if policies are changed, how much practical impact do the changes actually have on these same types of persons?

In some states there may not be the opportunity to investigate a field situation, and this reality itself can be turned into a research question. Using quantitative and/or qualitative techniques, the researcher might examine why progressive cadres do not develop in certain locales, or, if they do develop, why they are ineffective in recruiting from among the aggregates. For example, it may be that the degree of drift toward a nonconventional lifestyle is so extensive and rapid among aggregates that they may sense little or no imperative to participate in or lend support to a progressive interest group. Or certain judicial rulings may render concerted legislative political action relatively unnecessary. Regarding recruitment, recall Weitzman's (1981: xvii) observation that the people most likely to sense the inequities of conventional domestic laws and policies are those who have formally tried to alter their marriage arrangements or who have been involved in divorce. Perhaps it would be wise for investigators lacking a field situation such as the one described above to focus on these kinds of people and attempt to identify factors influencing the degree to which they do or do not become involved in progressive cadres or otherwise allow themselves to be recruited out of the ranks of the aggregates.

Note the common thread running throughout this series of research questions (and others of a similar nature that might be stimulated by this general problem). The thread emanates from the approach to macro-level phenomena taken by Dahrendorf (1959: 189-193), who in turn borrowed it from Max Weber. What aggregates have in common, according to Dahrendorf, is a shared set of *subjective* factors, interests, goals, and preferences. If and when aggregates are recruited into interest groups, it is because they sense that such organizations will enhance those shared goals. Hence, those macro-level transformations and the subsequent potential macro conflicts and changes are inseparable from micro- and meso-level phenomena. Dahrendorf's contention is brought up to date by Blalock and Wilken (1979: 1), who state that "subjective variables, or 'meanings' that actors attach to objective events, must be an integral part of any micro- or macro-level theory that purports to explain social reality." More bluntly, they say, "It is our fundamental assumption that macro-level theories will tend to be inadequate to the degree that they ignore that human motivations and behaviors constitute important driving forces or causes of social phenomena" (p. 3).

In brief, the larger social milieu that currently prevails in U.S. society (and promises to prevail for some time to come) provides a significant research opportunity for application of a Weberian approach to the macro-level study of family. While it may not have been entirely appropriate six or seven decades ago, its relevance is becoming increasingly apparent. Interest groups have formed in an attempt to preserve the conventional lifestyle, including their family. And although a growing aggregate of citizens is simply ignoring the conventional lifestyle, and thus sense little need for interest group formation, their casualness may not be impenetrable. Since the conventionals do not accept lifestyle pluralism as described by Stone (1977), but insist on the preeminence of their patterns, some aggregates may eventually come to perceive that their own lifestyle options are being limited. To the degree that this belief occurs, or is stimulated by progressives, the progressive cadre may become increasingly effective in recruiting from the aggregate ranks.

While it is extremely hazardous to try to predict the directions and outcomes of such wide-ranging (legislative, judicial, media, and religious) macro struggles, certain hypotheses seem fairly plausible. Should the struggles occur, large numbers of citizens who are now merely onlookers and/or aggregates are likely to become well acquainted via the media with the family-society synchrony issue. To the extent that the out of phaseness between morphogenetic society and morphostatic family becomes translated into household terminology, (1) it will become increasingly difficult for conventionals to enforce their lifestyle and family patterns by formal, legal, and policy means, and (2) it will become more likely that greater numbers of ordinary citizens will increasingly behave in progressive rather than in conventional terms.

The theoretical relevance of a Weberian approach to these macro events is apparent, expecially in identifying what is perhaps the key variable in this entire scenario: the extent to which aggregates actually do come to feel threatened, either because conventionals are, ironically, effective in enforcing their family and life-style, or because progressive cadres are effective in raising aggregates' consciousness to perceive the threat potential. The developmental and reciprocal nature (Blalock and Wilken, 1979) of these ongoing struggles is underscored when we consider that conventionals initially organized (see Chapter 6) in response to relatively mild organized efforts by a few progressives on behalf of ERA and abortion reform. In turn the conventionals' organization stimulates additional progressives to escalate the struggle by organizing further and by proclaiming not only the threats posed by the conventionals, but also the *superiority* of progressive perspectives. This in turn causes conventionals to feel even more threatened, and the escalating developmental cycle continues. A great virtue of the Weberian approach to these macro phenomena is that the researcher becomes theoretically prepared to validly describe and analyze them, however complicated they become.

A Micro Perspective

As unaccustomed as most researchers and applied professionals (and indeed most people) are to thinking about macro family matters in the terms described above, most of us are equally unfamiliar with viewing micro-level matters in the structural and processual terms described in Chapters 6 and 7. The research and theory over the past fifteen years regarding family changes have focused primarily on certain compositional matters: women entering the paid labor force, men doing more domestic work, lower birthrates, more divorces, more single parents, more single-person households, and so forth. It is, of course, vital that we continue this sort of research, but it is equally imperative that we simultaneously investigate the remaining dimensions of social life, namely, structure, preferences (culture), and processes. Indeed, if we accept the assumption (Levine et al., 1976; Buckley, 1967) that structure arises out of process (and preferences), we have no choice but to look more carefully than we have at these particular dimensions. A literature search (Scanzoni and Fox, 1980) shows that interest in these dimensions is growing.

Much more work is also needed on the critical issue raised in Chapter 7—namely, with the apparent proliferation of familylike structures, what is the possibility of identifying a "family form" or model that could operate as a societal "template?" Is it possible to unearth evidence that will help us determine whether the conventional *structure*, which once operated as that sort of template and thus served as a cohesive and integrative force in society, is or is not being replaced by a model that is equally compelling and as integrative? Significantly, if we remain at the level of the emerging variations in household composition such a task could appear impossible and perhaps even misguided.

As vital as composition is, the researcher needs to ask whether or not there is something fundamental underlying composition that gives meaning to its variations and that provides a framework under which many of those variations can be fitted. In probing this issue, the researcher would simultaneously be exploring the degree to which citizens have actually moved on the continuum from traditional to modern—

conventional to progressive. Both themes—unity among diverse categories and preferred family lifestyle—can be at least partially ascertained by investigating three matters discussed in Chapters 6 and 7: the nature and extent of the emerging moral norms; the nature and extent of demand and policymaking by women as well as men; and the nature and extent of emerging intimacy patterns. Ideally, the researcher would be able to probe these matters across varied household forms and would also be able to compare and contrast differences and similarities by sex, race and ethnic group, education, religious commitment, and so forth.

MORAL NORMS

In recent years there has been a growing body of research focusing on sex- (gender) role preferences (SRP; Scanzoni and Fox, 1980) in which the aim has been to document variation in the extent to which persons desire "traditional" or "modern" patterns both in family and in the marketplace. Generally, items used to measure preferences are quite specific regarding particular behaviors. In addition, it turns out that most of the SRP items reported in the literature tend to be most closely identified with the third moral norm, interchangeability. To the extent that authority matters are subsumed under the second norm of equity, these matters have also been addressed, but to a much more limited degree. In addition, investigations regarding whether parents value child obedience or autonomy (Kohn, 1978) may be connected with the fourth child socialization norm. Finally, many of these investigations have classified couples as to their degree of traditionalism-modernity (Bowen, 1981), or as to whether their marriages fit into categories such as head-complement, senior-junior partner, or equal partner (Polonko and Scanzoni, 1981).

However, implicit in those investigations has been the assumption that there is one basic family form in our society,

albeit with several variations. Based on the preceding
discussion of macro issues, investigations focusing on moral
norms would begin by questioning that assumption. They
would compare and contrast families in terms of the norms in
order to identify whether there is more than one basic theme or
form. Measuring these four dimensions would likely reveal a
continuum on which some families would fall strongly toward
the conventional end and others toward the progressive end,
with many at various points in between. In spite of the
likelihood that such a continuum could be found, one could
argue, on the basis of the substance of the moral norms, that
families falling clearly into the conventional plane represent a
very different family form (that is, morphostatic) than do those
falling clearly into the progressive plane (that is, morphogenetic).

Take, for example, the first norm regarding the sphere of
negotiable items. One could measure this dimension in at least
two different ways. First, we might assess respondents' degree
of acceptance *in general* of the idea that persons should not *a
priori* bring certain nonnegotiable expectations to their
marriages. Complementary to that technique would be to list
an array of specific areas, including economic provision, child
care, sexuality, leisure activities, and so forth. Respondents
could be asked to score (on a Likert-type scale) how strongly
they feel a particular behavior (such as the husband in-
tentionally remaining out of the paid labor force indefinitely or
the matter of either spouse's sexual fidelity) is totally outside
the realm of "discussion" (there is only one "right" and/or
"acceptable" way to do it) or is a matter that could be
negotiated and changed according to a couple's preferences at
any given time. There is likely to be a positive correlation
between general acceptance of non-*a priori* items and willingness to "discuss" specific matters. In any event, this would be
one approach the researcher might take to distinguish conventional from emerging marriages in terms of this first moral
norm.[3]

The second norm—equity in demand and policymaking—is extraordinarily pivotal for a variety of reasons, not least of which is that it requires behavioral measures as well as the obtaining of respondents' expectations. It might, in fact, constitute a behavioral check on the first norm, in that the researcher could inquire as to how many of the specific areas in question had ever actually been discussed or negotiated. Recall that Jancar (1978; see Chapter 6) forcefully argued that gender equality is a reality only to the degree that women and men actually participate jointly in shaping the arrangements that affect their own destinies. Consequently, it becomes essential to devise measures (see Scanzoni and Szinovacz, 1980; Hill and Scanzoni, 1982) that validly identify the *dynamics* of marital/familial decision making, including degree of power symmetry and amount of satisfaction with the outcomes of those dynamics. As above, marriages/families could be placed on a continuum according to degree of equality, equity, symmetry, and so forth. At this juncture, one could begin to construct a typology or "property-space" (Barton, 1955; Riley, 1963: 343-349), placing couples who are *most* flexible on dimension one, and simultaneously *most* symmetrical on dimension two, into the *highly* nonconventional or "emerging" category. Conversely, the least flexible and least symmetrical couples would be placed at the opposite or conventional end of that same property-space.

Applying this logic to dimension three means that couples already in the "emerging" space continue to remain there if they also simultaneously adhere most strongly to the norm of interchangeability, that is, that each person can and should be able to function "effectively" both at home (routine chores, child care) and in the marketplace. Once again, behavioral checks would be introduced to ascertain actual, as well as normative, interchangeability.

Turning to the fourth moral norm regarding children, it would seem that attempting behavioral measures of parent-child decision making among couples without children is prolematic. And even when a child is present, the age of the child of necessity becomes a factor in assessing the norm of participatory childrearing. However, whether children are present or not, couples who hold most strongly to that norm (as well as simultaneously hold strongly to the three remaining norms, as above) would be placed in that "emerging" space or category.

Reference to the fact that presence of children affects measurement procedures reminds us that single-adult households (with or without children) also introduce measurement complications. In these situations, behavioral checks of the types proposed above become problematic. In any case, the overall thrust of a "property-space" procedure would be to attempt to empirically place households on a continuum of adherence to the four emerging moral norms and, having done that, to argue that households falling within the extreme "emerging" space represent a very different family form from those falling within the extreme conventional space.

DEMAND AND POLICYMAKING

In making this argument special attention needs to be paid to certain aspects of the second normative dimension regarding decision making. In particular, the issues of women's behaviors and resources require considerable research. In exploring those matters, we must recognize the link between them and the intimacy question below. Gray-Little's (forthcoming) reasoning is that "power" has an impact on "marital satisfaction," but she fails to consider the alternative hypothesis that the intimacy or expressive realm may exercise even more profound influence on demand and policymaking (DPM). Bernard (1981b: 87), for instance, concludes that existing research reveals that women are "passive, dependent, fearful of success, unaggressive, unassertive." Explaining this conclusion, Bernard (1981b: 502) says that women are socialized to place expressiveness and emotional support of others above anything else. They specialize in "showing solidarity,...giving help, rewarding, agreeing, concurring, complying, understanding, passively accepting."

In sum, the conventional pattern has been for women to approach DPM with the overriding orientation that they must provide nurture at all times, including in decision-making situations. Hence, the research question becomes, to what degree does variation within the intimacy realm affect DPM processes? Bernard (1981b: 502) asserts that "the love-and/or-duty ethos is inherently nonegalitarian. It calls for a serving role. Anyone who lives by it must always be compliant, doing for others, 'stroking.'" Thus research is needed to determine if women who behave in this manner are, in reciprocal fashion, highly rewarded by their partners in terms of expressiveness (companionship, sexuality, empathy, and so on) and thus tend to avoid the risks that would inevitably accompany assertiveness during DPM processes. The risks are, of course, that the expressive rewards being received from their husbands might be undermined. In other words, the researcher would seek to determine if Bernard is correct: Does the conventional view of expressiveness and intimacy (Bernard's description is remarkably similar to Swidler's [1980]; see Chapter 4) tend to subvert symmetrical DPM processes? Indeed, is it basically incongruous to use terms such as "demand" or "policymaking" to describe decision making in conventional households?

On the other side, can the researcher discover instances in which intimacy is viewed in other than conventional terms (that is, other than Bernard's "love-duty ethos," or Swidler's four traditional conceptions)? If so, does that contrast result in significant differences from conventional households in decision making? In short, are there emerging situations in which concepts such as "demand" and "joint policymaking" do indeed take on considerable face validity in describing what is actually occurring?

Children and Demand and Policymaking. Throughout this book I have repeatedly made the point that one of the prime benefits for society and children of emerging family forms is the presumed socialization of children into these DPM processes. While some researchers have, for instance, examined adolescents' perceptions of whether their parents treat them in a "democratic" or "authoritarian" fashion, much less attention has been paid to the *dynamics* of parent-child and peer-peer decision making. Wheeler's (1982) research is an effort to move in the direction of measuring these types of complex dynamics, and more such investigation is needed. For example, what are the connections between the degree of actual involvement of both spouses in their own joint DPM and the degree of the child's (or adolescent's) actual participation in DPM regarding matters that affect his or her own life? Moreover, does the degree to which children and adolescents learn to become "effective problem solvers" at home correlate with their capabilities to solve problems with peers, in school, and in other types of activities?

It would appear that evidence contrasting the extent of "content-bound" with process-oriented socialization would, among other things, provide important clues regarding the speed with which emerging family patterns are actually, if at all, gradually replacing conventional ones. This is not to say that many children exposed to conventional socialization will not, as adults, shift their own preferences and behaviors. The point is simply that the greater the frequency and intensity of conventional socialization, the more gradual family changes are likely to be.

INVESTIGATING INTIMACY

To explore the intimacy issue the researcher will need to draw on and synthesize notions from several analysts discussed in this and prior chapters (for example, Gadlin, Yankelovich,

Swidler, and Bernard). The researcher could begin with the basic assumption that intimacy and DPM processes exercise feedback influences on each other over time. From there, it would be possible to delve into the nature of intimacy itself. For instance, one hypothesis might be that women's rejection of Bernard's (1981b) "love-duty ethos" is associated with acceptance of Swidler's (1980) emerging conceptions of love—indeed, it is difficult to expect it to be otherwise. Swidler's notions involve the sort of autonomy that would lead a woman to risk explicitness and assertiveness during DPM because her identity as a human being is not ultimately solely dependent on the expressive rewards and approval of her male partner. This is not to say that she would attempt to dominate or coerce or refuse to make any sacrifices—recall Yankelovich's notions. The researcher would look for evidence that women who define love and intimacy primarily in terms of *mutual* growth and development are also more willing to take DPM risks (even risking the relationship itself if need be) in order to enhance both autonomy and intimacy.

At the same time, the researcher would look for evidence that certain men may also be redefining expressiveness with women to include not just companionship and sexuality but also "mutual stroking" as one aspect of intimacy. One hypothesis might be that men in conventional households exercise greater assertiveness during DPM processes, not only because they possess greater tangible resources and thus wives are more dependent on them economically than they are on their wives, but also because of the situation just described. That is, even though women do the "stroking," they are more dependent on men for affirmation and validation as a result of the stroking than men are dependent on them to receive the stroking. Hence, the researcher would need to discover the extent to which certain men have redefined intimacy in terms described by Gadlin, Swidler, and Bernard. These are terms in which there is "mutual stroking," that is, men taking as much responsibility for the nurture of women as women do for the nurture of men.

The "causes" or conditions of this redefinition would be at least twofold: (1) such men would be related to women who insist on their own autonomy, thus to maintain their relationships men would have to learn to "stroke" effectively; (2) men would come to learn that intimacy based on mutual stroking is much richer than intimacy based on the sort of expressiveness open to them under conventional patterns, and would thus consider it a highly valued reward.

The research question then becomes, in addition to men becoming more vulnerable to women because of relatively increasing economic parity, are some men also making themselves more vulnerable to women because of gradually shifting definitions of intimacy? To the degree that this syndrome is actually developing, the researcher would predict increasing gender symmetry during DPM processes. The reason would be a growing convergence of vulnerabilities—women's being scaled downward, and men's being scaled upward. From both perspectives, the risks (for example, of impermanence) are increased compared to the risks in conventional situations, but so are the rewards, thus making the risk taking more acceptable.

Critical/Normative Theory or Positivist-Policy Feedbacks?

There are many additional empirical questions generated by the policy issues outlined in prior chapters. A major one, for example, is suggested by the Blalock and Wilken (1979) emphasis on linking macro and micro perspectives. Thus, for example, a vital research question would be how the sorts of interest group dynamics described early in this chapter stimulate, and in turn are stimulated by, the micro dynamics described in the preceding section (Scanzoni and Fox, 1980; Callon and Latour, 1981).

But what I wish to emphasize here is that this entire chapter has been grounded in what Boulding (1976: 75-76) calls "positive science," or positivism: It "is a science of constraints.... The study of what the constraints on the system are.... [It consists of] laws and correlations.... Positive science is the study of boundaries that divide the possible from the impossible." Positivism, as a means of describing and analyzing empirical phenomena (what is) attempts to maintain a value-neutral (what should be) position. We saw how difficult it can be to maintain such a position in Chapter 4. Indeed, some sociologists (Sewart, 1979) and family analysts contend that the effort is untenable and that "a critical perspective is needed" (Paolucci and Bubolz, 1980: 1), by which they mean that analysts take "a normative and ethical stance" in promoting their conception of the desirable and good, or "healthy," family. "A radical-critical approach," says Osmond (1981: 22), "requires that its proponents believe in the possibility of radical social change." Compare Boulding's (1976) description of positivism with Osmond's observation: "Most possible things were thought to be impossible at some time." Giele (1978: 14) contends that "the link between political consciousness and scientific endeavor is forged in the domain of...'normative science' [Boulding's label for critical theory]. Normative science relates fact to value and suggests ways to accomplish specific goals such as equality."

However, Boulding (1976: 76-77) cautions that

it is important to keep positive and normative science both separate and related, and it is very dangerous to confuse the two. It is very dangerous to say that because something should be, it is. And it is also dangerous to be too positive about positive science since one can be wrong. The limits may be wider than we think. Normative science can force us to widen the boundaries of the possible, for if something which is not now possible should be, we have an incentive to find out [empirically] how to make it possible.... [But] values are no substitute for positive knowledge. They have to operate under known constraints. Otherwise they are not fulfilled.

I concur with Boulding's assertion that positive and normative science must be kept both distinct and connected. Research and theory of the types suggested in this chapter are essentially positivistic because they seek to describe and analyze *what is*. But they are stimulated at least in part by policy or normative considerations, that is, *what should be*. Positivistic results from such investigations would help inform policy or normative considerations. It goes without saying that the research itself would be conducted under the strictest positivist procedural canons possible. Nevertheless, the researcher is not deluded into thinking that he or she has no vested interest in the outcomes of the investigations, anymore than medical researchers can assume that they have no personal interests in the outcomes of their investigations. In one way or another, we are all members of households, families, or past or future relationships affected by current family customs and policies. And since our research findings often tend to legitimate or invalidate those customs and policies, we are led to affirm or to question our own norms and behaviors.

Although there is this inevitable connectedness, the separateness that Boulding also urges can be fostered through use of the interest group conceptualization discussed above. Conceiving of family research and policy in interest group terms permits the observer the luxury of a certain degree of disengagement and detachment. Regardless of whether the observer is part of an active interest group cadre or merely part of the unaligned aggregates, viewing family phenomena as a struggle between opposing interests somehow enables one to step back and attempt, for a moment at least, to view the phenomena as though through the eyes of an objective outsider. Hence, the struggles become a drama to which the observer is temporarily audience. A crucial benefit of this momentary spectator role, besides whatever value it might have in enhancing research validity, is that it enables one to view any agenda for radical-critical change (including the one suggested in prior chapters) with a certain degree of healthy skepticism. Boulding (1976: 76), for instance, observes that many past agendas for change have "been appallingly costly to the human race. When one thinks of the constant failure of liberations, revolutions, reforms, and prohibitions to improve the human condition...one is tempted to formulate a law of political irony—that everything one does to help people hurts them." While Boulding himself acknowledges that his hyperbole results in unwarranted conclusions, the point is that adopting a radical-critical stance without first couching it in what sociologists know about interest group objectives gone awry can lead to a naive optimism; for example, faith may be placed in progressive objectives that is just a blind as conventionals' pessimism that unless family goes "back to" their way, all is lost.

On Being a Possibilist

Perhaps Lerner (1979) captures the essence of "normative science" that is effectively constrained by positivist knowledge when he says,

> I am neither optimist nor pessimist. I am a possibilist.... I believe in the possible. More options are open for us than we dare admit. Everything depends on our collective intelligence in making choices, and our will to carry them out.... I ask the women of every age: would you rather be living in the days of male power and swagger, with slim options for jobs and careers and meager life chances, or now?... I ask the code breakers who deviate from the narrow social norms of the part, and who have found new life-styles: would you rather have lived before society accepted your life-ways, and before the breakthroughs that gave you a new identity—or now?

He goes on to remark that "America...is the world's most revolutionary culture. It is in a phase of rapid change which belies the familiar charge of decay."

Hence, when it comes to family, contemporary social scientists can certainly opt for varying degrees of a positivist stance or for varying degrees of a radical-critical stance. Or perhaps they can opt for that uneasy balance between the two stances implied by Lerner. That is, they can maintain serious involvement in empirical research and systematic theory that both is informed by and informs policy issues that are intrinsic to the conventional-progressive struggle. Their degree of involvement in the actual struggle varies at any given point in time depending on a variety of life circumstances. The involvement may range from simply drawing implications from their own research findings that bear on the struggle to actually forming a cadre. In short, there is a vast middle ground between extreme positivism and an extreme radical-critical stance in which one, both as social scientist and as citizen, can contribute answers to Socrates' profound query, "How can social organization be made highly advantageous to a person, and a person be made so aware of these advantages that s/he will always act socially?"

REFERENCES

AARON, H. J. (1978) Politics and the Professors: The Great Society in Perspective. Washington, DC: Brookings.

ABBOTT, P. (1981) The Family on Trial: Special Relationships in Modern Political Thought. University Park: Pennsylvania State University Press.

ABT, C. C. [ed.] (1980) Problems in American Social Policy Research. Cambridge, MA: Abt Associates.

ALBIN, M. and D. CAVALLO [eds.] (1981) Family Life in America: 1620-2000. New York: Revisionary Press.

ALDOUS, J. (1981) "From dual-earner to dual-career families and back again." Journal of Family Issues 2 (June(: 115-125.

——— and W. DUMON [eds.] (1980) The Politics and Programs of Family Policy. Notre Dame, IN: University of Notre Dame Press.

ALDRICH, R. A. [ed.] (1976) Toward a National Policy for Children and Families. Washington, DC: National Academy of Sciences.

ANDRE, R. (1981) Homemakers: The Forgotten Workers. Chicago: University of Chicago Press.

BAKER, R. (1981) "And the New Deal gat no heat." New York Times Service; in Greensboro (NC) Daily News, August 3.

BALDWIN, W. H. (1977) "Adolescent pregnancy and childbearing: growing concern for Americans." Population Bulletin 31, 2.

BANE, M. J. (1976) Here to Stay: American Families in the Twentieth Century. New York: Basic Books.

BARDWICK, J. M. (1978) In Transition: How Feminism, Sexual Liberation, and the Search for Self-Fulfillment Have Altered America. New York: Holt, Rinehart & Winston.

BARTON, A. H. (1955) "The concept of property-space in social research," pp. 40-53 in P. Lazarsfeld and M. Rosenberg (eds.) The Language of Social Research. New York: Macmillan.

BECKER, G. S. (1981) A Treatise on the Family. Cambridge, MA: Harvard University Press.

BECKER, S. D. (1981) The Origins of the Equal Rights Amendment. Westport, CT: Greenwood.

BELL, D. (1968) "The measurement of knowledge and technology," in E. Sheldon and W. Moore (eds.) Indicators of Social Change. New York: Russell Sage,

BELL, N. W. and E. F. VOGEL (1968) "Toward a framework for functional analysis of family behavior," pp. 1-36 in N. W. Bell and E. F. Vogel (eds.) A Modern Introduction to the Family. New York: Macmillan.

BENDIX, R. (1962) Max Weber: An Intellectual Portrait. Garden City, NY: Doubleday.

BERARDO, F. M. (1981) "Family research and theory: emergent topics in the 1970s and the prospects for the 1980s." Journal of Marriage and the Family 43 (May): 251-254.

BERGER, B. and S. CALLAHAN (1979) Child Care and Mediating Structures. Washington, DC: American Enterprise Institute.

BERGMANN, B. R. (1981) "The economic support of 'fatherless' children," pp. 195-212 in P. G. Brown et al. (eds.) Income Support: Conceptual and Policy Issues. Totowa, NJ: Rowman & Littlefield.

BERNARD, J. (1982) The Future of Marriage. New Haven, CT: Yale University Press.

——— (1981a) "The good-provider role: its rise and fall." American Psychologist 36 (January): 1-12.

——— (1981b) The Female World. New York: Macmillan.

——— (1981c) "Facing the future." Society (January/February): 53-59.

——— (1974) The Future of Motherhood. New York: Dial.

——— (1972) The Future of Marriage. New York: World.

——— (1942) American Family Behavior. New York: Harper & Row.

BIRENBAUM, A. and E. SAGARIN (1976) Norms and Human Behavior. New York: Praeger.

BLALOCK, H. M. and P. H. WILKEN (1979) Intergroup Processes: A Micro-Macro Perspective. New York: Macmillan.

BLAUVELT, M. T. (1981) "Women and revivalism," pp. 1-45 in R. R. Reuther and R. S. Keller (eds.) Women and Religion in America, Volume I: The Nineteenth Century. New York: Harper & Row.

BOGARDUS, E. S. (1960) The Development of Social Thought. New York: David McKay.

BOHEN, H. H. and A. VIVEROS-LONG (1981) Balancing Jobs and Family Life: Do Flexible Work Schedules Help? Philadelphia: Temple University Press.

BOLES, J. K. (1979) The Politics of the Equal Rights Amendment: Conflict and the Decision Process. New York: Longman.

BOULDING, K. (1976) "Comment I." Signs 1, 3(Pt. 2): 75-77.

BOWEN, G. L. (1981) "Sex role preferences and marital quality in the military." Ph.D. dissertation, University of North Carolina—Greensboro.

BRONFENBRENNER, U. (1975) "The challenge of social change to public policy and developmental research." Presented at the meetings of the Society for Research in Child Development.

——— (1972) "Who cares for America's children?" in L. K. Howe (ed.) The Future of the Family. New York: Simon & Schuster.

BROWN, L. [ed.] (1981) Sex Education in the Eighties: The Challenge of Healthy Sexual Evolution. New York: Plenum.

BUCKLEY, W. (1967) Sociology and Modern Systems Theory. Englewood Cliffs, NJ: Prentice-Hall.

BYRNE, D. (1979) "Determinants of contraceptive values and practices," pp. 301-307 in M. Cook and G. Wilson (eds.) Love and Attraction. New York: Pergamon.

CALLON, M. and B. LATOUR (1981) "Unscrewing the big leviathan: how actors macrostructure reality and how sociologists help them to do so," pp. 277-303 in K. Knorr-Cetina and A. V. Cicourel (eds.) Advances in Social Theory and Methodology: Toward an Integration of Micro- and Macro-Sociologies. Boston: Routledge & Kegan Paul.

CAMPBELL, H. (1893) Women Wage-Earners. New York: Arno Press. (Reprint edition, 1972.)

CHERLIN, A. J. (1981) Marriage, Divorce, Remarriage. Cambridge, MA: Harvard University Press.

CHRISTENSEN, H. (1964) "The instrusion of values," pp. 969-1006 in H. T. Christensen (ed.) Handbook of Marriage and the Family. Skokie, IL: Rand McNally.

CLARKE-STEWART, A. (1977) Child Care in the Family: A Review of Research and Some Propositions for Policy. New York: Academic.

COLLINS, R. (1975) Conflict Sociology. New York: Academic.

Connecticut Mutual Life Insurance Co. (1981) The Connecticut Mutual Life Report on American Values in the '80s: The Impact of Belief. Hartford, CT: Author.

COOGLER, O. J. (1978) Structured Mediation in Divorce Settlement. Lexington, MA: D. C. Heath.

COTT, N. F. (1979) "Passionlessness: an interpretation of Victorian sexual ideology," pp. 162-181 in N. F. Cott and E. H. Pleck (eds.) A Heritage of Her Own: Toward a New Social History of Women. New York: Simon & Schuster.

——— and E. H. PLECK (1979) "Introduction," pp. 9-24 in N. F. Cott and E. H. Pleck (eds.) A Heritage of Her Own: Toward a New Social History of Women. New York: Simon & Schuster.

DAHRENDORF, R. (1959) Class and Class Conflict in Industrial Society. Stanford, CA: Stanford University Press.

DE BIE, P.J.L (1980) "The rationale and social context of family policy in Western Europe," pp. 3-28 in J. Aldous and W. Dumon (eds.) The Politics and Programs of Family Policy. Notre Dame, IN: Notre Dame University Press.

DEEM, R. [ed.] (1980) Schooling for Women's Work. Boston: Routledge & Kegan Paul.

DEGLER, C. N. (1980) At Odds: Women and the Family in America from the Revolution to the Present. New York: Oxford University Press.

DOBASH, R. E. and R. DOBASH (1979) Violence Against Wives: A Case Against the Patriarchy. New York: Macmillan.

DUMON, W. and J. ALDOUS (1979) "European and United States political contexts for family policy research." Journal of Marriage and the Family 41 (August): 497-506.

EISENSTEIN, Z. R. (1981) The Radical Future of Liberal Feminism. New York: Longman.

ELDER, G. H., Jr. (1981) "History and the family: the discovery of complexity." Journal of Marriage and the Family 43 (August): 489-520.

ELLIS, D. P. (1971) "The hobbesian problem of order: a critical appraisal of the normative solution." American Sociological Review 36 (August): 692-703.

FALLWELL, J. (1981) "The maligned Moral Majority." Newsweek (September 21): 17.

FARBER, B. (1964) Family: Organization and Interaction. San Francisco: Chandler.

FARBER, S. M., P. MUSTACCHI, and R.H.L. WILSON (1965) Man and Civilization: The Family's Search for Survival. New York: McGraw-Hill.

FELDMAN, H. (1979) "Why we need a family policy." Journal of Marriage and the Family 41 (August): 453-456.

——— and M. FELDMAN (1975) "The effect of father-absence on adolescents." Family Perspective 10 (Fall): 3-16.

FELSENTHAL, C. (1981) The Sweetheart of the Silent Majority: The Biography of Phyllis Schlafly. Garden City, NY: Doubleday.

FERGUSON, M. (1980) The Aquarian Conspiracy: Personal and Social Transformation in the 1980s. Boston: Houghton Mifflin.

FISHER, R. and W. URY (1981) Getting to Yes: Negotiating Agreement Without Giving In. Boston: Houghton Mifflin.

FOX, G. L. (1979) "Mothers and their teenaged daughters." Wayne State University. (unpublished)

GADLIN, H. (1977) "Private lives and public order: a critical view of the history of intimate relations in the United States," pp. 33-72 in G. Levinger and H. L. Raush (eds.) Close Relationships: Perspectives on Meaning of Intimacy. Amherst: University of Massachusetts Press.

GARY, L. E. [ed.] (1981) Black Men. Beverly Hills, CA: Sage.

GIBRAN, K. (1980) The Prophet. New York: Knopf.

GIELE, J. Z. (1978) Women and the Future: Changing Sex Roles in Modern America. New York: Macmillan.

GIRDNER, L. K. (1982) "Adjudication and mediation: a comparison of process and function in third party interventions." University of Illinois—Urbana-Champaign. (unpublished)

GLAZER, N. (1966) "Foreword," in E. F. Frazier, The Negro Family in the United States. Chicago: University of Chicago Press.

GOODE, W. J. (1963) World Revolution and Family Patterns. New York: Macmillan.

GOODMAN, E. (1980) "Out from under the rule of thumb." Washington Post (September 30).

GORDON, T. (1976) P.E.T. in Action. New York: Wyden.

GRANBERG, D. (1981) "The abortion activists." Family Planning Perspectives 13 (July/August): 157-163.

——— and D. DENNEY (1982) "The coathanger and the rose: comparison of pro-choice and pro-life activists in contemporary United States." Transaction/Society (May).

GRANBERG, D. and B. W. GRANBERG (1981) "Pro-life versus pro-choice: another look at the abortion controversy in the U.S." Sociology and Social Research 65, 4: 424-434.

——— (1980) "Abortion attitudes, 1965-80: trends and determinants." Family Planning Perspectives 12 (September/October): 250-261.

GRAY-LITTLE, B. (forthcoming) "Marital quality and power processes among black couples." Journal of Marriage and the Family.

GULLIVER, P. H. (1979) Disputes and Negotiations: A Cross-Cultural Perspective. New York: Academic.

HALEM, L. C. (1980) Divorce Reform: Changing Legal and Social Perspectives. New York: Macmillan.

HANNAN, M. T., N. B. TUMA, and L. P. GROENEVELD (1978) "Income and independence effects on marital dissolution: results from the Seattle and Denver Income-Maintenance Experiments." American Journal of Sociology 84: 611-633.

——— (1977) "Income and marital events: evidence from an income-maintenance experiment." American Journal of Sociology 82 (May): 1186-1211.

HANSEN, D. A. and V. A. JOHNSON (1979) "Rethinking family stress theory: definitional aspects," pp. 582-603 in W. R. Burr et al. (eds.) Contemporary Theories About the Family, Vol. I. New York: Macmillan.

HAREVEN, T. K. (1977) "The family and gender roles in historical perspective," pp. 93-110 in L. A. Cater and A. F. Scott (eds.) Women and Men: Changing Roles, Relationships and Perception. New York: Praeger.

HEITLINGER, A. (1979) Women and State Socialism: Sex Inequality in the Soviet Union and Czechoslavakia. London: Macmillan.

HILL, R. and D. A. HANSEN (1960) "The identification of conceptual frameworks utilized in family study." Marriage and Family Living 19: 89-92.

HILL, W. and J. SCANZONI (1982) "An approach for assessing marital decision making processes." Journal of Marriage and the Family 44 (November).

HIMES, N. (1970) Medical History of Contraception. New York: Schocken.

HOLMAN, T. B. and W. R. BURR (1980) "Beyond the beyond: the growth of family theories in the 1970s." Journal of Marriage and the Family 42 (November): 729-742.

IBSEN, H. (1970a) "Ghosts," in R. F. Jelde (ed.) Ibsen, Major Plays, Vol. 2, New York: New American Library. (First published in 1881.)

——— (1970b) "An enemy of the people," in R. F. Jelde (ed.) Ibsen, Major Plays, Vol. 2. New York: New American Library. (First published in 1882.)

——— (1970c) "The lady from the sea," in R. F. Jelde (ed.) Ibsen, Major Plays, Vol. 2. New York: New American Library. (First published in 1888.)

JAFFE, F. S., B. L. LINDHEIM, and P. R. LEE (1981) Abortion Politics: Private Morality and Public Policy.. New York: McGraw-Hill.

JAGGAR, A. M. and P. R. STRUHL (1978) Feminist Frameworks: Alternative Theoretical Accounts of the Relations Between Women and Men. New York: McGraw-Hill.

JANCAR, B. W. (1978) Women Under Communism. Baltimore: Johns Hopkins University Press.

JOHNSON, A. S., III (1981) "Preface," in H. H. Bohen and A. Viveros-Long, Balancing Jobs and Family Life. Philadelphia: Temple University Press.

KAHN, A. J. and S. B. KAMERMAN (1979) "Government structure versus family policy." Washington COFO Memo 11 (Spring): 2-7.

KAMERMAN, S. B. and A. J. KAHN (1981) Child Care, Family Benefits, and Working Parents: A Study in Comparative Policy. New York: Columbia University Press.

——— [eds.] (1978) Family Policy: Government and Families in Fourteen Countries. New York: Columbia University Press.

KANOWITZ, L. (1969) Women and the Law. Albuquerque: University of New Mexico Press.

KEHRER, B. H. and C. M. WOLIN (1979) "Impact of income-maintenance on low birth weight: evidence from the Gary experiment." Journal of Human Resources 14 (Fall): 434-462.

KELLEY, H. H. and D. P. SCHENITZKI (1972) "Bargaining," pp. 298-337 in C. C. McClintock (ed.) Experimental Social Psychology. New York: Holt, Rinehart & Winston.

KENISTON, K. et al. (1977) All Our Children: The American Family Under Pressure. New York: Harcourt Brace Jovanovich.

KJELLIN, B.T.M. (1980) "New trends and changes in Nordic Family law," pp. 123-148 in J. Aldous and W. Dumon (eds.) The Politics and Programs of Family Policy. Notre Dame, IN: University of Notre Dame Press.

KLEIN, D. M. and R. HILL (1979) "Determinants of family problem-solving effectiveness," pp. 493-548 in W. R. Burr et al. (eds.) Contemporary Theories About the Family, Vol. I. New York: Macmillan.

KOHN, M. L. (1978) Class and Conformity. Chicago: University of Chicago Press.

KOOP, C. E. (1980) The Right to Live, the Right to Die. Wheaton, IL: Tyndale.

KRAUTHAMMER, C. (1981) "The humanist phantom." New Republic 185 (July 25): 20-25.

LAPIDUS, G. W. (1978) Women in Soviet Society: Equality, Development and Social Change. Los Angeles: University of California Press.

LASCH, C. (1978) The Culture of Narcissism. New York: Norton.

——— (1977) Haven in a Heartless World: The Family Besieged. New York: Basic Books.

LASLETT, P. (1977) Family Life and Illicit Love in Earlier Generations. New York: Cambridge University Press.

LEIK, R. and S. A. LEIK (1977) "Transition to interpersonal commitment," pp. 299-322 in R. L. Hamblin and J. H. Kunkel (eds.) Behavioral Theory in Sociology. New Brunswick, NJ: Transaction.

LERNER, M. (1979) "On being a possibilist." Newsweek (October 9) 21.

LERNER, R. M. and G. B. SPANIER [eds.] (1978) Child Influences on Marital and Family Interaction. New York: Academic.

LEVINE, D. N., E. B. CARTER, and E. M. GORMAN (1976) "Simmel's influence on American sociology: I." American Journal of Sociology 81 (January): 813-845.

LEVINE, J. A. (1976) Who Will Raise the Children? Philadelphia: Lippincott.

LEWIS, R. A. and J. H. PLECK [eds.] (1979) "Men's roles in the family." Family Coordinator 28 (October): special issue.

LIPMAN-BLUMEN, J. and J. BERNARD [eds.] (1979) Sex Roles and Social Policy: A Complex Social Science Equation. Beverly Hills, CA: Sage.

LORY, B. (1980) "Changes in European family policies," pp. 69-122 in J. Aldous and W. Dumon (eds.) The Politics and Programs of Family Policy. Notre Dame, IN: University of Notre Dame Press.

McADOO, H. P. [ed.] (1981) Black Families. Beverly Hills, CA: Sage.

McCALL, M. (1966) "Courtship as social exchange," pp. 190-200 in B. Farber (ed.) Kinship and Family Organization. New York: John Wiley.

McDONALD, J. F. and S. P. STEPHENSON, Jr. (1979) "The effect of income maintenance on the school-enrollment and labor supply decisions of teenagers." Journal of Human Resources 14 (Fall): 488-495.

MARET-HAVENS, E. (1977) "Developing an index to measure female labor force attachment." Monthly Labor Review 100 (May): 35-38.

MARTIN, A. (1976) "I am one man, hurt," pp. 382-385 in J. Blankenship (ed.) Scenes from Life: Views of Family, Marriage, Intimacy. Boston: Little, Brown.

MASNICK, G. and M. J. BANE (1980) The Nation's Families: 1960-1990. Boston: Auburn.

MATHEWS, D. G. (1977) Religion in the Old South. Chicago: University of Chicago Press.

MAY, E. T. (1980) Great Expectations: Marriage and Divorce in Post-Victorian America. Chicago: University of Chicago Press.

MAYNARD, R. A. and R. J. MURNANE (1979) "The effects of a negative income tax on school performance." Journal of Human Resources 14 (Fall): 463-476.

MERTON, R. K. (1949) Social Theory and Social Structure. New York: Macmillan.

MILTON, J. (1963) "The doctrine and discipline of divorce," in W. Petersen and D. Matza (eds.) Social Controversy. Belmont, CA: Wadsworth.

MODELL, J. and T. K. HAREVEN (1978) "Transitions: patterns of timing," pp. 245-270 in T. K. Hareven (ed.) Transitions: The Family and the Life Course in Historical Perspective. New York: Academic.

MOHR, J. C. (1978) Abortion in America: The Origins and Evolution of National Policy. New York: Oxford University Press.

MONRONEY, R. M. (1979) "The issue of family policy: do we know enough to take action?" Journal of Marriage and the Family 41 (August): 461-464.

MORGAN, R. (1980) "The first feminist exiles from the USSR." Ms. 9 (November): 49-56, 80-83, 102, 107-108.

MOYNIHAN, D. P. (1965) "Employment, income, and the ordeal of the Negro family." Daedalus (Fall): 745-769.

New Republic (1981) "The new gilded age." Vol. 185 (August 15): 5-6.

NOVAK, M. (1977) "The family out of favor." Urban and Social Change Review 10 (Winter): 3-6.

NYE, F. I. and G. W. McDONALD (1979) "Family policy research: emergent models and some theroetical issues." Journal of Marriage and the Family 41 (August): 473-486.

O'DELL, F. A. (1978) Socialization Through Children's Literature: The Soviet Example. Oxford: Cambridge University Press.

O'NEILL, W. (1967) Divorce in the Progressive Era. New Haven, CT: Yale University Press.

OSMOND, M. W. (1981) "Rethinking family sociology from a radical-critical perspective: applications and implications." Florida State University, Tallahassee. (unpublished)

——— (1980) "Cross-societal family research: a macrosociological overview of the seventies." Journal of Marriage and the Family 42 (November): 995-1016.

PAOLUCCI, B. and M. BUBOLZ (1980) "Toward a critical theory of family." Michigan State University, East Lansing. (unpublished)

PARSONS, T. (1965) "The normal American family," pp. 31-50 in S. M. Farber et al. (eds.) Man and Civilization: The Family's Search for Survival. New York: McGraw-Hill.

——— (1951) The Social System. New York: Macmillan.

——— (1937) The Structure of Social Action. New York: Macmillan.

PEARLIN, L. I. (1980) "Life strains and psychological distress among adults," pp. 174-192 in N. J. Smelser and E. H. Erikson (eds.) Themes of Work and Love in Adulthood. Cambridge, MA: Harvard University Press.

PHILLIPS, M. H. (1981) "Favorable family impact as an outcome of income support policy," pp. 165-194 in P. G. Brown et al. (eds.) Income Support: Conceptual and Policy Issues. Totowa, NJ: Rowman & Littlefield.

PITTS, J. R. (1964) "The structural-functional approach," pp. 51-124 in H. T. Christensen (ed.) Handbook of Marriage and the Family. Skokie, IL: Rand McNally.

PLECK, E. H. and J. H. PLECK (1980) The American Man. Englewood Cliffs, NJ: Prentice-Hall.

PLECK, J. H. (1982) "Changing patterns of work and family roles." Wellesley College. (unpublished)

——— (1981) The Myth of Masculinity. Cambridge: MIT Press.

POGREBIN, L. C. (1980) Growing Up Free: Raising Your Child in the 80s. New York: McGraw-Hill.

POLONKO, K. and J. SCANZONI (1981) Patterns Compared for the Voluntarily Childless, Postponing Childless, Undecided Childless, and Mothers. Final Report, National Institute for Child Health and Human Development (Contract 1-HD-92805).

RAPOPORT, R., R. N. RAPOPORT, and Z. STRELITZ (1977) Fathers, Mothers and Society: Perspectives on Parenting. New York: Random House.

RAUSH, H. L., A. C. GREIF, and J. NUGENT (1979) "Communication in Couples and families," pp. 468-492 in W. R. Burr et al. (eds.) Contemporary Theories About the Family, Vol. I. New York: Macmillan.

RILEY, M. W. [ed.] (1963) Sociological Research, Vol. I. New York: Harcourt Brace Jovanovich.

RODGERS-ROSE, L. F. [ed.] (1980) The Black Woman. Beverly Hills, CA: Sage.

ROGERS, C. R. (1968) "Man-woman relationships in the year 2000." Journal of Applied Behavioral Science 4, 3: 270-272.

ROLOFF, M. E. (1981) Interpersonal Communication: The Social Exchange Approach. Beverly Hills, CA: Sage.

SACHS, A. and J. H. WILSON (1978) Sexism and the Law: Male Beliefs and Legal Bias. New York: Macmillan.

SAFILIOS-ROTHSCHILD, C. (1976) "A macro and micro examination of family power and love: an exchange model." Journal of Marriage and the Family 37 (May): 355-362.

——— (1974) Women and Social Policy. Englewood Cliffs, NJ: Prentice-Hall.

SCALES, P. (1982) "The front lines of controversy: sex education and public action in America." Planned Parenthood Federation of America. (unpublished)

SCANZONI, J. (1982) Sexual Bargaining: Power Politics in American Marriage. Chicago: University of Chicago Press.

——— (1979) "Social exchange and behavioral interdependence," pp. 61-98 in T. L. Huston and R. L. Burgess (eds.) Social Exchange and Developing Relationships. New York: Academic.

——— (1978) Sex Roles, Women's Work and Marital Conflict: A Study of Family Change. Lexington, MA: D. C. Heath.

——— (1977) The Black Family in Modern Society: Patterns of Stability and Security. Chicago: University of Chicago Press.

——— (1975) Sex Roles, Life Styles and Childbearing: Changing Patterns in Marriage and Family. New York: Macmillan.

——— and G. L. FOX (1980) "Sex roles throughout the seventies: a decade review." Journal of Marriage and the Family 42 (November): 743-758.

SCANZONI, J. and M. SZINOVACZ (1980) Family Decision-Making: A Developmental Sex Role Model. Beverly Hills, CA: Sage.

SCANZONI, L. D. and J. SCANZONI (1981) Men, Women, and Change: A Sociology of Marriage and Family. New York: McGraw-Hill.

SEELEY, J. R., R. A. SIM, and E. W. LOOSLEY (1956) Crestwood Heights. New York: Basic Books.

SEWART, J. J. (1979) "Critical theory and the critique of conservative method," pp. 310-322 in S. G. McNall (ed.) Theoretical Perspectives in Sociology. New York: St. Martin's.

SEXTON, L. G. (1979) Between Two Worlds: Young Women in Crisis. New York: Morrow.

SHORTER, E. (1975) The Making of the Modern Family. New York: Basic Books.

SHURE, M. B. and G. SPIVAK (1978) Problem-Solving Techniques in Childrearing. San Francisco: Jossey-Bass.

SKERRY, P. (1978) "The class conflict over abortion." Public Interest (Summer): 69-84.

SMITH, R. E. (1979) Women in the Labor Force in 1990. Washington, DC: Urban Institute.

SMITH, T. A. (1975) The Comparative Policy Process. Santa Barbara, CA: CLIO.

SOKOLOFF, N. J. (1980) Between Money and Love: The Dialectics of Women, Work, and the Family. New York: Praeger.

SPREY, J. (1979) "Conflict theory and the study of marriage and the family," pp. 130-159 in W. R. Burr et al. (eds.) Contemporary Theories About the Family, Vol. II. New York: Macmillan.

STAPLES, R. (1981) The World of Black Singles. Westport, CT: Greenwood.

STEIN, P. J. [ed.] (1981) Single Life: Unmarried Adults in Social Context. New York: St. Martin's.

STEINER, G. Y. (1981) The Futility of Family Policy. Washington, DC: Brookings.

STONE, L. (1977) The Family, Sex and Marriage: In England 1500-1800. New York: Harper & Row.

STRAUS, M. (1980) "Sexual inequality and wife-beating," pp. 86-93 in M. A. Straus and G. T. Hotaling (eds.) The Social Causes of Husband-Wife Violence. Minneapolis: University of Minnesota Press.

STRAUSS, A. (1978) Negotiations: Varieties, Contexts, Processes and Social Order. San Francisco: Jossey-Bass.

SWIDLER, A. (1980) "Love and adulthood in American Culture," pp. 120-150 in N. J. Smelser and E. H. Erikson (eds.) Themes of Love and Work in Adulthood. Cambridge, MA: Harvard University Press.

TALLMAN, I. (1979) "Implementation of a national family policy: the role of the social scientist." Journal of Marriage and the Family 41 (August): 469-472.

TATALOVICH, R. and B. W. DAYNES (1981) The Politics of Abortion: A Study of Community Conflict in Public Policy Making. New York: Praeger.

TAX, M. (1980) The Rising of the Women: Feminist Solidarity and Class Conflict, 1880-1917. New York: Monthly Review Press.

THWING, C. F. and C.F.B. THWING (1887) The Family: An Historical and Social Study. Boston: Lee & Shepard.

TOFFLER, A. (1980) The Third Wave. New York: Morrow.

TRAVERS, J. (1980) "The National Day Care Study," pp. 247-251 in C. C. Abt (ed.) Problems in American Social Policy Research. Cambridge, MA: Abt Associates.

TROELTSCH, E. (1931) The Social Teaching of the Christian Churches (D. Wyon, trans.). New York: Macmillan.

TROLL, L. and V. BENGSTON (1979) "Generations in the family," pp. 127-161 in W. R. Burr et al. (eds.) Contemporary Theories About the Family, Vol. I. New York: Macmillan.

TUCKER, J. G. (1980) "Chairman's message: agenda for action," pp. 8-16 in Report of the White House Conference on Families. Washington, DC: Government Printing Office.

TUFTE, V. and B. MYERHOFF [eds.] (1979) Changing Images of the Family. New Haven, CT: Yale University Press.

UDRY, J. R. (1981) "Marital alternatives and marital disruption." Journal of Marriage and the Family 43 (November): 889-908.

VEDEL-PETERSEN, J. (1978) "Denmark," pp. 295-328 in S. B. Kamerman and A. J. Kahn (eds.) Family Policy: Government and Families in Fourteen Countries. New York: Columbia University Press.

VROOM, P., D. FASSETT, and R. A. WAKEFIELD (1981) "Mediation: the wave of the future?" American Family 4 (June/July): 8-13.

WALLACE, P. A., L. DATCHER, and J. MALVEAUX (1980) Black Women in the Labor Force. Cambridge: MIT Press.

WALSTER, E., G. W. WALSTER, and E. BERSCHEID (1978) Equity: Theory and Research. Boston: Allyn & Bacon.

WANDERSEE, W. D. (1981) Women's Work and Family Values: 1920-1940. Cambridge, MA: Harvard University Press.

WARD, T. (1981) "The church and the Christian familly." Family Life Today 1 (Spring/Summer).

WEED, J. A. (1980) "National estimates of marriage dissolution and survivorship." Vital and Health Statistics 3, 19.

WEISS, R. L. and G. MARGOLIN (1977) "Assessment of marital conflict and accord," pp. 555-602 in A. R. Ciminero et al. (eds.) Handbook of Behavioral Assessment. New York: John Wiley.

WEISSTEIN, N. (1981) "Abortion rights: taking the offensive." Ms. 10 (September): 36-39.

WEITZMAN, L. J. (1981) The Marriage Contract: Spouses, Lovers, and the Law. New York: Macmillan.

WHEELER, V. A. (1982) "Reciprocity within first grade friend and nonfriend dyads in a conflict of interest situation." University of Illinois—Urbana-Champaign. (unpublished)

WHITE, B. L., B. T. KABAN, and J. S. ATTANUCCI (1979) The Origins of Human Competence. Lexington, MA: D. C. Heath.

YANKELOVICH, D. (1981a) "New rules in American life: searching for self-fulfillment in a world turned upside down." Psychology Today 15 (April): 35-91.

——— (1981b) New Rules: Searching for Self-Fulfillment in a World Turned Upside Down. New York: Random House.

——— (1981c) "Stepchildren of the Moral Majority." Psychology Today 15 (November): 5-10.

ZARTMAN, I. W. (1976) "The analysis of negotiation," pp. 1-42 in I. W. Zartman (ed.) The 50% Solution. Garden City, NY: Doubleday.

ZELNIK, M., J. F. KANTNER, and K. FORD (1981) Sex and Pregnancy in Adolescence. Beverly Hills, CA: Sage.

ZIMMERMAN, S. L. (1979) "Policy, social policy, and family policy: concepts, concerns, and analytic tools." Journal of Marriage and the Family 41 (August): 487-496.

——— (1978) "The family and its relevance for social policy." Social Casework 8: 451-457.

ZURCHER, L. A. and R. G. KIRKPATRICK (1976) Citizens for Decency: Antipornography Crusades as Status Defense. Austin: University of Texas Press.

ABOUT THE AUTHOR

JOHN SCANZONI is a member of the Family Research Center, and Professor of Family Relations and of Sociology at the University of North Carolina—Greensboro; he was formerly Professor of Sociology at Indiana University—Bloomington. His previously published books include *Sex Roles, Women's Work and Marital Conflict; Sexual Bargaining; The Black Family in Modern Society;* and *Family Decision-Making: A Developmental Sex Role Model,* with Maximiliane Szinovacz. His articles have appeared in *Journal of Marriage and the Family, American Journal of Sociology,* and *American Sociological Review.* His continuing research interests focus on the interplay between societal changes and family changes, with particular concern for the implications of the changing roles of women and men.